MODERNS
AND NEAR-MODERNS

MODERNS
AND NEAR-MODERNS

ESSAYS ON HENRY JAMES, STOCKTON, SHAW, AND OTHERS

BY

WILLIAM CHISLETT, Jr., Ph.D.

Essay Index Reprint Series

Originally published by:

THE GRAFTON PRESS

BOOKS FOR LIBRARIES PRESS, INC.
FREEPORT, NEW YORK

First Published 1928
Reprinted 1967

LIBRARY OF CONGRESS CATALOG CARD NUMBER:
67-30180

PRINTED IN THE UNITED STATES OF AMERICA

TO
ELSIE KING

CONTENTS

CONTENTS

FOREWORD

THE essay on Shaw and the second note on Dunsany were inspired by the Drama League of Tacoma; most of the notes on the Irish Renaissance by W. W. Lyman, Jr., whose beautiful work in Celtic poetry at the University of California some of us will not soon forget. *New Gods for Old* is reprinted from the University of California *Chronicle*, Vol. XXI, 1918.

I have added to my studies of James and Stockton a number of notes on the past, present and future of the American novel—a matter of endless fascination and speculation.

The last part of the book is given over to certain aspects of other literary enthusiasms, English, Hindoo, Russian, American.

MODERNS AND NEAR-MODERNS

HENRY JAMES: HIS RANGE AND ACCOMPLISHMENT

IN this brief study I want to survey all of Henry James; sometimes carefully, sometimes more cursorily. Here, again, is "a Baedeker to a continent," to borrow Ezra Pound's phrase in his illuminating but incomplete studies of James in *Instigations*. Indeed, every book and essay on James does something for him and omits much else: even Pelham Edgar's *Henry James: the Man and His Work* (1927), is not quite comprehensive. Mr. Edmund Wilson, in *The New Republic* for March 16, 1927, calls for an exploration of James; we should know, says he, just what James means to convey to us in each of his stories and novels. Far be it from me to say I have in each case disclosed just that. But I have regarded him as a story-teller in his stories as much as a psychologist and character-drawer; I have striven perhaps primarily to see what his story is. Then I have read his plays; and I have made much of his *American Scene*. But enough of an Introduction—

"Look at my works, ye mighty, and despair," cried James himself, about to die. Yet "I want to leave a multitude of pictures of my time," he wrote to Stevenson in 1888, in a passage now widely quoted, "projecting my small circular frame upon as many different spots as possible and going in for number as well as quality, so that the number may constitute a total having a certain value as observation and testimony."

I

Is this man European, English or American? I ask myself
again as I sit in a Berkeley summer, in sunshine, amidst flowers,
or in cool University stacks, or stroll over a campus the crowds
of which are gone on vacation or to the Southern Branch, Los
Angeles,—sit reading Henry James, again, as I used to read
him at home in Southern California, slowly, away from apart-
ment houses and automobiles and restaurants and universities
and small colleges; as I have read him since in New York and
Washington; as I have viewed his *scene* in Europe.

American, to be sure—the English so regarded him, Ford
Madox Ford so considers him. And so does the present hopeful
essayist—hopeful of saying something of the range of Henry
James,—but differently from those writers. They trace disil-
lutionment with Europe; Brooks *dittos*, but carries him to
America, to find him horribly disappointed with that; to return
shuddering to Lamb House, Rye.

O folly of their view! Professor Pelham Edgar's new sober
book of exposition is better, a credit to our sister Canada. It
is fitting that a Canadian should understand James, that
Scotch-Irish combination of American and European. And
Miss West's book is true, too; his was a life of art, and Europe
was the better field for his art. Yet how little he relinquished
his Americanism even at the last, with his citizenship. "His
genius is not the less American for presenting us, before all
things, this vision of a bride rushing to the arms of her bride-
groom: vision of the mystic marriage (shall we say?) of new-
world faith and old world culture," says Joseph Warren Beach
in *The Cambridge History of American Literature.*—Take his
The American Scene. Do all his critics realize the importance
and fascination of this book? It "totals" over six hundred
pages and its interest is amazing. It is art, mature art. It
is wordy, yes; it wants humor often; sometimes it is snobbish;
it is at moments unkind; but the art of it! "I shall do, verily,

a lovely book," he wrote to Gosse (October 27, 1904. "I am interested up to my eyes—at least I think I am." Think of being born in America, then of returning to it after twenty years, equipped as James was; yet foregoing, as far as in him lay, odious comparisons and yielding himself to impressions old and new.   True, he was less affable on the subject in his letters, but he wrote them as letters, not as art,

But I have the way to enjoy Henry James on America, letters and all: to be sectional, for the moment, and to be a bit critical, oneself, of one's own section: but to be all for the South, so as to contradict him there.   Let a Californian, then, lead off with James on California, "with its deliciously simplified social state to make me taste the charming sweetness and comfort of this spot."   (He is writing in April of 1905, from the Hotel Coronado, and to Mrs. William James).   "California on these terms, when all is said (Southern C. at least— which, however, the real C., I believe, much repudiates), has completely bowled me over—such a delicious difference from the rest of the U. S. do I find it.   (I speak of course all of nature and climate, fruits and flowers; for there is absolutely nothing else, and the sense of the shining social and human inane is utter).   The days have been mostly here of heavenly beauty, and the flowers, the wild flowers just now in particular, which fairly *rage*, with radiance, over the land, are worthy of some purer planet than this.   I live on oranges and olives, fresh from the tree"—one assumes that he is not referring to the olives— "and I lie awake nights to listen, on purpose, to the languid list of the Pacific, which my windows overhang."   He is then to go back to Los Angeles to lecture "to a female culture club of 900 members," then to the Del Monte.   "It breaks my heart to have so stinted myself here—but it was inevitable; and no one had given me the least inkling that I should find California so sympathetic."

There is more (and less) of California in *The American Scene;* for formally speaking, the Far West doesn't figure in that

mighty book: it was to have done so. But in Florida he antici-
pates: "California was to have—if I may be decently premature
about it—her own treachery; but she was to wind one up much
higher before she let one down. I was to find her, especially at
the first flush, unlike sweet frustrated Florida,[1] ever so amiably
strong: which comes with the art with which she makes the
stoutnesses, as I have called them, of natural beauty stand you
in temporary stead of the leanness of everything else (everything that might be of an order equally interesting)." She
"belongs to the handsome side of the continent"; her Nature
is aristocratic; she braces herself "against the assault of a
society so much less marked with distinction than herself." And
again in Florida:[2] "I had the foretaste of what I was presently
to feel in California—when the general aspect of that wondrous
realm kept suggesting to me a sort of prepared but unconscious
and inexperienced Italy, the primitive plate, in perfect condition, but with the impression of History all yet to be made."

But if James is gracious to California, he is offish and off in
the South. Yet if that isn't one of the most American things
in him may I dwell in eternal snows. He wanted to join the
Northern forces and fight, but was prevented. Here he somewhat unchivalrously stabs, with his pen, a fallen foe. Yet even
one phrase like his "the wide-eyed smile of the South" is enough
to restore him to our love, artistically. And of course he has a
word of praise, if grudging, for the social graces of the Old
South. Indeed Dr. Herbert Leland Hughes, in his *Theory and
Practice in Henry James* says "there is something in James that
identifies him with the old Southern code: at least we Southerners like to think so." But we do expect him to rise somehow
higher to the beauties of Charleston, and to love the people, and
the pines in the country. His letters, though, be it noted, show
a taste for St. Augustine. But he says Richmond is blank and

---

[1] In the *Letters* he regrets Cuba: "I am heartbroken not to have a
sniff of that flamboyant flower"—that flower Hergesheimer has sniffed in
The Bright Shawl.

[2] Yet still again (*Letters*): "In the heart of golden orange-groves I
yearned for the shade of the old L. H. mulberry tree."

void, hovered over by a sort of intellectual bankruptcy. Slavery he handles with positive prejudice: the South, says he, is futile without it or with it—it is adorably weak, played upon and betrayed by slavery. He misses European churches—the aesthetic appetite goes unassuaged. Yet he is charmed at last by a little Southern lady in charge of a depressing museum. But "the illiteracy seems to hover like a queer smell; the social revolution has begotten neither song nor story—only, for literature, two or three biographies of soldiers, written in other countries, and only, for music, the weird chants of the emancipated blacks," sighs this anticipator of *The Desert of Bozart.* And if James ever hated anybody it is the young Southerner he meets, who'd like to fight 'em again, and is as haughty about "niggers" as if his people hadn't been properly trounced by New Englanders, New Yorkers and Father Abraham. He sees a French statue of Lee to praise, but says it looks down on futility—not on a lost cause, but on a cause never to be gained. He notes the South's *bled* condition, but never pauses to note who bled it. Even the girls are noisy and empty. He casts himself upon Nature; he says one always has to in America: "natural beauty must stand you in temporary stead of the leanness of everything else"; and he retreats precipitately into libraries, they alone being charged with anything beyond arithmetic. "I remember comparing them," says he, "inwardly, after periods of stress and death, after long, vacant stretches, to the mastheads on which spent birds alight in the expanses of ocean." Prejudice, prejudice! Yet presently we shall find him pummeling his own town, New York, which, however, needs it, can stand it, and doesn't much care.

New England comes off better, and Baltimore and Washington, and Philadelphia best of all. Philadelphia doesn't *bristle.* Its past looms squarely and substantially through it. The old order is there. There's an intimacy, a kindness about it—an absence of New York. His letters reiterate this liking for "dear queer flat comfortable Philadelphia," so "materially

civilized." Wonderful little Baltimore, too, like a sweet, good
child: the quiet charm of its dignified houses; its unobtrusive-
ness; its green boughs! And "the sustained low pitch of Mt.
Vernon!" In Washington proper, though, he prepares to resume
his offensive armor. Here is the City of Conversation. Nobody much is in business. He likes the White House and
"adores" the Capitol. But what, in the future, will Washington
have to say, and what apart from stone, marble, trees, will it
say it with? Will a true society develop in which American
men, as well as women, will figure? Will American men catch
up with American women in the amenities? (We may recall here
that at this same time he was writing two series of articles for
Harper's Bazaar on *The Speech* and *The Manners of American
Women;* to say nothing of lecturing on *The Question of Our
Speech* before the women of Bryn Mawr). He reminds American women that whereas in other countries the man's standards
"color the whole air," in America language, manners and social
usages are in the keeping of women.

His chapter on Boston is not enthusiastic; he says he misses
the past in the new Boston; and he finds its modern language
Italian. But Concord appeals to him, sitting back there like a
widowed New England matron of old days. He likes Salem,
too, but finds it less Hawthornesque than he had hoped. (He
enjoys motoring through the Adirondacks with the Whartons:
a car can "rope in, in big free hauls, a huge netful of impressions," he observes in the *Letters*). But the prize chapter in the
book is *New England: an Autumn Impression.* Again the disappointment in the American scene; but again the delight in
American scenery. He is entranced by the New Hampshire
mountains; New England rivers and lakes rest his baffled eyes.
And Harvard is still of the gods, albeit a roaring stadium has
the place of a Lowell and a Howells. Yet after all, he muses,
there is a possible drama in the waiting spectacle of America.
The women's faces, at least, are less commercialized than the
men's—

But New York! "New York," says the author of *The Pilgrimage of Henry James*, "was practically a huge, continuous, fifty-floored conspiracy against the very idea of the ancient graces." "Appallingly, fantastically charmless; altogether unspeakable" are James's own words in his letters; yet his *American Scene* chapters on New York are fascinating, are thrilling. "I suppose I am much interested, for the time passes inordinately fast," he writes in the *Letters*. Yet this town, this New York: Take Washington Square, Ellis Island and the Waldorf-Astoria. An old charm clings to the first, yet his home is torn down, an index of the city's perpetual change. (Newport, his other boyhood home, is all "white elephants"; its fine old houses closed; its charm and leisure fled). And Ellis Island: Americans can never be the same after visiting it: it warns us that we no longer possess our country; New York itself convinces us. As for the Waldorf—one scrambles up the bank out of the roaring tide of the street and is inducted into the social free-for-all, into that hotel spirit which is the American spirit. Yet he whispers a liking for the old town—his boyhood town. And hotels do have bathrooms. But the alien: what one liked about him in Europe is washed out here. He has shed his sociability, his manners. Will these return some day? Yet our analyst paints the Jewish quarters glowingly—the New Jerusalem, where the New Poverty flourishes. And the new accent—how long shall we know it for English? Yet to the traveler returning from the Far West (and the Middle West which he liked less) the East shows marks of established customs. It is Irving's Sunnyside, though, that "carries the last faint echoes of a felicity forever gone." New York society he finds a court function with no one to curtsy to; the St. Gaudens statue glorifies war, the Metropolitan Museum is all money, "for *all* the most exquisite things except creation." Yet in the Bowery he falls into an almost bacchic fit of artistic delight. "O remarkable, unspeakable New York!"

II

Another reader may value James's foreign travel books more than his *American Scene:* I do not, though one of them, *English Hours,* is perhaps more perfect, even as England is more perfect, in finish, than we. On the other hand, America and *The American Scene* are more perfect, because unfinished. "James revealed how much Europe needed American eyes to intellectualize, even discover, her beauties," says Mrs. M. Sturge Gretton handsomely. His *Transatlantic Sketches* gives far most space to Italy: there are thirteen Italian, four English, three Swiss and two German pieces, and one French, Dutch and Belgian. Germany is *good* for one; it is nutritive, is one remark of his. *Portraits of Places* gives England eight, France six, America (one of them Quebec) four, and Italy two. (Who would think the same man wrote this limpid book and the later *Golden Bowl?*) One passage is to the effect that it takes a great deal to make a successful American; but to make a happy Venetian takes only a handful of quick sensibility—Mussolini having mercifully not yet ascended. *Italian Hours,* 1909, chiefly compiled from his former books, has the additional glory of being illustrated in color by Joseph Pennell. *A Saint's Afternoon* (in the *May Book,* 1901, contributed to by many writers and artists in behalf of Charing Cross Hospital) is a charming account of a visit to Capri, of its dreamy beauty and of its Festival of St. Anthony. In 1905 he issued *English Hours.* The whole of that book, if he had written it alone, would have justified that pilgrimage and that exile so deplored by Mr. Brooks. The beauty in it, of his *North Devon!* And *Winchelsea, Rye and "Denis Duval"* explain, through Thackeray, some of the fascination that district James was later to call home long had for him.

His family books dovetail in here. *A Small Boy and Others* is a fascinating if wordy account of his education, in Europe especially. Verily, it explains his later life and work: he was

indeed schooled all over Europe and liked it—always—except
Germany during the war. The *Notes of a Son and Brother* paint
effective portraits of his father, and, in particular, of his mother.
He does less well for his adored brother: he seems to feel that
himself. But at least his cousin, Mary Temple, he adds, has
pertinence (she of *The Wings of a Dove*). As for *The Middle
Years*, there we have restaurants, the National Gallery,
George Eliot, Mrs. Greville, "as summing up an era," Lowell,
Tennyson's reading and Browning. In Liverpool our passionate
pilgrim long feels "the incomparable truth to type of the waiter;
truth to history, to literature, to poetry, to Dickens, to
Thackeray, possibly to Smollett and to Hogarth."

III

"The critic's first duty in the presence of an author's collected works is to seek out some key to his method, some utter-
ance of his literary convictions, some indication of his ruling
theory," observes our author in *The Novels of George Eliot*
(in his volume *Views and Reviews*). As a writer of fiction himself, he naturally shows most interest in other writers of fiction,
and what he looks for in them is "saturation" and impersonality.
That is the upshot, too, of his lecture, *The Lesson of Balzac*.
He writes to H. G. Wells (*Letters*, Vol. II) praising him for the
former quality in *The New Machiavelli*, but criticizing the
first person narrative. "A particular detachment" must inter-
vene before the artist's report becomes authentic, interesting and
beautiful. An air of reality, however, is the chief virtue of a
novel (*The Art of Fiction*). In *Views and Reviews* he praises
Arnold for his seriousness; for "the writers who are willing to
resign themselves to this obscure distinction are in our opinion
the only writers who understand their time." In the same volume he commends George Eliot when she is simple: but not when
she tries to be modern and complex. As for Dickens, he is a

great observer and humorist, but nothing of a philosopher; and "a novelist very soon has need of a little philosophy." He is hard on Whitman, calling his an essentially prosaic mind. In *Notes and Reviews* he expresses a liking for Trollope but not for his *Miss Mackenzie*, which he is reviewing. "Why should we follow the fortunes of such people?" he cries, much as if they were one type of American. "They vulgarize experience and all the other heavenly gifts." He criticizes Swinburne, this time for the peerless *Chastelard*. In *Epictetus* (in the same volume) he denounces Stoicism for paralyzing the sensibilities: for "it is through our sensibilities that we suffer, but it is through them, too, that we enjoy."

Notes on Novelists and Some Other Notes is an interesting mixture of Scotch, English, French, Italian and American. D'Annunzio and Serao meet with only moderate approval: Sex plays too prominent a part with them: it masters them. *The Future of the Novel* (in *The Universal Anthology*, 1899, Vol. 28) foresees an enduring place for fiction and notes the oncoming freedom of women. And "it is the opinion of some observers that when women do obtain a free hand they will not repay their long debt to the precautionary attitude of men by unlimited consideration for the natural delicacy of the latter."—*The New Novel* (one of the *Notes* again) is the saturated novel; Stevenson is himself again in *Catriona* and *Weir of Hermiston*. Flaubert has genius, but his characters are too small affairs; Charles Eliot Norton is a true lover of the life of art. But it is Zola now who has his interested examination. *His* work has nothing to fear from sailing too light! He praises his healthiness and heartiness. Yet how handle so much material without some larger subjective consequence? As for the Dreyfus Affair: Zola's "outbreak in connection with it was the act of a man with arrears of personal liberty to make up, the act of a spirit for which life, or for which at any rate freedom, had been too much postponed, treating itself at last to a luxury of freedom." Compare with that James himself and the Great War! Note his awakening in *Within the Rim and Other Essays*—But we antici-pate.

His famous *Partial Portraits* swings from Emerson to Du Maurier, with spotlights on his friend Stevenson and his idol Turgenieff. The Turgenieff essay places him high as a literary portrait painter. He likes Daudet, too, and Maupassant's economy of means, but dislikes his women. Indeed his *French Poets and Novelists*, Ford Madox Ford (in his *Henry James*) calls more an expression of likes and dislikes than a display of criticism. "In this volume" says he, "our author desperately belauds Balzac, places Turgenieff at the top of the tree, damns Flaubert by bracketing him in the same paper with Charles de Bernard, an even then forgotten scribbler who hopelessly imitated but in some respects improved upon Balzac. He writes about Musset with great justice and very little sympathy; about *ce pauvre* Theo with a great deal of sympathy and not much critical justice; about George Sand with relish as a wicked old woman, and about Mérimée with pity for his physical ills and not much feeling for his clear, hard diction." It is in this book that James finds Turgenieff "a cosmopolite whose roots have never been loosened in his native soil."

IV

But James's range (quite apart from his short stories and novels) is not yet circumscribed. There is his readable life (mostly the letters) of *William Wetmore Story*, who abandoned law for art, and lived chiefly in Rome; there is his *Hawthorne*, a Hawthorne concerned with conscience, but with something good enough, withal, in *The Scarlet Letter*, to present without em-barrassment to English Literature; there are his appreciations of Crackanthorpe, of Walcott Balastier, of Rupert Brooke (prefacing *The Average Woman, Last Studies* and the *Letters* of these young friends); there is his Introduction to *The Art of the Actor* by Coquelin: there are hundreds of minor pieces in periodicals (see Mr. Le Roy Phillips' *Bibliography of the Writings of Henry James*, 1906, pp. 87–163). Among these are papers and notes on painting which Ezra Pound says (in his remarkable studies of James in *Instigations*) he understood little enough beyond the Renaissance, but which, judging from a number of letters he wrote to the New York *Tribune*, he understood, along with current politics in France, very well; there is *The Progress of Anthropology* (Mr. Phillips says it is by him) in the *Nation*, Feb. 6, 1868; a translation of Daudet's *Port Tarascon;* an interesting review of Hardy's *Far from the Madding Crowd* (*Nation*, Dec. 24, 1874) in which he praises the sheep and dogs, observes that the book is too long, and thinks the English novel in general should acquire some Aristotelian rules; and finally there is *In After Days*, to which he contributes an essay on the future life,—speaking still as an artist; probing, observing, feeling in communication with *sources; desiring* immortality—a life better and more beautiful to apprehend and enjoy.

Finally, did we say? Not so, for there are the *Letters*, still, and his Prefaces—the first a joyous flood of informalities; the second a rockier stream, but one wherein we fight up to the head and source of his different stories and novels, learning of his pains to make them more and more artistic, even to the extent of rephrasing some of them; and of his greater and greater tendency towards the dramatic in them. His observations on men of letters in the *Letters*, concern us here: admiration of Meredith's work and discomfiture in its presence, too, and in its author's; letters to Hugh Walpole *not* approving the formlessness of Dostoievsky and of *War and Peace;* enthusiasm for Kipling and for Wells; and (to Gosse, Dec. 13, 1894) a beautiful expression of his feeling for Pater, to whose style and devotion to Art he owed not a little. Nor is *The Question of Our Speech* without importance, commending, as it does, the conservative element of English as *core*, with innovations adhering thereto: a composite true of his own style, at once so stately

and so idiomatic: so English and so American.   And lastly his
address before the Academic Committee of the Royal Society
of Literature in commemoration of the centenary of Robert
Browning on *The Novel in "The Ring and the Book"* (see the
Living Age, August 24, 1912) is a resplendent appreciation of
the great poem, which he knew thoroughly.   Browning works
over his material, says he; we work over Browning, and from
the process emerges Caponsacchi, "the tried and tempered and
illuminated *man*."   But he talks as much of the poem as a drama
as a novel; and the present play *Caponsacchi* lays just the
emphasis he does on Caponsacchi and his pure and perfect love
for Pompilia.   There's the difference: to Browning the girl
Pompilia was the "hero"; to James, the worldly but noble
Caponsacchi.

v

Though he appears not to have essayed any poetry, our
subject, as Mr. Ford is always calling our restless analyst, as
James calls himself, took more than one "shot" at the Theatre.
(Note too a collection of letters on the Drama, *A Most Unholy
Trade*, chiefly in praise of *Little Eyolf*, who is indeed a sort of
Jamesian child).   *Guy Domville* failed and wasn't resurrected
by its author; *Still Waters, a Farce*, mentioned by Mr. Phillips
as appearing in *The Balloon Post* (six numbers in Boston) is
still indeed; as also *The Saloon* [3] (what, what, not *Salon?*),
dated 17 Jan. 1911, by Mr. H. M. Walbrook (*Nineteenth
Century*, vol. 80, pp. 141–5).   *Pyramus and Thisbe* (*The
Galaxy*, April, 1869) is a twelve-page dialogue between Stephen
Young, a journalist, and Catherine West, a music teacher,
separated by a wall.   She objects to his smoking, he to her
playing (for they *have* windows), but they win each other in
the end, wall or no wall—or windows.   Meanwhile *A Change*

[3] This is *Owen Wingrave* dramatized, says Miss Bosanquet, in *Henry
James at Work*, Hogarth Press, 1924.

of Heart (*Atlantic*, Jan., 1872) comes to Robert Stanley, who wants to break off an affair between his cousin Margaret and Charles Pepperel, and to make use of Martha Noel to effect it. But he finds he loves Martha too much, and leaves Margaret to her sad fate, if it really is that. *The High Bid*, according to Mr. Walbrook, won acceptance and a few performances by the Forbes-Robertsons. It is *Covering End* in play form. *The American*, dramatized, had its little day, too. *Daisy Miller*, which we can still read dramatized, though with a happy ending, apparently did not. *The Outcry* had a production by The Stage Society of London, and *The Other House* (now a short novel or long short story) was gotten ready for one,—"an Ibsen play with Jamesian ramifications," Mr. Edgar calls it.—Meanwhile James had somewhat shamefacedly published two volumes of *Theatricals*, containing four apparently unactable plays, *Tenants, Disengaged, The Album* and *The Reprobate*. The titles are good, but apparently no critic has read beyond them. In *Tenants* a Mrs. Vibert, her son Claude and Captain Lurcher, his tutor, take a lodge on the estate of Sir Frederick Byng, in Dorsetshire. Sir Frederick has a son Norman who is in love with Mildred, an heiress and the ward of Sir Frederick. Sir Frederick packs Norman off to India so that he will not appear to encourage him to marry Mildred and her money. Meanwhile Lurcher plots to marry her to Claude so he, Lurcher, will get some of it. Meanwhile it comes out that Claude is Sir Frederick's natural son, and that his mother and father now plan to marry. But Mildred steps in and produces Norman, back from India. The brothers face each other. At the end Mildred and Norman are to be united and Claude is to look after his mother, though there is still a possibility that she and Sir Frederick may be united. In *Disengaged* Captain Prime is impressed by two other men and a matchmaking mother into proposing to Blandina Wigmore; but disengages himself to wed Mrs. Jasper, who wants him, only, of the several who want her. In *The Album* two cousins are the prospective heirs of a Mr. Bedford: Sir Ralph

Damont turns out to be the lucky one. But at the end he makes over his fortune to the other because by so doing he loses Lady Bassett, who is trying to marry him for his money. The now lucky cousin (Mark Bernal) wins Grace Jesmond, and Maud (something of a fortune-hunter herself) contents herself with Teddy Ashdown. *The Reprobate* discloses the machinations of a Mrs. Freshville, who by means of a picture of Paul and some letters of Captain Chanter is trying to marry the latter. But Mrs. Doubleday gets the Captain and Paul weds Blanche Amber, who thinks his bad reputation (though undeserved) is "cute."

Finally, in the London *Mercury*, vol. VI, 1922, we may read James's monologue for Ruth Draper. It is spoken by an American girl and is all about her Presentation. Word comes that a certain quota must have husbands, so she sends out for one,—*the* one. 'Tis rather clever fooling.

VI

And now for the short stories.

The Story of a Year (1865) is laid in Revolutionary times and concerns Jack, who dies of wounds, and Lizzie, his sweetheart, who is also loved by Bruce, and whom Jack charges her to marry, but whom she perhaps will not.

A Day of Days (1866) is a summer day in New England. Adela Moore, society girl, has returned to the country to keep house for Herbert Moore, her brother, who is a scientist. Thomas Ludlow, an uncultured New Yorker, appears seeking Herbert: he finds Adela. They walk: he tells the girl he is going to Europe the next day to study for five years. She half tempts him to stay, but neither is sure enough of the other. He departs, and Adela will presumably listen further to the protestations of Madison Perkins, a young Unitarian minister.

A Landscape Painter (1866) is the diary of a young artist

who is hiding a wounded heart in a fishing village. But an old sailorman's daughter marries him; then informs him she has read his diary.

"*Poor Richard* (1867) deals with the conscience of a man very much in love with a woman who loves his rival. He tells the rival a lie which sends him away to his death on the field, but Poor Richard's lie does not win his love." (Howells' summary, *Century*, Nov., 1882).

My Friend Bingham (1867) has accidentally shot a widow's only child. He is so overcome with sorrow that the mother pities, esteems, then loves him.

In *The Romance of Certain Old Clothes* (1868) a girl loves her sister's husband, waits for her to die, gets a key to a chest of the wife's old clothing and is found dead by the chest with marks of fingers on her.

A Problem (1868) has to do with a young married pair and two fortune tellers' prophecies. The first one foretold that the young man would marry twice; the second that the young couple's child, a girl, would die. The wife gets jealous and leaves her husband, the child dies, and the pair are reunited:— they *are* married twice, according to the excellent *Julia*, now the friend of both.

De Grey, a Romance (1868) concerns a curse upon an old family. Within a month after a girl is engaged to a De Grey she dies, unless the engagement is a loveless one. That had been the case with the father and mother of Paul, the present De Grey. Paul becomes engaged to Margaret, to whom Father Herbert, who also loves her, discloses the family curse and whom he begs to break off her engagement. She refuses, preferring to give her life. But first she curses the curse. Paul is thrown from his horse and dies.

Osborne's Revenge (1868) tells of Robert Graham, who kills himself for love of Henrietta Congreve; and of his friend Osborne who hopes at first for revenge upon her. He learns instead that his friend really persecuted her—that he was a

monomaniac—and that Miss Congreve is not a flirt but a fine
person indeed. He marries a woman resembling her.

A Most Extraordinary Case (1868) has to do with Colonel
Mason, who is taken out of a hospital by his aunt, Mrs. Mason,
and carried to the country where she and her niece Caroline
Hoffman are living. The Colonel falls in love with Caroline, but
she favors Dr. Knight. The Colonel dies when he hears of their
engagement, and the doctor thinks it all a most extraordinary
case. It is.

In *The Story of a Masterpiece* (1868), Baxter, a young
artist who has been engaged to Marian Everett in Switzerland
—she is now to marry the rich Mr. Lennox—has been com-
missioned by Lennox to paint Marian's portrait. He does so
too well (she has loved too often) and though Mr. Lennox
marries her, he first cuts the portrait to pieces.

A Light Man (1869) has for "no hero, I confess," a young
man returned from Europe and introduced into the household
of an old Epicure, Mr. Sloane, by one Theodore. Quite unin-
tentionally, evidently, he supplants Theodore in the old man's
affection, but tries to rewin Theodore's regard. He gives up
a claim to the old gentleman's fortune, but even at the end
doesn't seem to have Theodore back. The piece is less than
sophomoric.

Travelling Companions (1870) is redolent of Milan, Padua
and Venice, and has for characters two young Americans who
marry, but not because they miss their train and are left alone
in Padua.

At Isella (1871) is chiefly Swiss and Italian scenery; but
for story has a young American who gives money to a handsome
Italian *marchesina* to hasten her departure to Milan to marry
her lover. The next morning her husband appears and is
assured by the inn-keeper that his wife has not been at Isella.

A Passionate Pilgrim (1871) is Clement Searle, an American
with a nostalgia for England. When the story opens he is over
there with a vague claim to an English estate, and thanks to

the narrator meets its owners, two very distinct cousins of the Pilgrim, a brother and sister. The brother later drives him out, but as he lies dying at Oxford Miss Searle comes to him to announce the death of her brother. She loves him; the property is to be hers; it might have been his, too. Ere he goes, he gives the little he has left to an Englishman to remove to America.

Master Eustace (1871) is a haughty youth whose governess is the recorder of his story. His mother is a widow, and a silent one. When Eustace is seventeen a Mr. Cope returns from India and marries the mother. The boy is frightfully jealous, there is a flare-up, and Eustace is disclosed as the illegitimate son of the bride and groom.

In *Guest's Confession* (1872) the narrator and his invalid step-brother Edward have sought a watering-place for the brother's health. One day the writer enters the little Episcopal church. A girl—she turns out to be Miss Guest—comes there: it reminds her a bit of Europe. A storm blows up: the writer talks with the girl and falls in love with her. But later it comes out that his brother Edward has been done out of money by the girl's father, and he exacts a written confession from him. Still later Edward dies, leaving his brother the confession. Meantime, in New York, the writer woos Miss Guest, but her father will have nothing to do with him. The lover now threatens him with the confession and gives him two hours to make up his mind. When the time is up, however, he burns the confession, thereby winning over the father and getting his consent to the marriage.

The Madonna of the Future (1873) is to be poor Theobald's masterpiece: he spends his life in Florence adoring an Italian woman and planning to paint all she means to him artistically and spiritually. He dies, leaving only a cracked and discolored canvas.

The Sweetheart of M. Briseux (1873) is a bit ironical in title, for the original of M. Briseux's *The Lady in a Yellow*

Shawl was a model to him, and no more, as she explains to the writer. This lady had gone abroad with a Mrs. Staines, a friend of her mother; and Harold, the son; and she became engaged to him. In Europe, she agreed to set the wedding day,—when Harold should finish a portrait of her. Once only, when he was out, she saw the picture, and she was dissatisfied with it. Suddenly a poor artist came in to borrow money. He at once begged to do our lady's portrait, or to touch up Harold's. Harold now appearing, refused, broke with his sweetheart and left M. Brieux to paint her far into the night: at the opening of the story the writer and the lady are both in the town of M—— gazing at this masterpiece of the now famous Briseux.

Professor Fargo (1874) is a medium who has come to P—— with Colonel Gifford and the latter's deaf and dumb daughter. The narrator is a very intelligent commercial traveler who is putting in three unwelcome days in the little American town. He finds Professor Fargo to be a noisy charlatan, Colonel Gifford an accomplished but unpractical and impecunious mathematician and his daughter an enigma with a genius for figures. Later he encounters the three in New York, where their performance is a failure. It is now time for the Professor and the Colonel to part, but as he leaves, Professor Fargo carries off the girl, who goes with him readily.

Madame de Mauves (1874) is a prim young American married to a Frenchman. She is outraged by her husband's infidelities; he wishes she would be untrue so he wouldn't have to look up to her. But in the end he kills himself because he is hopelessly in love with his cold life.

In *Eugene Pickering* (1874) a pair are engaged to each other by parents; they resist; but come to like and love each other.

Adina (1874) is engaged to Scrope, an American in Italy who has worried Angelo, an Italian youth, out of a valuable topaz intaglio found on the Campagna and displaying a full length portrait of Tiberius. Angelo tries to recover the topaz but is refused it; whereupon he elopes with Adina. Scrope throws the unlucky gem into the Tiber.

In *The Last of the Valerii* (1874) Count Valerio falls in love with a disinterred Juno, and can't come back to his wife until Juno is buried again.

Benvolio (1875), half scholar, half poet, was bored. "To get entangled, therefore, pondered Benvolio, should be the wise man's aim. . . . He would entangle himself, at least, in a mesh of work—work of the most profound and elaborate sort." Then follows a double love affair with a countess and Scholastica, a professor's daughter. The countess gets Scholastica appointed to teach "at the Antipodes"; *he* parts with the countess and devotes himself to poetry. If this were a fairy story, 'twould have ended differently, says James: Benvolio would have married Scholastica.

In *The Ghostly Rental* (1876) a father receives rent from the ghost of his daughter, presumably. For she has really only pretended to be a ghost in order to scare him away and to keep him from marrying her to a man she didn't care for.

In *Four Meetings* (1877) an American schoolmistress gets to Havre, is relieved of her money by an American cousin whom Europe has demoralized (he has been tricked into a marriage, he says, to a countess), returns to America without seeing Europe and is later descended upon, for life, by the "Countess."

Longstaff's Marriage (1878) tells of two cousins—women —traveling in Europe, who stop at Nice for a time and encounter Mr. Longstaff, an invalid. About to die, he persuades Diana to marry him. She does; he settles his property upon her. Later the cousins return to Europe and find Mr. Longstaff still alive. But Diana is now failing; and calling upon Mr. Longstaff to help her in turn, she marries him again, and dies.

Théodolinde (1878), or *Rose-Agathe*, is the story of a young art fancier who falls in love with a hair-dresser's model.

He buys it and takes it home. But first the author tries to keep us in suspense for many pages by pretending it is the hair-dresser's wife that his friend is infatuated with.

An International Episode (1878–9) concerns two English cousins, Lord Lambeth and Percy Beaumont, who visit New York and Newport, and Mr. and Mrs. Westgate and Bessie Alden of Boston, sister to Mrs. Westgate. When Lord Lambeth shows signs of getting engaged to Miss Alden, his cousin has him called home. Later, while the sisters are visiting England, Lord Lambeth returns to the siege, but Bessie does not think he takes his responsibilities seriously, and goes back to America, apparently quite through with him.

A Bundle of Letters (1879) is chiefly from Miss Miranda Hope to her mother. Miranda is fond of William Platt, back in Bangor. Meantime, her impressions of Europe are conveyed to us. So are other impressions of the international scene, by a Frenchman, a German and a young American.

The Diary of a Man of Fifty (1879) relates an affair that didn't come off with an Italian countess. Now a young English friend is in love with her daughter and marries her, while the man of fifty wonders if he was fair to her mother.

The Pension Beaurepas (1879) discloses an old American being held in Europe by an extravagant matchmaking wife and daughter, while his business goes to ruin in New York.

In *The Point of View* (1882) Aurora Church and Louis Leverett are kept tantalizingly from marrying each other, while the story spins itself out by means of a half dozen reactions of as many persons to America vs. Europe, and *vice versa*.

The Impressions of a Cousin (1883) are the reactions of a woman who prefers Europe but who is back visiting her cousin Eunice in America. Her views of outer New York, however, are soon swallowed up in inner relationships. Eunice loves the clever Mr. Caliph, her guardian, who has just lost her fortune for her. The narrator prevails upon Eunice's half-brother, Adrian, to make over most of his money to Eunice: the narrator will marry *him*, she says, when Caliph marries Eunice. The story so ends.

The Siege of London (1883) is conducted by Mrs. Headway, a Westerner several times divorced, against the family prejudices of Lady Demesne, whose son is nevertheless destined to be the next and perhaps the permanent husband of our adventurous countrywoman. Even Littlemore, an American who knew her in San Diego and intends her no good, doesn't prevail against her.

A New England Winter (1884) is Florimond Daintry's vacation in Boston (from Europe) with his mother,—who gets Rachel Torrance brought up from Baltimore to amuse him. She stays with the Meshes and Florimond comes often—but, as it transpires, to see Pauline Mesh. Mrs. Daintry is upset and goes off to Paris with Florimond. Rachel likes Florimond, but Florimond likes Pauline, who is only amused by him.

Lady Barbarina [4] (1884) tells of a peer's daughter who marries an American millionaire and who goes most reluctantly to live in America; and of her sister, Lady Agatha, who comes too and then elopes with a Californian, Herman Longstraw. "Lady Barb" and her husband end up in England.

The Path of Duty (1884) is the road followed by a man and woman who love each other but remain apart, he having already promised (just before his true love becomes a widow) to marry another.

The Author of Beltraffio (1884), Mark Ambient, is disapproved of by his wife Beatrice, who fears their child Dolcino will be contaminated by his books. The boy falling ill, she lets him die. Then later, remorseful, she does read some of her husband's work. A young American admirer of Ambient tells the tale.

Georgina's Reasons (1885) studies a young American girl who marries a naval officer against her parents' will, keeps it all a secret, secludes their child in Europe, marries a Mr. Roy

---

[4] Originally appearing as *Lady Barberina*.

without obtaining a divorce first, and "gets away with it."
Meanwhile Kate Theory has fallen in love with Georgina's first
husband and he is tempted to marry her and say nothing:
but hasn't done so for some years when the story ends.

Pandora (1885) of Utica is engaged to a fellow-townsman
whom she gets the President to make Minister to Holland. Her
effrontery and "push" are the amazement of Count Otto Vogel-
stein, of the Germany Embassy at Washington.

Mrs. Temperly (1887, as *Cousin Maria*), a wealthy New
Yorker, takes her three daughters to Paris. Her nephew,
Raymond, is in love with her daughter Dora, but the mother
has decided Dora is an old maid—or at least that she'll marry
off the two younger girls first. So Raymond must wait long
(though Dora cares for him) and perhaps will not get her at
all.

In *The Modern Warning* (1888)—also called *Two Countries*—Agatha Grice marries Sir Rufus Chasemore and returns
to America. Here her husband writes a book unfavorable to
our country, and Agatha is so afraid that it will shock her
brother Macarthy, that she begs him not to print it. On seeing
how set he is, however, she gives her consent, then takes poison.

The Patagonia (1888), a liner, is carrying the gossipy
narrator, his friend Mrs. Nettlepoint, her son Jasper and Mavis
Allen to Europe. Mavis is to meet a Mr. Porterfield at Liverpool and marry him. But she falls in love with Jasper, and
when he at last ceases to go about with her on the ship, she
slips over the side and leaves the narrator the task of breaking the news of her death to Porterfield.

The Reverberator (1888) is the title of an American paper
which causes a crisis in the lives of Francie Dosson, living
abroad with her well-to-do family, and of Gaston Probert, also
"over" with his, but thoroughly Gallicized. George Flack, Paris
correspondent of the *Reverberator*, who is running hard after
Francie, learns some secrets of the Probert family and prints
them as news. The Proberts, who don't want Francie one of

them anyway, now threaten in good earnest to break up the match, but unsuccessfully.

The worldly *Louisa Pallant* (1888) has many years since jilted the narrator. She now breaks off a budding affair between her icy-cold daughter Linda and the writer's nephew. Linda marries money, and the nephew, when the story ends, is like his uncle still a bachelor.

In *The Aspern Papers* (1888) Juliana Bordereau (Jane Clairmont) sits in an old palace in Venice with the memory of her love affair with the great poet Aspern (Byron). A young American comes to wheedle away her lover's letters; she coaxes money out of him for them, to provide for an old spinster niece.

In *The Lesson of the Master* (1888) Henry St. George fires Paul Overt with devotion to their art of novel writing; then, when Paul is consecrating himself abroad, marries Paul's *fiancée*, Miss Fancourt, whom Paul has earlier inspired with his enthusiasm for the Master.

In *The Liar* (1888) Oliver Lyon paints Sir David Ashmore, husband of a lady Oliver has once loved. He soon discovers that Sir David is an unconscionable liar, and so portrays him. When his wife sees the picture, she weeps; her husband cuts it to pieces; then says an old woman who has visited the studio destroyed it. His wife backs his story, and the painter sees that she, too, is now a liar.

In *The Solution* (1889) two young diplomats (American and French) play a trick on another young diplomat (from the West). They persuade him he should marry an English girl he has mildly compromised. But the young American diplomat's conscience hurts him, and he gets the woman he loves to break the affair off. She does, but she then marries the chivalrous Westerner instead of her lover.

In *A London Life* (1889) Laura Wing, an innocent American girl, is living with her sister and brother-in-law, an Englishman. They, especially her sister, are "fast," and Laura is much distressed over them and their neglect of their children. She keeps going about with Mr. Westover, a nice young American, and on being seen with him often, is, according to the rules of her day, compromised. So one evening, left alone in an opera box with him, she endeavors to get a declaration from him, obtains a very weak one, is heartily ashamed of herself, and runs off, avoiding him thereafter and returning to America. He follows, and may or may not win her, for he is now much interested, thanks in part to Lady Davenant, Laura's sister's mother-in-law, who is bent on the marriage.

The Pupil (1891), Morgan Moreen, is son of parents who carry their family about Europe, leaving debts everywhere. They get a tutor for him: he stays long with them in spite of receiving very little pay, for he likes the boy. But at last he takes another place—only to be summoned back. Presently the Moreens go quite bankrupt, and deliver Morgan over to the tutor to have always. Morgan is so glad that he dies of joy.

In *The Marriages* (1891) Adela Chant, reverencing the memory of her mother, works hard to prevent her father's marrying again. When he doesn't, it is largely through loyalty to his daughter, rather than to her mother.

The Chaperon (1891), Rose Tramore, is a beautiful girl who sets about restoring her discredited mother to society. She overcomes all opposition; and she marries Bertram Jay, who has been nice to her mother during the struggle.

Brooksmith (1891) is the name not of a country house but of a butler. The master of the house, Mr. Oliver Offord, dies, and the narrator encounters Brooksmith here and there as butler, then once as waiter: till he finally disappears, a remnant of a vanishing order.

Collaboration (1892) occurs between a German and a Frenchman—on an opera that will be startlingly good. But the Frenchman loses his French sweetheart because he has taken up with a German. Yet the author one day hears her picking out one of the German's tunes on the piano.

Sir Dominick Ferrand (1892) as *Jersey Villa* tells in

eighty-odd pages how a young writer buys an old davenport writing-desk; finds unpublished damaging letters in it by Sir Dominick Ferrand, is about to sell them, and discovers just in time that Mrs. Ryves, who lives in the same lodging-house and whom he admires, is Sir Dominick's natural daughter. Her little boy is a bright, real child, not like the later wise ones of James.

Lord Beaupré (1892), a desirable catch, has suggested to Mary Gosselin that, for his protection, they pretend an engagement. But her mother has anticipated them and spread it as a fact. Later Beaupré falls in love with Mary in earnest, but Mr. Bolton-Brown, American, makes off with her and leaves the noble lord to a cousin.

In *The Wheel of Time* (1892) Maurice Greywood runs off from the plain Fanny Knocker and marries. He brings back his motherless daughter Vera. Fanny meanwhile is a handsome widow with a son Arthur. Maurice now wants to marry Fanny, but she is giving all her life to her son. Then history partly repeats itself: Arthur, whom Vera loves, runs off from her, and she dies.

"He (Lord Mellifont) was all public and had no corresponding private life, just as Clare Vawdrey was all private and had no corresponding public one" is James's thesis for *The Private Life* (1892). The real Clare is found writing at his desk while the sham one is talking elsewhere; the real Lord Mellifont shines forever *with* people but is observed to vanish entirely when left alone (as he thinks) upon an open hillside.—Mrs. Adney, an actress, is trying to get at the real Clare, and while the narrator keeps the apparent one out walking, does find him in his study and does possess herself, apparently, of a great dramatic part from him—but only apparently. For the real and the sham— the public and the private in him—are never in harmony. (James felt some of this disparity in Browning and Meredith).

Sir Edmund Orme (1892) is a ghost that haunts Mrs. Marden, who had jilted him. Especially when her daughter is wooed does he show himself. The narrator is one of the wooers; he sees the ghost, too. But when Mrs. Marden dies, Sir Edmund departs, leaving the lovers in peace.

Nona Vincent (1892) is the heroine of a successful play by Allan Wayworth, a part inspired by and modeled in part on his friend Mrs. Alsager. Violet Grey is assigned the title role and fails in it. But the second night and thereafter she succeeds, for Mrs. Alsager comes to her and helps her by merely showing her herself. Violet and Allan marry at the end, as Mrs. Alsager intends—though she likes Allan much herself. There are a few subtle touches and some interesting remarks on the drama as a form.

Owen Wingrave (1893) is a young Englishman of military descent who is considered a coward by his loved ones because he wants to get out of the family profession of being a soldier. A girl in the house tells him he is afraid to sleep in a room haunted by a deceased murderer. He takes the dare; in the night the girl, screaming, rouses the household. Owen Wingrave is dead.

In *The Visits* (1893) Louisa Chantry wastes away of shame because she has declared her love to a man who has responded just to please her.

In *The Real Thing* (1893) an artist endeavors to use an impoverished major and his wife as models; but finds that the Real Thing is not they but Miss Churm, "a freckled Cockney" and Oronte, a fruit-vender.

Greville Fane (1893) is the pen name of Mrs. Stormer, whose life story the narrator (a journalist) tells with cleverness and bitterness. She is shown turning out reams of cheap and unseemly fiction, getting her daughter married to an insignificant title and assisting her son write novels. When she dies her precious children fight over the proceeds of such unpublished papers as they find in her desk.

The Middle Years (1893) concerns "poor Dencombe," a writer who holds his last book, a work of genius, in his hands but is unable to fathom its contents. He dies alone at the seaside, save for one friend.

The Coxon Fund (1894) is set apart by a Mrs. Coxon for the care of genius, and Mr. Saltram (whose resemblances to Coleridge are patent), is the first beneficiary. Under its provisions he is now so comfortable that he produces less than ever, and all the people who used to look after him suffer for lack of their old occupation.

The Death of the Lion (1894), Neil Paraday, occurs at one of the houses of Mrs. Weeks Wimbush, a celebrity-hunter. He has come to read from a new manuscript; but even that gets lost, so that the narrator, his ardent admirer, cannot publish it for him. In contrast to the Master appear "Guy Walsingham" and "Dora Forbes," successful writers and vulgarians, who are contrasted with the dying Paraday, now practically deserted.

In *The Next Time* (1895) Mrs. Highmore, sister-in-law of Ralph Limbert, is introduced as a writer of popular successes. The bulk of the story, however, goes to Ralph, who makes the barest living writing novels of high quality but of little market value. He *tries* to come down, but dies still writing well. A wife and children, with bills to be met, make the comedy of his fate a tragedy.

The Altar of the Dead (1895) is kept alight with candles by George Strassmore, in memory of his Dead. Before his shrine a woman kneels; she has loved Acton Hague, his enemy, once his friend, for whom he lights no candle. His refusal to do so parts them for a time: he is haunted by her need for one more. But in the end she is content with *his* number: only to have him sink in death beside her, a last candle for the Altar.

Glasses (1896) is told by a painter to whom Flora Saunt has sat and whose beauty conquers Lord Iffield and Geoffrey Dawling. Lord Iffield is eliminated, however, when she is forced sadly to wear glasses. Then much later the painter sees her in a box at the opera, comes to her and finds her blind, but with

Dawling, now her husband, ever at hand, and her beauty as great as ever. At times she sweeps the house with her opera glasses!

In *The Way It Came* (1896), also called *The Friends of the Friends*, the author finds a story among a dead woman's papers. Another woman has seen the ghost of her father in a picture gallery; a man has had a like experience with his mother at Oxford. The narrator thinks the two should meet, but time and again something prevents. Both know each other well by description, neither by photograph, for each, though handsome, refuses to be "taken." Then the narrator becomes engaged to the man and prevails upon *him* to be taken. The woman sees the photograph and the address of the man on its back; and once she almost encounters him, for the narrator aims to bring them together. As they are about to meet, though, fear and jealousy possess the narrator, and she prevents the encounter. But that night the woman comes to the man, remains speechless with him for a time, goes home, and dies. The narrator is made unequivocably aware that they love each other: that in death the woman returns to the man nightly. She breaks her engagement: the man lingers some years, then goes to join his dead love.

The Figure in the Carpet (1896) is the illusive design or purpose that underlies the fiction of Hugh Vereker (and Henry James). A critic writes an article on him; Vereker discovering him an author, tells him there is an intention in his work that people do not divine. Meanwhile Corvick, another critic, discovers the secret, but dies before revealing it to anyone except his wife Gwendolyn; who in turn dies without disclosing it to Drayton Deane, her second husband. The critic, who is telling the story, is left with no real clue and only one consolation— Deane is now fiercely wondering what Vereker (and James) is all about.

In *In the Cage* (1898) a telegraph operator who gets the love affair of a handsome Englishman through taking his messages, loves him herself, but marries Mr. Mudge, a grocer, while the Captain marries the subject of his affair, Lady Bradeen, whose husband dies opportunely.

In *Covering End* (1898) Clement Yule, heir to Covering End, may have it from Mr. Prodmore, mortgagee, if he'll marry Prodmore's daughter Cora and stand for Parliament on the Conservative side. But Cora loves another and Mrs. Gracedew loves Clement—so she pays off his mortgage and all live happily.

In *The Turn of the Screw* (1898) a governess and butler corrupt two children and then keep re-appearing to try to get them to join them in the other world. Their new governess is "the point of view." The children are amazingly clever in getting away from her and meeting their tempters. The girl, Flora, departs; the boy, Miles, defies the butler, but dies, as he does so, in the new governess's arms.

John Delavoy (1898) is a deceased author whom the editor of *The Cynosure* commissions a critic to write up and a sister (of Delavoy) to paint. He then refuses the critic's article—it is expository and will prove objectionable to readers because Delavoy wrote of Sex—and tries to get the sister to write a personal one instead. She declines and tries to call back her portrait; but it is given to the public, accompanied by an innocuous little study. The critic publishes *his* study in another magazine, but it attracts no particular attention.

The Great Condition (1899) is a worrisome tale of two young Englishmen who haven't met any women they care for in America, but who both fall in love with a Mrs. Damerel, an unattached American, on the way home. Both men suspect she has a past; she agrees to marry one of them on condition that he ask her nothing for six months thereafter. His faith is too weak: he goes off to Hawaii and California, trying to unearth something, but unsuccessfully. Meanwhile, the other man has married her, on the same condition—only he gives her a year. It turns out she has no past, but is enjoying her husband's exaltation over what he thinks his chivalry. (She tells this to the doubtful one).

"Europe" (1899) is another *Three Sisters*. A mother, Mrs. Rimmle, lives much in the memory of a trip to Europe she had taken in early days with her husband. Her spinster daughters hope to go, but the mother is forever falling ill—and recovering. At last one daughter breaks away and departs, the second dies and the third is left alone with her mother.

In *The Given Case* (1900) two women yield to lovers; but one is married, the other engaged,—the first to a man she hates, the other to one she dislikes. Yet the first will not get a divorce nor the second break her engagement: they will do no more for their lovers than admit they'll suffer without them, and with their husbands.

The Third Person (1900) is a smuggler ancestor of two old maiden ladies. He reappears in self-defense when the local vicar discovers that he has been hanged for his offenses.

Miss Gunton of Poughkeepsie (1900) is engaged to a Prince, but grows impatient because his mother fails to write to her. She sails to America and calls off the affair, though the Princess meantime has indited a letter. The narrator (Lady Champer) informs the Prince that Miss Gunton has inherited a large fortune and is going to marry Mr. Adam P. Bransby, an American.

Maud-Evelyn (1900) is told by a lady of some years who hoped that "Lavinia" and "Marmaduke" would marry. But when Marmaduke asked her and Lavinia refused, Marmaduke went traveling and presently took up with an English couple who had lost a daughter Maud-Evelyn. So under their sway he falls, that he even *marries* her, and then wears mourning for her and devotes the rest of his life to her memory. And he gets Lavinia to do the same! The parents have died now and left him their money; and presently when he dies, he leaves it to Lavinia.

In *The Great Good Place* (1900) George Dane, weary of

this world, its successes and its duties, has in for breakfast another Duty—a young man who, however, hypnotically wafts
him to the Great Good Place, where all is ordered and polished
—a Jacobean Paradise, a Christian Heaven. At the end of the
day Dane awakes.

The Tree of Knowledge (1900) discloses a sculptor who
believes himself an artist; his wife, who knows he isn't; and a
son.

In *The Tone of Time* (1900) Mary J. Tredick is commis-
sioned by a woman she has not seen to paint a portrait of one
dead, her husband, presumably. Mary paints with art and
hatred the image of a man she has once loved and whom another
woman has taken from her. When Mrs. Bridgenorth sees the
portrait she wants it so badly that she agrees (through the
narrator) to double the price. But the painter discovers that
her patron is the other woman and will not part with her work
to her rival. After both are dead, the narrator possesses himself of it, never learning the name of its original.

The Two Faces (1900) has to do with Mrs. Grantham, to
whom Lord Gwyther had paid attention, and his young bride.
Lord Gwyther asks Mrs. Grantham to induct his wife into London society. Mrs. Grantham makes her ridiculous by overload-
ing her with clothes. However, the bride's charming face and
her hard one are not lost on the company.

In *Paste* (1900) a young governess receives from her cousin,
a young man whose father and stepmother have just died, some
old jewelry of the latter, who was an actress before she married
a vicar. The governess produces her treasures later at Bleet
(where she has the care of several children) to let Mrs. Guy
use them in some theatricals. Mrs. Guy immediately discovers
that one piece, a string of pearls, is genuine. The girl returns
them to her cousin, who is much confused and vows they're
paste: that he will dispose of them, at least, as such. Later the
governess encounters Mrs. Guy wearing them: she has obtained
them from the young man, or, as she claims, from a shop in

Bond Street. He, knowing the pearls are real, knows that their genuineness reflects on the early morals of his stepmother.

In *The Real Right Thing* (1900) George Withermore begins the biography of Ashton Doyne, a deceased writer, working in the great man's study, fairly reliving his life and getting him down to the letter on paper. Then of a sudden the ghost of Doyne appears and lets the biographer know that he has left enough of himself for the world in his own writings.

In *The Abasement of the Northmores* (1900), Mrs. Hope, wife of a brilliant and unknown man, overshadowed in life by the pompous Northmore, has one copy of her husband's love letters to herself set up and printed that they may be given to the world after her death. Northmore's letters have just been published and show what a nobody he really was. After the world sees Hope's, his wife is certain what the verdict of posterity as to the two men will be.

Broken Wings (1900) presents a man and a woman, one a painter and the other a writer, each of whom discovers that the other is no longer successful, whereas it was in the old days each other's success that kept them apart. Hesitantly but inevitably they now come together, but with the words "And now to work!"

In *The Jolly Corner* (*c.* 1900?) Spencer Brydon returns to New York after thirty-three years in Europe. He amuses himself hunting himself as he might have been had he remained at home as a business man.

The Beldonald Holbein (1901) is (in portrait form) an American, Mrs. Brash, companion to Mrs. Beldonald, and successor to Mrs. Dodd, deceased. Mrs. Brash becomes so popular in London art circles for her beauty that Mrs. Beldonald ships her home, while *she* goes to the artist who all this time has been awaiting a sitting from her. The painter, however, is now likely to put more of her real character into her portrait than she bargains for.

Flickerbridge (1902) is one of those perfect old English places that James and his offspring adore. Frank Grainger, an

American artist, convalescing, is introduced by letter to Flickerbridge and itₛ charming hostess by Addie Wenham, to whom he
is halfway engaged. Suddenly news comes to him that she too
is coming from Paris to Flickerbridge. He flees—with its
memories.

The Papers (1903) is an endless "story" (it's more like a
tract) of two young writers, a man and a girl, in London, and
how newspaper publicity, through such as they, fairly screams
for some persons, like Sir A. B. C. Beadle-Muffet, and as in-
variably passes others by, like the shy but hopeful Mr. Marshal.

The Birthplace (1903) has some fun with the human frailty
of booming shrines. Morris Gedge and his wife are stationed
at the birthplace of England's greatest poet, and expected to
peddle exaggerations to the gullible visitor. At first Morris is
backward and ironical, and is reprimanded by the Board; later
he goes to the other extreme, and gets his salary raised.

Mrs. Medwin (1903) is to be engineered into society by
Mamie Cutter, social secretary, through the special favor of
Lady Wantridge. But Scott Cutter, big American brother,
turns up and sister is afraid the crude boy will upset things.
However, it is just he that Lady Wantridge likes, and through
him Mrs. Medwin gets invited into the charmed circle.

In *The Story in It* (1903) Colonel Vogt says that romance
implies a developed relation which cannot spell innocence. Mrs.
Blessingbourne takes the view that romance may consist in a
suppressed relation. She herself, we learn, has for the Colonel
just such an innocent feeling.

The Beast in the Jungle (1903) concerns a man who once
told a woman that he lived under a fear of some undefined
calamity. They meet again after a dozen years, and are constantly together, he, however, feeling only friendship for her.
She dies, but not before letting him know unmistakably that the
"beast" he fears has leaped upon him: the beast being the
realization that he is the one man of all time to whom nothing

is going to happen—and to whom ere she died his friend vainly offered herself.

The Special Type (1903) was Alice Dundene, with whom one Brivet went about some to give his wife cause for divorce, that he might marry Mrs. Cavenham. All is well: the wife marries someone else, the husband marries Mrs. Cavenham. Meanwhile Alice gets the narrator's portrait of Brivet—to live with alone, for she's never been alone with him alive. Mrs. Cavenham is ungrateful: she would have the picture, too, but the artist refuses her even a copy of it.

In *Fordham Castle* (1904) an American meets a country-woman at Geneva: *his* wife and daughter and *her* daughter are "getting in" at *Fordham Castle*. He is going under a false name, his wife under another. His countrywoman's daughter and his daughter are fellow climbers. A telegram comes saying that *her* daughter is to marry Lord Dunderton, and that *his* wife and daughter will be acceptable to them. She is now at liberty to go over to Fordham, and asks him if he'll come, too, if she sends for him: but he continues to say ironically that he's dead.

Julia Bride (1908), six times engaged and daughter of a woman three times divorced and living apart from her fourth husband, desires to marry the aristocratic Mr. French. She appeals to Mr. Pitman, one of her stepfathers, to aid her, but he, wanting in turn to marry Mrs. Drack and her millions, pre-vails on her to help *him* (Julia wants him to say *he* was in the wrong; *he* wants her to say her mother was in the wrong). She next meets with Murray Brush, the most serious of her old suitors: but Murray is now engaged to the perfect Miss Lin-deck, whom Julia fears. Murray wants her to arrange a meet-ing for all four: Julia sees how anxious he and his intended are to get in with French. She goes home from the Park (the story is laid there and in the Metropolitan Museum) and despairs; but is proud through it all of the wonderful French.

Crapy Cornelia (1909) is the unexpected figure that White-Mason walks in upon in Mrs. Worthingham's drawing-room. Though he has come to woo Mrs. W. he is fascinated by his old friend Cornelia and thereafter frequents *her* house.

In *The Bench of Desolation* (1909–10) Herbert Dodd, seller of prints and old books, and Kate Cookham become estranged; but to ward off a breach of promise suit, he agrees to pay her four hundred pounds. He marries, his wife and his children die, he is bankrupt, and only two hundred and seventy pounds are paid. He sits on a bench overlooking the sea. One day some-one else—no other than Kate Cookham—is there before him. She has invested his money and more than quadrupled it; she has always loved him; each has wrongly suspected the other of a transfer of affection.

In *A Round of Visits* (1910) Mark Monteith, returning from Europe, finds everybody nervous in New York. Mrs. Folliott and Mrs. Ash pour out troubles. Newton Winch, how-ever, seems more hopeful. Mark tells him why he has come over —to look into the case of Phil Bloodgood, who has absconded. At this Winch gets excited and confesses he is in the same plight. The bell rings, and, as officers enter, Winch kills himself.

The Velvet Glove (1910) concerns the sweet revenge of one Berridge, a literary lion, with whom Amy Evans flirts that she may get him to write a preface to one of her boring books. He appears to yield, but kisses her goodbye instead.

Mora Montravers (1910) leaves the dull household of her relatives, the Traffles, and establishes herself in the studio of Mr. Puddick. Mrs. Traffle offers to settle four hundred and fifty pounds a year on Mora if Puddick will marry her. He is embarrassed, but Mr. Traffle (whose drab life with Mrs. Traffle has been agreeably jarred by Mora) learns later that the two *are* now married. But Mora wishes to be free, gets the money settled on her husband and seeks a divorce so that she may marry Sir Bruce Bagley.

VII

As a novelist James leads off with *Gabrielle de Bergerac* (1869), a brief essay at historical fiction. An old French baron who has survived the Revolution tells how his aunt Gabrielle married his tutor Coquelin, against the wishes of her family and her suitor Vicomte de Trevil, only to die later, with her husband, among the Girondists. In *Watch and Ward* (1871) Roger Lawrence loses a woman he has never won, adopts Nora Lambert, a child of twelve, and in the end wins her, but not before her refusal of Hubert Lawrence (a cousin of Roger) has led to some complications, solved by Hubert's engagement to and marriage of Amy.—Then (in 1875) with *Roderick Hudson*, James becomes an international novelist. A rich American sends Roderick, a promising young sculptor temporizing with law, to Paris. His family feels that the life of an artist will be easy for him, but he is not up to its rigors and consecrations. And Christina Light, daughter of a scheming American woman and a worthless Cavaliere, gets him in her toils, from which even his mother and Mary Garland, and Christina's marriage to a Prince, do not fully extricate him. At the end, he falls over a cliff. In *The American* (1876–7) Christopher Newman, an American of means and worth, woos a French lady but is prevented from marrying her by her family. *Daisy Miller* (1878) is an independent American girl of much charm, who is dispatched by her creator because she has gone out after dark in Rome with a Roman; her American admirer learning from him what we all know well enough already—how innocent she is. *The Europeans* (1878) brings Eugenia, a morganatically married Baroness, and her brother Felix, a painter, back to New England to visit some cousins. Felix wins Gertrude; but Eugenia tells white lies and loses Robert Acton, for whom she would have sacrificed her noble husband. In *Confidence* (1879–80) Bernard Longueville, man of wealth, lover of Europe and amateur artist, marries Angela Vivian, also an American abroad. His boyhood friend Gordon Wright marries Blanche Evers. In *Washington Square* (1881) a plain girl, Catherine Sloper, is jilted by Morris Townsend when he discovers she will be disinherited if she marries him. Much later he returns, to be in turn rejected. *The Portrait of a Lady* (1880–81) is the divine semblance of Isabel Archer, who refuses good offers, American and English, and settles her affection and her wealth upon an apparently deserving object, Gilbert Osmond, an American expatriate of perfect taste and no means. In time she finds that Osmond, abetted by Madame Merle, his mistress, has married her for her money and that the two are further scheming for her to help marry Pansy, their child, to Lord Warburton, one of Isabel's rejected suitors. Isabel, horrified, leaves her husband—and returns to him. *The Bostonians* (1885–6) is a humorous picture of the New Woman movement in Boston, and the story of how Basil Ransom, a young Southerner, carries off Verona Tarrant, whom the suffragettes are hoping to wed exclusively to their cause. *The Princess Casamassima* (also 1885–6) is Christina Light again, now living apart from her husband, the Prince, but still enjoying his wealth. The "lead," however, is Hyacinth, son of a peer and an unfortunate milliner: in Hyacinth this double inheritance wars, for now he is attracted to the great, the cultured and the beautiful, now to the unfortunate and the poor. The Princess, also, and an English aristocrat or two, are revolutionary. But like Roderick Hudson, Hyacinth, assisted by the baleful Christina, goes to pieces. *The Tragic Muse* (1889–90) affords James opportunity to revel, as far as in him lay, in things theatrical. Miriam Rooth is an actress of ideals and attainment; in the end she marries, without sacrificing her career— but she does not marry Nick Dormer, the hero, who has abandoned politics for art. He is not much of a success,—but marries comfortably. *The Spoils of Poynton* (1897) are the beautiful possessions of Mrs. Gereth, who so fears that they will fall into the hands of some vulgarian her son Owen may marry, that she invites Fleda Vetch to her beautiful house and tries to throw this fine girl and Owen together. Owen, however, has his own favorite in Mona Brigstock. His mother now withdraws from Poynton to Ricks, and through Fleda negotiates for the transfer of some of the spoils: later, indeed, she gets the pick of them. Fleda feels sorry for Mona: indeed is most honorable throughout; for Owen now falls in love with *her* and she with him; but she bids him keep his word with Mona. Mrs. Gereth, meanwhile, has heard that her son is smitten with Fleda, so she returns the spoils to Poynton in the belief that Owen will now marry her favorite. But Mona, now that Poynton is itself again, experiences a revival of regard for Owen (it had died down with the absence of the Spoils), and fixes her wedding day. But in the end Poynton catches fire and the spoils burn.

In *The Other House* (1896) Rose Armiger lets the child Effie drown, so that Tony Bream may be utterly hers—and loses him. What *Maisie Knew* (1897) has for heroine the amiable, and for long unsuspecting child of divorced parents. These pass her back and forth for six-month periods; they are chiefly interested to know what the one may be saying of the other. Then Miss Overmore, a governess, is installed for the mother's six months; but at the end she transfers herself and her affections to the child's father. When Maisie returns to her mother a new governess, Mrs. Wix, is provided. Meanwhile Mamma is running about with Sir Claude,—and marries him. So does Miss Overmore marry—Maisie's father, Beal Farrange. Later still the mother, the new Lady Claude, welcomes a succession of lovers, as does her former husband a string of mistresses, settling finally upon Mrs. Cuddon. As for Maisie, through Sir Claude, who is a decent fellow, Maisie goes to live with Mrs. Wix, her young eyes at last opened to the wickedness of her parents—and the whole crowd. *The Awkward Age* (1898–99) stars a somewhat more sophisticated child than Maisie—Nanda Brookenham, who is growing to be a young lady and before whom her mother and her intimates now hesitate to speak frankly. Besides, we have Aggie and her husband, Vanderbank, whom Mrs. Brookenham wants for herself and whom Nanda likes and doesn't get, and Mitchy Langdon, a rich old fellow with high character who in the end adopts Nanda. In *The Sacred Fount* (1901) a week-end visitor to Newmarch finds that the brilliant Mrs. Brissenden is absorbing the life and youth of her husband. He then looks around to see why Gilbert Long, once so surly and unintelligent, is now all fire. The attractive but mentally drained May Server, and not Lady John, is finally discovered to be his sacred fount; only the narrator is loth to believe ill of this lady, who somehow enchants him. *The Wings of the Dove* (1902) opens with Kate Croy and Merton Densher, lovers, and English, and with Mrs. Lowder, Kate's rich aunt, who has adopted her and presently chooses Lord Mark as her future husband. But Kate plots to marry Densher, a poor journalist, and still have money. Enter now the means thereto, and the real heroine—Milly Theale, a rich and ailing American girl. Kate, Mrs. Lowder and Mrs. Stringham make much of her; they throw Densher, to whom she is strongly attracted, in her way. Kate's scheme, of course, is for Densher to marry Milly so that upon her early death he will have her money and can then marry *her*. Milly leaves him her money *without* his marrying her; but Densher is through with the nefarious Kate. In *The Ambassadors* (1903), Lambert Strether, a middle-aged American, has been sent over to Europe by Mrs. Newsome, a wealthy widow, to break off an affair her son Chad Newsome is having with Madame de Vionnet and to win him back to America and his interests there. But influenced by Maria Gostrey, a Europeanized American, Madame de Vionnet herself, who is winsome and beautiful, and by Chad, Strether insensibly but surely gives way, surrenders his Puritanism and Americanism and is only sorry he is not European as these charming people are. He returns to New England content to leave Chad in his immoral but beautiful life; even though he, Strether, has, in failing in his mission,

lost the hand of Mrs. Newsome. In *The Golden Bowl* (1904)
Maggie Verver (married to Prince Amerigo) and Mr. Verver,
her father (married to Charlotte Stant), are confronted with
the problem of how, politely and genteelly, to go about breaking
off an affair between the Prince and Charlotte. Maggie is not
only a noble and wellbred person; she is also adroit. In the
end she gets her father and Charlotte off to America, and peace
presumably reigns in two households. *The Outcry* (1911) is
raised in England over the projected sale to an American of a
great English picture. Its owner, Lord Theign, is determined
to sell it: his daughter Kitty owes card debts. But Hugh
Crimble, the *connoisseur* who has started the outcry, loves Lady
Grace, the younger daughter, and diverts the attention of Mr.
Bender, a rich American dealer, from the famous picture to a
rare Montovano, thus saving the international situation and
winning Lady Grace. In the unfinished *The Sense of the Past*
(1917) the author evokes Ralph Pendrel, a New Yorker with
a craving for Europe, who is about to marry Aurora Coyne,
who feels she must live in America. Just then a cousin Pendrel
in England is found to have left Ralph a family house in London. Ralph goes over, exchanges identities with a long *deceased*
cousin (who had always craved things modern) and begins living the life of the eighteenth century, including the wooing of
Molly. But an unsuspected sister, Nan, appears and so charms
Ralph that he grows discontented with the thought of living for
good in the past with Molly. In the end, James would have
rescued him for the *present*, aided by Nan, Aurora and an
ambassador (i.e., James Russell Lowell). *The Ivory Tower*
(1917) survives in part complete, in part in elaborate notes. It
is laid in America (Newport and New York, with Boston or
California later, perhaps), and was the result of the author's
final visit here. Graham Fielder, whom Rosanna Gaw had persuaded, some years since, to remain in Europe rather than
return to America to be brought up by his rich uncle, now does
return, to be made his uncle, Mr. Betterman's heir, to find Mr.

Gaw, his uncle's partner estranged from his old associate, and to further find Rosanna still devoted to him, Graham. Cissie Foy, however, is destined to attract him; but she and Horton Vint are in together to fleece him. Whether Rosanna and he will at last be united is somewhat uncertain; her great wealth may stand in the way—and his own lukewarmness. Ezra Pound and Pelham Edgar both give the book and its notes considerable attention and analysis.

VIII

James was all wrought up over the War and became an English citizen in 1915 because we came in too slowly. "His most devoted contribution to the war had been the sacrifice of his artistic life," says Pelham Edgar. During his last illness he summoned Miss Bosanquet. "He then proceeded," continues Mr. Edgar, "to dictate as of yore what purported to be an autobiographic relation of episodes in the great Napoleon's life. The fragment contains a letter couched in the genuine Imperial style, succinct and dictatorial, with comment in the most highly developed Jamesian manner on the complexities of the Napoleonic problem."

But if this remains unpublished, we have his affectionate Preface to *The Letters from America* of Rupert Brooke, and his *Within the Rim and Other Essays* (1914–15). He is impressed by Brooke as in the best sense modern. "This ideal image of English youth at once radiant and reflective . . . expressed us *all*, at the highest tide of our actuality." *Within the Rim* thrills with his love for lovely England. At Lamb House, Rye, he looks forth on that Channel across whose waters is happening *that*. He is glad for our Civil War—glad to have had it to familiarize him with the calamity loosed upon the world. That this England he adored, that he had made his life, that now *was* his life, should be destroyed or even shaken—

unthinkable! His love for every English person—that England
that had made his days sweet—how it glows and shines! And
then, at the end of the little essay he looks west to his own
countrymen—"on the whole unquenchable association" of England and America, on which the enemy had "laid his unholy
hands." *The Long Wards* is an appeal to America for ambu-
lances, a measured eulogy of France, and a meditation on men
in hospitals. *Refugees in Chelsea* (final paragraph) is about
refugees in Rye, and is one of the finest things the War has
called forth. "The resonance through our immemorial old
street of her sobbing and sobbing cry was the voice itself of
history," he says of a young mother. And the picture of the
English gathering her in, and the others, and whisking them to
safety *and out of sight*—well, James knew what it was to have
English hearts about him, too, and English eyes that stared
not. "On the 28th February, 1916," says one of them finely
(Rebecca West in *Henry James*), "he died, leaving the white
light of his genius to shine out for the eternal comfort of the
mind of man."

IX

There are the usual critical differences of opinion over James.
"His greatest appeal is perhaps to those whose lives have yielded
the minimum of realization," says Joseph Warren Beach in
The Method of Henry James, after pointing out that the combi-
nations of good taste, social grace and spiritual discernment
were desired by him, and that for subjects he liked things slight,
off the common track and neglected. "In James," says Ezra
Pound in *Instigations*, "the maximum sensibility, compatible
with efficient writing was present." Yet "there was titanic volume, weight, in the masses he sets in opposition within his work.
. . . His art was great art as opposed to overelaborate or over-
refined art by virtue of the major conflicts which he portrays.
In his books he showed race against race, immutable;—the

essential Americaness, or Englishness or Frenchness—why men
of different races are not the same. . . . And this communication is not a leveling, it is not an elimination of differences. It
is a recognizing of differences, of the right of differences to exist,
of interest in finding things different." "Only an American who
has come abroad will ever draw all the succulence from Henry
James's writings," adds Pound. Which may lead to some
remarks from *Expatriate—Vintage 1927* by Louis Bromfield in
The Saturday Review of Literature, March 19, 1927:

"It was Henry James, himself so thoroughly of that era of
snobs and expatriates, who set down the tragic story of one of
those American girls who, brought to Europe by an ambitious
and vulgar mother, languished and died in Rome. It is a beautiful story, fixing an epoch and a type, but one couldn't do it
today because even by searching Europe with a microscope, one
couldn't find a Daisy Miller. And she couldn't fall a victim to
malaria in Rome because American sanitary methods have done
away with malaria. It is unromantic, to be sure, and hard upon
novelists looking for the aid of malaria in·their romances, but
Rome is almost clean and if Mussolini succeeds in evading bullets
long enough he will, in his energetic American way, perhaps make
certain quarters smell less like a garbage can from which the
lid has just been lifted.

"If one were to set down the history of the Daisy Miller of
today, one would probably find the young creature alone in
Europe, roaming about, freed of the ambitious and vulgar
mother. She would be quite on her own, clad in a minimum of
clothing, all cut in the most beautiful style by Chanel or
Vionnet or Lanvin, with shingled hair and an air of independence and *savoir faire* sufficiently strong to rout whole regi-
ments of Roman noblesse. One is likely to see her entering the
bar at the Ritz or Ciro's, more elegantly dressed than the best
of Parisian demi-mondaines (who are as a rule the best dressed
women in France save for their sisters among the noblesse who
have similar leanings). One would see her tossing off the cock-
tail which marks the beginning of her day—a steel-clad Diana,
the confusion of European men who cannot fathom the manners

of a demi-mondaine in the body of an Artemis. As to the Italian dukes and princes—they come just the same seeking her fortune, but the new Daisy Miller is not easy. "Why," she asks herself with brutal realism, "shall I marry that wop?"

At any rate anyone who has lived abroad for a month or a day can *not* agree with Professor Pattee [5] (though he has lived there much longer) that James wrote without a message, for he paints the Europe that ostensibly collapsed—the corrupt and overcivilized part of it—with the War.

James's work was not "a thing alone of the intellect" (I find myself still attempting to counter Professor Pattee's criticisms). Repression of feeling does not signify total lack of it. His letters and war essays show how deeply he felt; we contrast their expression at once with his usual repression.

"You can't be a great artist without a great passion," says Professor Pattee. But James *had* a great passion—Europe! [6] and the upper classes of Europe, which he liked but by no means always lauded in his fiction. Their acts in his books often convict them out of hand.

James does not, as Professor Pattee would have us think, make only perfect external likenesses and fail to reach the springs of life. How can one of the world's three or four foremost psychological novelists fail to get below the surface? Sometimes he gets too far to keep us comfortable: certainly he gets far.

Surely the criticism that James has not felt what he observed does not sweep over the *whole* of his fiction, as his critic declares. Again, his undoubted conviction (except in California, whose beauty enchanted him) of the unsuitability of America as a residence for persons of culture, has done America good. We are raised not alone by praise. Finally James's "last manner" is not classicism at all; it is the most arrant modernism; a veritable futurism that is, of a verity, overstrained. So much

[5] *American Literature Since 1870.*
[6] After the war started he had a mistress, says Violet Hunt—France. His work was his passion, according to Miss Bosanquet.

for Professor Pattee: who, it is only fair to add, is fairer to James in his *The American Short Story*.

Action, in the sense of anybody's doing anything, is singularly rare in Mr. James's *nouvelles*," says Ford Madox Ford,[7] "but what the French call *progression d'effet* is never absent from the almost apparently negligible of them." His stories are stories, he continues, not sketches or studies. The "treatment of mental progression" is rare in fiction, that is all, but common in him. Ford finds him a master of Impressionism.— Elisabeth Luther Cary says his aim is tactile values plus the greatest amount of spiritual truth. As for his women, Mr. Howells grew lyric over them: "No other novelist," says he [8] (ignoring Meredith, as usual), "has approached Mr. James in his appreciation of women and in his ability to suggest the charm which is never wholly absent from them, whether they are good, bad or indifferent in looks or in behavior."

Clever and independent observations on James crowd M. Abel Chevalley's *The Modern English Novel* (translation by Ben Ray Redman, 1926). James was "a reversed Christopher Columbus"; he became a *bourgeois* of cultivated Europe; his novels are "built and scaffolded with the solidity of a scientific work"; the first portion of his work displays social conflict between the New World and the Old; the second, almost entirely, that between the Victorian Age and the new generation of Edward VII. As for his psychology, "his psychology, apparently profound and learned, is really superficial." It *has* been overrated by some, as it has been underrated by others.

Edmund Wilson, in *The Exploration of James* (*New Republic*, Mar. 16, 1927), says that while James was bold in some ways he yet wrote his fiction under heavy inhibitions, the result both of personal shyness and the peculiar moral timidity of his race and day" . . . James and his

[7] *Henry James.*
[8] Introduction to *Daisy Miller* (Modern Library).

spectator-narrators, says he, are spectators, not doers, and his women are sensitive and intelligent. The critic thinks his real psychology lies beneath the lines. "At bottom, James was as scientifically modern and as 'tough-minded' as his brother William." Mr. Wilson sees quite a bit of sex repression in James and his people—but thinks him conscious of it. *Was* he especially? At least that repression didn't come hard to him. Expression of it was harder. "Without accidents he had loved her, without accidents everyone had loved her; she had made the passions about her as regular as the moon made the tides," is George Strassmore's memory of Mrs. Kate Creaton in *The Altar of the Dead.*

x

We have seen (to return from our brief excursion among James's critics) that James could write a biography on occasion, turn out a fair reading play (one of them, *Tenants*, should also act well), paint distinguished literary portraits, write interestingly of his travels in Europe and America, show great enthusiasm for Art and its theories, especially as applied to fiction, compose glowing letters, display a real feeling for British politics, and live in the present and pray for the future of England.

But it is as a writer of stories and novels, national, international and Anglo-Saxon, that he lives. In *The Special Type* (1903) the painter-narrator says, "I cared only to be out of it. I may as well say at once, however, that I never *was out* of it; for a man habitually ridden by the twin demons of imagination and observation is never—enough for his peace—out of anything." Can't one see James looking, imagining, seeing stories everywhere just crying out to be told—stories not of everyday happenings, but of happenings that don't "get happened"—to society people, artistic people, retired persons, disturbing American girls, noble American women? And as he grew older be became more and more a stately time spirit, stopping, looking, listening, dictating, recording.

In *Nona Vincent* (1892) he observes that "the dramatic form had a purity which made some others look ingloriously rough. It had the high dignity of the exact sciences, it was mathematical and architectural. It was full of the refreshment of calculation and construction, the incorruptibility of line and law." There you have James in so many of his stories: he works like a mathematician soberly solving a problem, or a philosopher giving laborious thought to Truth, or a modeler shaping shapeless clay, or a painter evoking a picture out of a blur of pigments; but seldom, how seldom, as a mere straightforward narrator or describer. Someone calls Santayana an artist in philosophic revery. We might say James is a philosopher or scientist in artistic revery. He walks round and round an idea, however small, examining it from many angles with field glasses. Why did so and so do so and so? Come, let us not be obvious: she did it for some reason not too farsighted—nor too simple. Verily James posits his own world and his people are all caught in it. Do they ever get free and act quite naturally? Always, always he is directing them. He is the prompter at an opera he has written: there are his voice and his hands telling them what to do and think: *pointing* them what to do. A sort of servitude for his people—a devotion demanded of his reader. One's mind must never slip: every sentence grows out of every other; every paragraph out of every other; and ever that insistent voice demanding attention, seldom epigrammatic, seldom witty, rarely humorous.

The evolution of James as a novelist has been clearly enough pointed out, technically speaking, by Mr. Beach in *The Method of Henry James*. In our own study, we have seen him passing from historical romance to American artists, business men and

American girls and women abroad—to a weak American like
Roderick Hudson, a strong and straightforward one like
Christopher Newman, an innocent one like Daisy Miller, a
scheming one like Christina Light, an adorable one like Isabel
Archer, a pathetic one like Milly Theale, a good and *able* one
like Maggie Verver. In America itself, we have Catherine Sloper
of Washington Square, jilted but unbroken, and some charming
expatriated Americans returning in *The Europeans*. Then we
have the English stage in *The Tragic Muse*, and the effect of
beautiful worshipped *things* in *The Spoils of Poynton*, and
stark tragedy in *The Other House*, and the effect of European
high life on the child Maisie and the girl Nanda Brookenham,
and the question of English ancestral possessions passing to
Americans in *The Outcry*, and the giving way to European
morals as opposed to ours in *The Ambassadors*, and the rescu-
ing for the present of a dweller in the past in *The Sense of the
Past*, and the case of two pleasant Americans, man and woman,
whom a second pair are bent on fleecing in *The Ivory Tower*.
And even so, there are the humors of *The Bostonians*, the
intricacies of *The Sacred Fount*, and the background of English
social change in *The Princess Casamassima*.

London, Paris, Rome, New York! This great writer of fiction is at home in all of them, and so are his creations. He
wrote twenty-three novels. And they are not always of cities.
His countrysides are justly famous.

His short stories number one hundred and nine: I think
there are no more to be accounted for! And artificial as the
classification is, I have been interested to view them by decades.
His stories begin in 1865 and close in 1910.

Needless to say his 1860 period is youthful, even naïve. *The
Story of a Year* (1865) [9] and *A Light Man* (1869) are in-
credibly so: as for subject matter, we have the Revolutionary
War, a family curse, avenging ancestors, fortune tellers'
prophecies, capricious boys and girls, quite a bit of dying for

[9] About "Elizabeth (as I shall not scruple to call her outright)."

love; but also, in *The Story of a Masterpiece* (1868), a painter story; and already in 1866, in *A Day of Days,* a hero off to Europe for Culture, or perhaps more accurately, for study. The stories number twelve.

Those for the 70's total twenty-one. Of these *Guest's Confession* and *Professor Fargo* are pleasantly American, and *The Ghostly Rental* (like *The Romance of Certain Old Clothes*) harks back to Hawthorne. But otherwise Europe is italicized and capitalized. *Travelling Companions, At Isella* and *The Passionate Pilgrim* lead the way in 1871: *Master Eustace, Madame de Mauves, Adina, Four Meetings, Rose-Agathe, A Bundle of Letters,* and *The Diary of a Man of Fifty* follow. And *An International Episode* has charming New York and Newport scenes through British eyes, and English scenes through American eyes.

In the 80's European scenery (*or* American) is not emphasized quite so much *as* scenery. Europe and America are now stages for stories that become more human, more dramatic; at times even tragic. Yet the first story, *The Point of View* (1882), is full of opinions on Europe and America. But *The Impressions of a Cousin,* brimming as it is with New York, is more interested in plot than in atmosphere. And the Texas heroine of *The Siege of London* lives. So does the scheming *Mrs. Temperly. A New England Winter, The Path of Duty, The Reverberator, The Liar* and *The Solution* are well plotted. True, *A London Life* is silly, *Georgina's Reasons* are strained and *The Modern Warning* is overdone; but *Lady Barbarina* and *Pandora* are jolly. And there is poignancy in the endings of *The Reverberator, Louisa Pallant, The Author of Beltraffio* and *The Lesson of the Master.* The stories are nineteen in number.

Twenty-eight stories adorn the 1890's. Here James shines in full glory. We have the James child in *The Pupil,* to open the decade, and the tragedy of the three sisters shut away from *Europe* to close it. We have French-German relations in

a music story, *Collaboration,* the passing of the English butler
in *Brooksmith,* a sort of Hawthorne reversion in *Sir Dominick
Ferrand,* and schemings and counter-schemings in *The Mar-
riages, The Chaperon, Lord Beaupré* and *Covering End.* In
The Wheel of Time history repeats itself; while in *The Visits*
James has a return of pity for a girl who has made love to a
man: she must die. And ghosts are loose in this decade. *Sir
Edmund Orme* is a rather nice ghost. A bad ghost gets *Owen
Wingrave* and punishes thereby a girl and his family. Ghosts
motivate *The Way It Came,* and a ghost concludes it. *The
Turn of the Screw* has those two infamous ghosts and the two
English children they still pursue. Then in *The Private Life*
artists are examined, as they are, and as they appear; in *Nona
Vincent* an actress is taught to act by an enlightened rival in
the dramatist's affections; in *The Real Thing* models are
studied; in *Greville Fane* a hack writer is redeemed by devotion
to her children; in *The Middle Years* a pathetic writer is viewed
in his dotage; in *The Coxon Fund* a modern Coleridge is
analyzed; in *The Death of the Lion* a writer is pictured dying
neglected; in *The Next Time* a writer is worried to death writing
masterpieces that don't pay bills; in *The Figure in the Carpet*
an author's intent puzzles and tantalizes person after person;
in *John Delavoy* a dead writer is resurrected who has dared to
write of Sex. Meanwhile *The Great Condition* wins its case for
a woman, in spite of appearances: I mean she doesn't even die!
Finally, *The Altar of the Dead, Glasses* and *In the Cage* are
intensely fine work, the first poetic, the second pathetic, the
third dramatic *and* pathetic—a pathos noble and chastened,
though, and with even a touch of humor.

From 1900 to 1910, his final period as a short story writer,
James published twenty-eight pieces. Twelve of these are dated
1900, and one, *The Jolly Corner,* about a New Yorker returning
from Europe after thirty-three years, is, presumably, to be
placed about that year. In this 1900 group appear a pleasant
story (except for him) of a rather vain and hasty girl and a

more conscientious prince—in *Miss Gunton of Poughkeepsie,* a self-deceived artist in *The Tree of Knowledge,* a skit in *Maud-Evelyn,* a vision of a better world in *The Great Good Place,* a portrait study in *The Tone of Time,* a dramatic contrast of two women in *The Two Faces,* the adventures of several people and some old jewelry in *Paste,* a new ghost in *The Real Right Thing,* a noble picture of a wife's devotion to an unappreciated husband in *The Abasement of the Northmores,* and two middle-aged "successful" artists in *Broken Wings.* The remaining years of the decade are made notable by *The Beldonald Holbein:* besides, James stars English country places in *Flickerbridge* and *Fordham Castle* and laughs at tourist shrines in *The Birthplace* and at journalism in *The Papers.* Finally, *Mrs. Medwin* gets engineered into society; *The Beast in the Jungle* is fear and futility; *The Bench of Desolation* brings two troubled souls together and to peace; and *A Round of Visits, Julia Bride* and *Crapy Cornelia* do their bits for the American scene.

XI

After so many summaries one need hardly further labor the point that James could plot: his stories, if one will be patient with them, always have story.—His people have a few objects in life, too: to win someone for husband or wife, to get away from marrying someone, to abandon (rarely) someone one has already married. Then there is Money, a fairly Balzacian if not Zolaesque pursuit of Gold, chiefly in Europe, not by right of American conquest but by way of American bequest. But social prestige, climbing to Fordham Castle, towers over every thing else. Oh, to be in with the best people of Europe and to live in their beautiful country houses! No wonder Chevalley calls James *bourgeois* and Rebecca West once nearly spells him Jeams. But "granted his *donnée,*" what modern has combined plot, character, purpose, art, better? No one denies him his Scene, and a score of his characters live. His plots tantalize one, if nothing more, into having patience with him to know "how they'll turn out." And for that fullness of life he sought he had to be *bourgeois*. Compare him with Turgenev. Turgenev keeps aristocratic, but his range suffers. And James, not being a Turgenev lover, just couldn't have written love novel after love novel of the poignancy of Turgenev's. Nor had he the epic sweep of the aristocrat peasant Tolstoy, nor his intense convictions and fanaticisms. And lacking Meredith's comedy, he couldn't stand laughing at men's follies; nor could he paint them a more glowing future. It was his time he wanted to leave —"a multitude of pictures of my time"—a certain value accruing from the very number of his pictures as observation and testimony, to revert to his opening words in his paper, and it is noticeable how little he repeated.

Love is a motive force in him, not a passion. James in a tumult is unthinkable. As for his psychology, that is the psychology of his people, of ordinarily cultivated persons systematically studied. I have said in a book on Meredith that Meredith's psychology is applied, James's, pure—in the sense that Meredith had the object, always, of improving the present for the future, James no further end than of painting the present for the future. Meredith was a reformer, James a recorder. But if his psychology is "pure," it is not laboratory psychology. His subjects do not just yield themselves aimiably to experimentation. They perform not for Professor William James, psychologist at Harvard, but for Henry James, novelist of New York, London, Rome and Paris. And he is one of them. For when I complained on an earlier page that he was forever directing his people, I failed to add that they are as much directing him. His is a delectable slavery. To say with Professor Pattee that "he studied life without contacts with life and he recorded what he saw, himself as totally detached from his material as if it were a laboratory record," is to exaggerate his impersonality. For slily he *tells*. *They* are clever or good or bad or unusual or commonplace, all together, and he with them is en-

gaged in the game of European society. Author and fellow-
characters interpret one another from acts, but as much from
hints. His characters are so often hiding themselves away.
They are close-mouthed. They tantalize with monosyllables:
their author follows them up with an army of explanatory poly-
syllables (or he does in *one* manner). What do they mean?
can I penetrate beneath their polished surfaces? asks their
creator. Who are their real loves? Where are their real selves?
What is in their hearts? What only in their scheming heads?
How much real feeling, honor, beauty, grace, culture have these
people? How much are they just playing games to better themselves financially or socially?

His Americans especially are always interesting us. His
older Americans abroad, especially his men, are likeable enough,
with sometimes a touch of pathos. His goodly company of
artists over there with nieces (or daughters) are agreeable
travelers and climbers: they are much the same as at home.
But his *young* women? I seem to note a difference there. His
girls in *America* are capricious, changeable and unaccountable.
But in Europe they are constant: the Europeans are now the
fluid ones. One thinks of Isabel Archer (who first had to get
rid of her American girlishness), of Maggie Verver, of Milly
Theale. And Christopher Newman is a young male of the
species. And James is all against the unconventional woman,
at home or abroad. That sort ruin their own lives and hurt
their men: they are not swept by love, or excused as evolving,
or studied with affection or sympathy: they just plainly or
frankly come to a bad end, or if they succeed and then reform,
they at least get no bespiced and perfumed coat of whitewash
from *him*. He can't let himself adore such people: he doesn't,
from his own country, yet he studies doubtful Europeans with
zest if not approval.

Such is our "bachelor novelist." There is much unrequited
love in him, many bachelors and old maids,—inevitably, for he
was much of each himself. And he apparently loved his own

cousin best, the original of Milly Theale. Cousins, male and female, appear even oftener in him than in Poe. There are rival cousins in *Watch and Ward:* in *The Portrait of a Lady* Isabel Archer numbers a cousin among her admirers: in *The Europeans* two cousins marry and two others don't: in *The Sense of the Past* there is an exchange of identities between two men cousins, one dead. *A Passionate Pilgrim* has two distant living cousins and more that are dead. In *The Album* there are two male cousin heirs: in *A Change of Heart* two cousins of opposite sex: in *Four Meetings* a cousin abroad gets his American cousin's money away from her: in *Longstaff's Marriage* two ladies abroad are cousins: in *An International Episode* two English cousins visit America together: and *Lord Beaupré* marries a cousin, having lost the woman he loved.

There you are: bachelors, old maids, cousins, exotic rarefied children, subtle Continentals, simplified Americans (but how complex and complicated when they become Europeanized!); and in addition to these special types, perfectly normal persons, American and European. A civilized society,—with some primitive traits: an author of beautiful kindness who yet believes in Empire and War!

Perhaps for the good of his stories James got too much interested in the drama and in fiction as Art. His longing to be dramatic makes him less natural as he grows older. And his predilection for Art grew so strong that he became almost more interested in that than in life.[10] The ponderosity of his later sentences and the attenuation of some of his scenes will remain long the amazement of mankind, futuristic or otherwise. However, that's the way he grew, from the very simple to the fairly complex: and underneath it all, he is telling a story, painting his time, creating men and women. Who ever yet has quite fathomed him, exhausted his genius? The answer to that is,

[10] Van Wyck Brooks would have it that he grew so disillusioned with people, English and American, that he withdrew into his Ivory Tower. But why try to make out that if he had lived his life in America he wouldn't have retired into an even higher and thicker one?

who has ever fathomed Europe, America, England, New York, California, or Gopher Prairie? "Can we draw out Leviathan with a hook, or his tongue with a cord which we let down?" asks the brilliant director of *The Pilgrimage of Henry James.* Fathom any race, nation, city or individual to its last nerve and tissue, and you have sounded Henry James. Not that he did that much himself: but certainly he labored at it, in his fashion.

THE STORIES AND NOVELS OF FRANK STOCKTON

SIR ARTHUR T. QUILLER-COUCH remarks in his *Adventures in Criticism* that the stories of Stockton "only need time to ripen them into classics. . . . Originality, good temper, good sense, moderation, wit—these are classical qualities: and he is a rare benefactor who employs them all for the amusement of the world." Moreover his stories seem to him "the most genuinely American things in American fiction."

On the other hand Professor Fred Lewis Pattee, in his fascinating *American Literature since 1870*, has the following disconcerting observations:

"It is undoubtedly true that Stockton's personality was so interfused with his writings that the generation who knew him and loved him were too kind in their judgments. Behind his every story they saw the genial, whimsical creator and they laughed even before they began to read. But a new generation has arrived to whom Stockton is but a name and a set of books, and it is becoming more and more evident that very much that he wrote was ephemeral. . . .

"Stockton, indeed, is one of the half dozen writers of the period to whom may be applied the now old-fashioned term stylist. There is grace and character in his every sentence, a dignity despite the whimsical content that never descends to vulgarity or to what James has termed 'newspaperese'. . . . Instead of using dialect and curious provincial types, he dealt always with refined gentle folks amid surroundings that seem to have little to do with the actual, solid earth. . . . He was content to be a mere entertainer, aware undoubtedly that the entertainment that delights one generation all too often is obsolete in the next."

What is Stockton, then, an American classic, or an obsolete entertainer? If he is little read today, that might argue him either. But are not Aristophanes, Lucian, Petronius and Pope both classic and neglected? (No invidious comparisons intended). And is Stockton little read?

Enter at this point Professor Edwin W. Bowen, contributing to the *Sewanee Review,* July-September, 1920, a study entitled *The Fiction of Frank R. Stockton.* Professor Bowen's tone is not in the least controversial: he takes Stockton's permanence, in some of his work, for granted, and his popularity, again in part, as unquestioned. *Rudder Grange,* he says, is still selling well, with *The Late Mrs. Null* or *Kate Bonnett* second, and with *The Lady or the Tiger?* among his short stories, easily first.

Professor Bowen points out Stockton's "kinship to Lowell and Holmes as against Brown and Clemens." Later he shows how Stockton, though with a Defoe-like realism, lives in a world of his own, that illogical realm in which things nevertheless happen so logically. "His characters," says he, "are, without exception, moral men and women who are strict observers of the decalogue, who nevertheless have no compunctions about breaking the great commandment of realism."—"In truth," said a reviewer in the *Atlantic* in 1901, "Mr. Stockton is really an exceedingly clever juggler, who rolls up his sleeves, places his apparatus under a calcium light, puts on an innocent face, deprecates the slightest appearance of deception and then performs his extraordinary feats. There is a nimbleness of movement, an imperturbable air, and the thing is done." . . . Yet "where, indeed, in our literature shall we find such a body of honest humor, with its exaggeration deep in the nature of things, and not in the distortion of the surface? The salt which seasons it, and may be relied on to keep it wholesome, is the unfailing good humor and charity of the author."

Writing back in 1900, in Vol. XX of the *Bookbuyer,* Mr. Howells declares himself frankly unable, or unwilling, to

dissect the genius of his friend. "Never was a personality more
elusive, more shrinkingly reluctant from the approaches of
analytical criticism," says he. "You feel yourself hopelessly
baffled by this aroma, this pervasive essence, this subtle prin-
ciple. . . . He is of the last refinement." If the world is forgetting him, then the world is missing something rare, and should
be reminded. "He carried his fooling to an extravagance
and tenuity which have punished him with impermanence," says
Carl Van Doren in *The American Novel*, "the fate, indeed, of
most lighter comedy. But in his three or four genuine successes
he achieved more with merry farce than any other American
novelist."

There is very little written about Stockton personally. His
wife contributed a charming sketch and appreciation to *The
Captain's Toll-Gate* and to the last volume of the Shenandoah
edition of his works, and E. F. Harkins' *Little Pilgrimages*,
1902, is instinct with the spirit of the gentle story-teller. He
had been criticized, according to Mr. Harkins, for being igno-
rant of the way young people make love. "It is much more to my
liking," Stockton is quoted as replying, "to write about middle-
aged women than young women. The older ones have more character; you can make them do most amusing things." Stockton
was born in Philadelphia, lived for three years in Bucks County,
was brought back to the city for schooling and graduated
from the Central High School there. First cause for gentle-
ness, then. Then both his mother and wife were Southerners;
he lived latterly in West Virginia; he understood Southerners
and darkies—gentle people all to this gentleman. But his
"creations" are apt to be middle-aged New England women:
so he should have New England blood in him; but I do not find
that he had. His father was a religious writer, and at least one
of his brothers was a minister. On his father's side he was of
pure English descent, according to Mrs. Stockton, his ancestors
having settled early in New Jersey. His mother was of English-

French-Irish blood, and she, too, was of New Jersey descent. In *The Widow's Cruise* we find a widow living in New Jersey, but reading Mary E. Wilkins in the evening and expressing doubts as to the realism of her characters. Stockton, too, saw something additional in them: humor. He lived much in New Jersey and New York: then for his five last years at Claymont, a beautiful colonial house near Charles Town and Harper's Ferry, West Virginia. *The Home: Where It Should Be and What to Put in It* (1873) written with Mrs. Stockton, is of course inspired by the author's own earlier experiences in home making. And a book for New Jersey to prize is Stockton's *New Jersey from the Discovery of Scheyichbi to Recent Times*, a series of sketches about early New Jersey,—of the first Indian settlements, the adventures of several pioneer girls, of Joseph Bonaparte at Bordentown, of General Charles Lee and Washington, of the patriotic Lord Sterling, the warlike Mollie Pitcher, etc., etc.

Edmund Clarence Stedman once wrote some pleasant verses to Stockton. Here are the first eight lines:

> "I have roamed in the Squirrel Inn
> (With my vouchers from Germantown),
> To the House of Martha I've been
> And more than once have gone down
> In the queerest of all queer wrecks
> And have argued and taken my tea
> With Mesdames Aleshine and Lecks
> All up to our necks in the sea."

"If his fame seems in a momentary abeyance," says Howells confidently in his *The Great Modern American Stories*, "it is because this sort of eclipse must come to all." So welcome back, Elders and Youth Movement, to the goodly Stockton company.

In *My Favorite Novelist* (*Munsey's Magazine*) Stockton nods to Thackeray, Goldsmith, Cervantes, Hugo, Dumas, Balzac and Daudet; but bows low to Defoe and Dickens. "In front of

all who have created fiction stand, firm and unmoved, Defoe and
Dickens, who, as I look upon it, have established the great prin-
ciple that the author who believes in his story will tell the best
story and the author who believes in his characters and loves
them will make them real beings who shall live with his readers
and be held by them always as companions and friends." He
points out how flimsy and artificial Dickens' plots often are, but
how real his characters are.   Much of the machinery and other
properties "would not interest him were it not for the personages
to whom they serve as backgrounds or opportunities."

Stockton sets all novelists who follow him an example of
good temper. He is never shrill. It is not that he could not
have been aware of the weighty problems that concern Phillips,
Herrick, Dreiser, Mrs. Wharton, Whitlock and Mrs. Austin.
But sex, fighting, pushing, drinking, grabbing and gossiping
did not occupy him (except the gossip be harmless and the
fighters, pirates) and he knew they did not other Americans
necessarily, except as they were whipped up to these things by
novels, plays, cocktails and war patriots. To him America was
a gentle place. (He was harmless, amusing and much petted
by the minor critics, according to the brilliant Thomas Beer!)
Let us rejoice that one of our authors found it consistently so,
in book after book. Since his death the world is too much with
us. Even California is getting strenuous, if not serious, each
eye dilated with money or movies.

Stockton was essentially a spinner of tales. The Orient
would have liked him. As a professor he would have delighted
our weary college classes. He wrote first for children and then
went on explaining things to the same children grown up. He
was born to teach and expound—to tell the world it was a good
world full of stories and wholesome pleasures.

Stockton's story ingredients are varied: but given the sea
and some middle-aged or near-old New England women and we
are off on adventures good enough for anyone. What we

remember from *The Adventures of Captain Horn* (1895) is less
Captain Horn than Mrs. Horn, *née* Edna Markham, a teacher,
and Mrs. Cliff, from Plainton, Maine. To prove it, read the
sequel, *Mrs. Cliff's Yacht* (1896), in which Mrs. Cliff, made rich
by the golden hoards of the Incas, acquires a yacht in a most
reasonable manner, but soon finds herself, with a company of
clergymen, pursuing certain pirates bent upon robbing the
Peruvians of their proper share of the treasure. The immortal
Mrs. Lecks and Mrs. Aleshine at once occur to us—much of
them and the sea, too, in the *Casting Away* (1886) of the two
ladies. As for *The Dusantes*, here we have our same friends
in a snowdrift and the discovery, in the same plight, of the
people at whose house they've stayed on the island, and much
discussion of the rent the ladies have left in the ginger jar and
its final equitable distribution among the sailors who helped
them. Then think of *The Great Stone of Sardis* (1898)—how
Mrs. Black dominates the scene, refusing to let her husband seek
the North Pole without her, even though she make the thirteenth
aboard. In this story, incidentally, the voyagers use a
submarine, journeying under the ice, and, secondly, the centre
of the earth is found to be a great crystal. It's a glassy sub-
stratum, anyhow, according to Professor Daly in *Our Mobile
Earth*.

Among the sober volumes listed as collateral reading for
History 1 at one of our Universities in California stands Stockton's *Buccaneers and Pirates of Our Coasts*. There is a quiet
relish to the book. Stockton says that as a boy he wanted to
be a pirate, lured by the independence of the life and the means
its booty offered for doing good. As for women pirates—their
natures carry them too far. Women, says he, have been too
long debarred from professions to which they are admirably
adapted: but as pirates they are unduly cruel. Pirates figure
in his fiction, too—in *Kate Bonnet* (1902) for instance, the
story of a pirate's daughter. Captain Bonnet was a respect-

able planter who turned pirate and came to an ignoble end, having first tried to drag his spiritual guide down with him. But Blackbeard, another pirate, gets him to convert him, Blackbeard, back to respectability, and Kate marries the brave boy Dickory and is *not* held blameworthy for her father's deeds. The mingling of refinement, swashbuckling, story and burlesque is inimitable.

It may not be widely known that Stockton has done his bit for the Father of Our Country. To the Association of New Jersey Publications, Vol. I, 1887–98, he contributed *The Spirit of Washington*. Here we see Washington back on a visit to modern Morristown, viewing the things kept there to honor his memory and passing his grave comments on them.

It is not surprising that the gentle Stockton was an enemy of war, for even in his fiction he takes no joy in killing. He is not called upon, as was that other white soul, Virgil, to fill half an epic with slaughter. It seems that his first published piece, *A Northern Voice for the Dissolution of the Union* (New York, published by the author, 1860 or '61), was "an attempt to avert the impending conflict between the States by suggesting a form of compromise." [1] Then *The Great War Syndicate*, ridiculous as it is, is no more ridiculous than war itself, and really offers good suggestions. If warring nations will not let their disputes be settled by arbitration or a bout at quarter-staves, then why not by the enlightened procedure of *The Great War Syndicate?* In our own day Will Rogers in his *Illiterate Digest* suggests that we lay off on rainy days—and then move to Portland, Oregon. In Stockton's yarn, a war over Northern fisheries is taken on by a syndicate of our prominent citizens. They agree to bring the trouble to a rapid conclusion, or forfeit a huge guarantee. They use "Crabs," speedy little vessels that rush up and tear away the enemy's rudders and propellers;

[1] See *The Captain's Toll-Gate*, or vol. XXIII of the Shenandoah edition, Bibliography, Item 1. Also C. C. Buel, *The Author of "the Lady or the Tiger,"* *Century Magazine*, July, 1886. Stockton believed in freeing the slaves gradually, indemnifying their owners, and permitting secession.

and an instantaneous motor launching so terrible a projectile
that England allies herself with America to prevent future
wars. "Reduction of military and naval forces and gradual
disarmament" became the new policy of the new friends. One
life was lost, that of Thomas Hutchins. A derrick fell on him;
but Britons and Americans united to contribute a monument to
him and a pension to his family. For the fun Stockton poked at
the Spanish-American War, see our summaries later of *Afield
and Afloat*.

As for a formal travel book, Stockton has that too, in
Personally Conducted (1889). France, Italy, England, Holland and Germany are visited in even flowing narrative, though
not rivalling Mark Twain, nor Stella Benson, nor Karel Čapek.
But *Pomona's Travels*—how different! When Pomona, the
priceless housemaid of *Rudder Grange*, sees Europe (part of
it) and writes back home to Euphemia of it, how original indeed.
You remember *Rudder Grange* (1879)—how the author and his
wife Euphemia and a boarder inhabit a houseboat, and how they
acquire Pomona, who sits far into the night reading high-flown
romances. Then how Pomona marries Jonas, a young farmer,
and how Jonas has money left him and how they can now go to
Europe. By this time Pomona is rather well educated, explains
the author, so she indites pretty smoothly. Moreover, "I am
not going," says she, "to write about things and places that you
can get much better descriptions of in books." And instead of
floating all over the Continent, our friend limits herself and
Jonas to England and Scotland, and settles down and becomes
a little Stockton corner in the "old land." She stops a stag
hunt, routs pigs that are eating pictures and rides into a
clothes-line, well filled. And she says Hannah's (a servant's)
English is "like drops of molasses falling on a gong," and she
mentions a London square—or crescent—"where about half the
inhabitants were pervaded with all the solemnities of the past
and the other half bound down by the dolefulness of the present."
Then, in *The Rudder Grangers Abroad*, she calls on an Earl;

and great is the fun thereof, for us, and presumably for the Earl. *Pomona's Daughter* is another adventure. Here two-year old Corinne pushes another baby out of its carriage and is lost to our friends until Pomona hears her call "Mamma" at the Opera in Paris. In *Euphemia Among the Pelicans* Euphemia and her husband are cruising in Florida waters. Euphemia catches a pelican and all three nearly sink into a bog together. Finally, in *John Gayther's Garden*, Pomona and Jonas make a farewell appearance and contribute another story.

Stockton is a born short-story teller. Take *The Griffin and the Minor Canon*, for instance. A griffin having heard of an image of himself on a church comes to town to view it. He sits before it day after day, the Minor Canon having conducted him to it. The people send the Minor Canon away and the Griffin takes over his school. But having learned of the removal of the Minor Canon, the Griffin goes and carries him home sleeping. Then he bears the image off, too, and lying down before it, gazes at it till he dies.

The Queen's Museum (to include another fairy tale or two) concerns a dictatorial ruler and her pet hobby, a museum that she insists that her subjects like. They just don't, so they have to go to jail. But a Deliverer appears. With a robber gang he makes off with the Museum's exhibits; then steals things from a magician to put in their place. The people like the new objects. The Queen is delighted, releases them, and marries the Stranger. The *Clocks of Rondaine* is about a little girl who wanted all clocks to strike the hour together, especially for Christmas. But when she compared her own watch with a dial and found it, too, didn't agree, she preferred to keep her own time and receive Christmas when it came—approximately. *The Lost Dryad* is the tale of a sprite that lost her oak tree. She meets a constable and a cruel stepmother and by kissing them makes them children, for every one of her kisses takes off ten years. She is careful, though, not to kiss the charming little girl that befriends her and whom the others are persecuting. In the end she finds her oak tree. The better known *Old Pipes and the Dryad* is of an old shepherd who is kissed by a dryad and made younger, and his mother too; but when he comes to free the dryad from her tree later, he finds it blown down, and therefore no dryad. Then there are *The Bee-Man of Orn* and *The Philopena*. The Bee-man is told that he has been transformed from something and should return to his rightful being. After many mistrials, he decides he has been changed from a baby, so he is given that form. But in time he grows, and becomes the same tough-skinned old man he was before. *The Philopena* is all about a Prince and a Princess "who when quite young, ate a philopena together." Much later, after they have wandered far looking for each other, the Prince wins the Princess by saying Philopena, reaching out his hand to her, and having his hand taken by her. *The Banished King* discovers he is a better traveler and explorer than a king; *The Battle of the Third Cousins* doesn't come off, for one gets the kingdom, the other the Princess; *The Accommodating Circumstance* is a spirit that helps marry a Baron to a heroine; *Prince Hassak's March* is very direct, but turns out to be the longest way; and *The Christmas Before Last* is about a Captain and some ship-wrecked boys who get some marvelous nuts off the Fragile Palm and spend Christmas Before Last all together with the Captain's son. Then there are boy books, *The Story of Viteau*, *A Jolly Fellowship* and *Captain Chap;* and *Round-about Rambles* and *Tales Out of School*, those amazing potpourris for children, and *Ting-a-ling Tales*, of giants, dwarfs and fairies.

To this day everyone knows *The Lady or the Tiger?* but no one knows which came out of the door when the Princess "moved her hand to the right," indicating to her lover her choice for him. Did she therewith deliver him to the tiger or to her hated rival? such being her dilemma. Indeed it seems that a visitor from a foreign land was so stirred by the question that troubles us to this day that he ran away home before it was decided. We learn this from *The Discourager of Hesitancy, a Continua-*

tion of "*The Lady or the Tiger?*" He, however, reported the situation to his people at home, with the result that a deputation was sent to find out what did happen. The gentlemen dispatched on this mission were told that they would be informed if they would guess the following somewhat puzzling riddle. A Prince came to the same court, lured by the beauty of its fair women, and requested a wife. The king attired him beautifully, blindfolded him, married him to a girl with gentle hands and a rapturous voice, then whisked her away, faced the youth with forty ravishing maidens and bade him say which was his wife. He finally decided upon two, one of whom frowned, the other smiled. Were he to choose the wrong one, he was to die. But did the smile not welcome him, the frown upbraid him for passing it by? He could not say—now if the deputation could say which he fixed upon— But "At the latest accounts," says our story-teller, "the five strangers had not decided."

Stockton liked ghost stories; and of these *The Transferred Ghost* is well-nigh perfect. The narrator is in love, but fears his sweetheart's uncle. He finds that a ghost is about the place, a ghost that was gotten ready for the uncle, who thereupon inconveniently lived on. The ghost wants a transfer and gets it in the end: a Russian nobleman is murdered; meanwhile he appears to our lover and talks to him in the presence of the girl Madeline. His replies once drive the girl off (she thinks he is speaking to her), but the second time what he says to the ghost happens to be what she longs to hear *him* say to her. "I *am* yours," says Madeline, and all ends happily. *Amos Kilbright, His Adscititious Experiences*, is a ghostly tale told by a lawyer, to whom Amos comes, divulging his strange secret. At a spiritualist meeting he has been materialized; he has been long dead, but on being summoned, and left standing about too long, has regained his earthly form. The lawyer is interested and helps him. Amos gets engaged and is just ready to be married, when a German scientist arrives and dematerializes him. But the lawyer's wife gives the scientist several pieces of her mind, and the great man rematerializes him. The wedding comes off, the scientist goes home satisfied with his powers; and Amos and his wife live happily ever after. *The Spectral Mortgage* is about a ghost that makes love to the narrator's sister-in-law, delays her marriage to Will Crenshaw for a time—though she knows the ghost's a ghost—and causes a strain between the author and his wife, who thinks his words "vile interloper," addressed to the ghost, were meant for their child Pegram. In *The Bishop's Ghost and the Printer's Baby* the Bishop's and the other ghosts, including that of a girl who died of love, are out of their tombs. Meanwhile, a mason has sealed up the Bishop, so he dispossesses the young girl (she is staying, during his absence, in Sir Geoffrey's tomb). The girl hears a printer in the church praying for his sick baby: she goes to his home and when the child dies, enters its body. She later comes to visit the Bishop and gets him back into his own tomb. And she promises him not to die again of love. *The Philosophy of Relative Existences* is the title of a book in process of completion by the teller of the tale. He and a poet friend see a city in the distance and go to it. It is inhabited by ghosts of the future, and one of these is discovered reading the conclusion of our philosopher's unfinished book.

The Christmas Wreck (to return to the sea) tells of three men floating about the tropics in a disabled ship; of another wreck that comes along, and of how among them the crews blow the first wreck to pieces and raise a Christmas dinner of canned meats, pigeon pie and peaches from her hold. *The Remarkable Wreck of the "Thomas Hyke"* was caused by a collision with another vessel. Water entered her and she settled, bows under, stern in air. The Captain and some of his men left her and were picked up, but others returned in their boat and lived in the "Thomas Hyke" till they were taken off her. Her cargo of pig-iron had shifted and caused her to assume her upright position: later it was shaken back and the ship righted itself. In *The Water-Devil, a Marine Tale*, a mariner tells a company of being on a ship that suddenly stopped in the Bay of Bengal. The story thereabouts was that in those living waters lodged a water-devil with an arm that seized vessels, shook out their passengers and drowned them. But first the monster must carefully grasp the bottom of the sea with his million toes. So when this particular ship stops, the crew steals off and leave the passengers with the mariner in virtual command. Suddenly another ship is upon them. It is busy winding up a broken cable. But what has happened to the mariner's ship is that one end of the cable has risen up and gripped it. There is good by-play of a Miss Minturn. As soon as she gets on the cable ship she drops the gallant mariner, whom she before hailed as her deliverer. In *The Widow's Cruise* four captains tell a New Jersey widow four tall tales, but she counters with one that leaves them gasping. Among other things, she stills a raging sea by pouring oil on it. *Derelict* has to do with two wandering vessels, the narrator on one of them and his sweetheart and her friend Mary on the other. They come within hailing distance, are separated and later are united in England, largely owing to Mary. "Nobody knows what may happen on the ocean," said she; "but if you're once fairly married, that much is accomplished anyway." In *The Vizier of the Two-Horned Alexander* the writer meets a New Yorker on shipboard. The ship is run into by a derelict and all leave but the two men. They come off better than the rest. But the story in the main concerns the New Yorker, who invites the narrator to his home several times and recounts his story, which is always backed by his Quaker wife. He was with Alexander when the latter was hunting the waters of eternal life, and unwittingly drank down the whole spring himself. He was in his fifties then, and is so still. Throughout Time he has known everybody worth knowing, ancient, mediaeval and modern, including the Oriental. *Captain Eli's Best Ear* tells of two old sea captains who agree to celebrate Christmas together and invite Mrs. Trimmer and an orphan child to share it. On Christmas Eve Captain Eli's best ear detects trouble at the shore. He and

Captain Cephas go down and find a man stranded in a catboat. He asks for Mrs. Trimmer, and Captain Eli has palpitations. But the stranger turns out to be Mrs. Trimmer's brother, so Eli marries Mrs. Trimmer and adopts the orphan, while Captain Cephas continues to live alone, shipshape, as he loves to do, cooking sailor-fashion.

As for Southern stories, *That Same Old Coon* is full of coon lore, in Virginia dialect. The coon himself is known as Haskins', and has no rings on his tail. The hunt for him is long—but unsuccessful. "The fun in a coon hunt ain't so much in gettin' the coon as goin' arter him," concludes Martin. *Dusky Philosophy* tells of a darky preacher who increases his congregation by declaring that all women have seven devils, and mollifies them (the men especially) by showing that the Lord cast Mary Magdalen's out—but hers only; also of a darky who tries to pay for a piece of land by selling some of its owner's apples. *An Unhistoric Page* is another delightful darky sketch. An old negro has a son who has heard at the crossroads that pages at Washington get seventeen hundred dollars. He asks his father if he may go. His father tells him the story of the city and country mouse,—how the former lives so "high" he spends all his money and tries to borrow from the latter, but how the sheriff sells them both as slaves and keeps the property. "Dey can't do dat now," continues the sage, "but yuh 'll find yuhse'f gobbled up some way wuss dan dat plantation mouse was." However, he presently announces he will go himself and with the seventeen hundred he'll give up driving oxen and buy a "wine-yard." He departs and isn't heard of for some time. Then he returns—with another story—about the giraffe and the kangaroo, who were both fools. "I reckon de plantation mouse done gin up he wine-yard," mutters the boy Dick. The *Cloverfields' Carriage* was driven before the war by Uncle 'Lijah, but after it by a cobbler, 'Lijah feeling that he must show the neighbors he is as free as the best of them. But one day he sees the carriage coming down the hill with a chained wheel and is indignant. He banishes the new man and takes the reins. But he comes to a fork in the road and has to ask his mistress the way. The voice that answers him is Montague Braxton's, the new coachman's, who has been sent to get a seamstress. The two negroes drive along to the station where they unexpectedly pick up Master Charles and return him to his estranged family. 'Lijah remains as coachman—though it is really Montague who has blundered into finding Charles. The dialect, parables and situations are immensely amusing.

As for the wonders of science, *A Tale of Negative Gravity* concerns a machine that makes objects lighter. By means of it a middle-aged gentleman and his wife frisk about Switzerland. They have a son much broken up over a love affair with a girl whose father forbids their marriage. The boy's father treats the girl's father to a bit of lightning and enlightening and lets his machine float off into space. The lovers are united and the son is left with the secret of negative gravity. *The Magic Egg* discloses a hypnotist, his audience and his sweetheart. Herbert Loring invites a selected group, hypnotizes them with some "fireworks," and persuades them that they see him take a chick out of an egg, make him grow up, then return to chickhood and soon back into the egg. But his Beloved, who arrives after the fireworks, isn't hypnotized, and that evening dismisses him forever for trying to deceive her as he had the others.

Love Before Breakfast is a triumph of the Stockton love story. A young man, owner of a pleasant country house, a gentleman, his wife and daughter, an agent, the miller's wife who puts the young man up after he has rented his house to the old gentleman and his family, and the neighbors in general, who think the young man is lingering behind to watch his tenants instead of going to Europe, as he wants them to think he has, are all skilfully characterized. Our young friend wins the young lady; abetted by her parents and the agent, all of whom, including the young lady, have been aware of what he has been up to. But no summary could do half justice to the skill with which

Stockton unfolds these delightful situations. *The Staying Power of Sir Rohan* has reference to a horse that takes a young doctor off the road in a snow-storm and brings him to Sir Rohan's former home and the young man's sweetheart. The complications are amusing. So are Uncle Beamish and the girl's aunt. *My Unwilling Neighbor* concerns a young man with a house at the top of a hill, and tells how it slides down and stops near the home of Mrs. Carson and her daughter. The young man marries the daughter and the mother is pleased, because now the two houses can be joined together into one large one. *A Story of Assisted Fate* concerns a young man, who, by his own admission, has brains. He keeps a diary, just one page a day, and he lives with a household of admiring sisters, who tell him he needs a wife. He is twenty-eight. Suddenly he decides to do a bit of diary-keeping for the future; so turning ahead to September 14 marks that as the day for meeting his Fate. His sisters invite Kitty Watridge to visit them on the 16th; our hero goes after her earlier, is prevented by her older sister from taking her with him on his 14th, suffers a runaway and is brought home by a young man who turns out to be Kitty's cousin and sweetheart. The cousins court under his nose: he resigns himself. But his sister suddenly informs him that on September 14th a new baby has entered the world— Grace Anna. In Part Two we hear our hero calling the baby Francesca and waiting for her to grow to be nineteen. Meantime, he and Kitty tag it around together. Then one day as he apostrophizes Francesca he finds Kitty around his neck. It seems that unknown to our scholar Kitty's affair with her cousin is off. So Fate presides at their fate, and our hero can only feel sorry for poor little Francesca.

Under *My Terminal Moraine* is a glacier and it proves an ice mine. The hero falls into it and the heroine helps rescue him and they are married and grow rich ever after. *The Reverend Ezekiel Crump* is the name a florist has given to a remarkable pelargonium. The Reverend Ezekiel is intended to take a prize, but it is the means instead of bringing together the florist and his housekeeper and two young people, Clara and Leonard. The florist has tumbled into a cistern in his greenhouse and overhears Leonard proposing: he thereby learns the technique of proposing himself. *The Christmas Shadrach* concerns a man and two girls, one of whom marries some one else. This leaves our narrator to the other. The piece of shadrach which he gives her for a paperweight is hard to keep or lose, but it knocks down a bull and assists in straightening out several destinies. *Stephen Skarridge's Christmas, an Archaism*, is a delightful burlesque on old-fashioned Christmas stories. Stephen is a cruel and grasping landlord and even takes away an eight-cent mackerel which is all a poor family has for Christmas dinner. But he has a dream and thinks the mackerel comes to life, and with a dwarf, giant and fairy proceeds to sign away half of his wealth. He awakes, and next day gives food, bonds and other presents away wholesale. *Asaph* is the story of a good-for-nothing New Jerseyite who gets two suits of clothes, one from his sister, one from her rejected suitor; also the latter's Centennial pipe: also a wife, the village dressmaker, who will presumably support him. *The Baker of Barnbury* wins the Widow Monk, who alone of the village was giving him no Christmas order. She bids him go get ready his baking for Barnbury's New Year. *Mr. Tolman*, a rich business man, goes off on a vacation to another city and takes over a shop. He is the means of marrying off a night druggist and a teacher who are drawn together by a learned book on the mathematics of music in Mr. Tolman's circulating library.

A Borrowed Month is spent in Switzerland by an artist who finds himself disabled, but who at the suggestion of a supposed crank throws his ailments day by day on friends in America, and enjoys a pleasant time after all, especially with Beatrice. The *Watchmaker's Wife* has refused to let her husband go up alone to test the effect of altitude on time pieces; so when two men in a stranded "yacht" awake one morning and discover a balloon containing an old man clamped to their boat, they find Mrs. Pocock, too. One of the men is engaged to the other man's girl. The second man finally decides to sail in the balloon to the mainland (they are fast to a New England island) and carry a letter for his companion to the young lady. But Mrs. Pocock cleverly includes an epistle from herself (fastening up both letters in a bathing cap) telling Jeannette how much she thinks of the bearer and how little of the other man. All turns out well for the true lovers. *As One Woman to Another* is concerned with a young lawyer who pulls down a small balloon with a kite string, goes to see a young woman who is being mewed up by an erratic uncle, rescues her, but has to turn her affairs over to another lawyer, because his own *fiancée* is growing restive at his interest in the unhappy captive. *Our Archery Club* includes Pepton and Miss Rosa, bad shots; but they win the badge finally: at least Pepton does, and therefore Miss Rosa; for he bestows the badge and himself upon her. *My Bull Calf* is a picture that brings one thousand dollars—after some complications—to two young artists and enables them to set up housekeeping. Moreover, the story almost registers a Stockton kiss: "She looked up, as she said this, with a smile as bright and fresh as any daisy, and I—But never mind."

In *Our Story* a man and a woman writer collaborate. He makes her his heroine: she chooses another man for hero. The latter is a writer too. But the original collaborators marry. "Our story was never finished," says the narrator. "His was. This is it." *His Wife's Deceased Sister* is the title of a story so remarkable that editors refuse to publish any more of the author's usual work. He writes it under the stimulus of his first week of married life. So he has to change his name to get his other things accepted. Then a child is born and so happy is the father that he writes another masterpiece. He places it in a strong box and seals it. After his death and then only, may it be revealed. He doesn't even take the risk of publishing it under his true name. *Every Man His Own Letter-Writer* meets certain contingencies not provided for in Complete Letter-writers. *On the Training of Parents* contains further suggestions to the young. *Plain Fishing* is about a city man in the country who doesn't bring his fishing tackle along, but leaves it to old Peter to supply him.   He goes fishing, first buying some fish from an old fellow because he thinks he needs the money: then catches a large trout.   Returning, he is laughed at by Peter's daughter, who has heard of the sale and won't believe he caught the trout. *A Piece of Red Calico* retails the troubles of a suburbanite who attempts to match his wife some red calico.[2] He brings home Turkey red instead and his wife is unexpectedly pleased. *My Well and What Came Out of It* is an amusing and protracted search for water, with the neighbors' comments thrown in.   After everybody has given up hope and the well has been dug deeper and deeper, an operator finds that by this time the original thirty-foot well yields water. "Leave well enough alone," is his moral. *Our Fire-Screen* was a new article of furniture, very tasteful, but which threw the rest of the room out of tone.   So that room was changed and presently all the rest, and brother Tom bought the old things. The man and his wife buy Tom's house, and rent him theirs.

Afield and Afloat is a group of stories "related only by the bonds of love or water."   The author bids them godspeed "into that vast region marked 'Unknown' on the maps of good and bad fortune."   They deserve the kindest of fates, and have it: they bring good cheer.   Eleven tales make up the volume.   Of these *The Buller-Poddington Compact* is an agreement between Mr. Buller, who loves the sea, and his old friend Mr. Poddington, who fancies horses, to at last visit each other.   Mr. Buller comes first, and goes out driving with his friend, is carried down stream, horse, buggy and all, and does his friend some service in

---

[2] Stockton liked this story. He included it and eight others—*A Tale of Negative Gravity, Asaph, His Wife's Deceased Sister, The Lady or the Tiger? The Wreck of the "Thomas Hyke," Old Pipes and the Dryad, The Transferred Ghost* and *The Philosophy of Relative Existences* in his *A Chosen Few.*

his watery element. Mr. Poddington then visits Mr. Buller by
the sea. The pair go driving in a boat up the canal, have a
runaway and effect a standstill by throwing out an anchor.
Both agree to visit again—if not required to drive or sail. *The
Governor-General,* a Spaniard who rules amiably over the
Pacific island of Mañana, uses his powder to shoot parrots,
whose plumage he collects for a new chromatic scale. Suddenly
a warship from Cabotia steams in and destroys a widow's cot-
tage. The little war that follows has no fatalities and the
widow's house is restored. The Governor and his people sur-
render to Cabotia and are, as far as we know, never visited
again. 'Tis a delightful skit on war throughout, which is "stern
and grim, no matter how we look at it," as he observes in his Introduction. But the man's everlasting good nature and good
temper! A second tale, *The Skipper and El Capitan,* carries on
the fun. An American merchantman captain and a Spanish
captain are friends, and the American's daughter and the
Spaniard are in love. Sailing into a Russian port, they learn
that their countries are at war. The Russian Commandant tells
them they are enemies, and may fight outside his harbor. The
Spanish captain then plots to capture the American boat, so
that he can carry off the daughter and marry her. But when
he proceeds to ram the "enemy," the latter lowers a mast and
pins him—I mean his ship—through. There are numerous complications and no bloodshed, and peace between the two countries brings all to a romantic conclusion.   •

"*Come in, New Year*" is the invitation uttered by a young
girl as she opens the door—and admits another uncle. For she
is already living with one uncle—and aunt—and rather tired of
so much age. The new uncle fortunately fetches a son Arthur
the next morning, and the cousins fall in love. *The Romance of
a Mule-car* is really more sentimental than humorous. But
then, 'tis laid in New Orleans and its heroine is a Creole. She
and her lover see the town, especially the cemeteries, then climb
into a mule-car, and when all others are providentially out,

pledge their love with eyes and hands.   The mule understands, and when his days of usefulness are over, he comes to live in their back yard. *The Boomerang* is a near-murder story. The narrator is a lawyer in love with a girl a relative of whom has unaccountably left his money to a doctor. The lawyer and the whole town are curious: a certain Farris, one of the witnesses, on being called back from a distance, is struck down and badly wounded. Suspicion falls on the father of the girl, but the lawyer decides that a fishing-tackle sinker he has himself thrown out of a window at a cat did the deed. He goes to confess and is laughed at; for the wounded man has recovered and charges the crime to the doctor, who presently admits his guilt. Wedding bells ring. *Old Applejoy's Ghost* doesn't care for his old grandson, but he does like Bertha, his grandson's niece. He gets her to help him give (perhaps we should say throw) a fine Christmas party, and brings her and Tom together. *The Ghosts in My Tower* were such revelers that the owner greased the lightning-rod whereby they got up there. That kept them away for a time, but soon they were back again. However, a demon arrived and one by one they disappeared. *The Great Staircase at Landover Hall* concerns the present owner of an old country place who is sitting alone one Christmas, whereupon the ghost of a beautiful lady comes to him. He falls in love with her and tells her so; then visits the lady's living great-granddaughter and marries her with the beautiful ghost's blessing.

A Sailor's Knot is almost serious: the author's ingenuity is tasked but does not fail him. "A well-tied sailor's knot has nothing Gordian about it," says he in his Introduction. "It may appear difficult, or even be impossible to untie it, but, if one knows how to give it the proper pull, the thing is done; the knot disappears." In saying which the author is praising that "marine angel," Captain Slopper. The story is of a young man in love with a girl who strongly reciprocates, but who loses her fortune if she marries anyone but a sea captain. Now the young

man is a linen merchant, and none too successful. He writes to
his sweetheart and breaks off the match, and she marries Captain Slopper, who is seventy-eight, and who proposed earlier
that she marry him and pay him two dollars a day till he died.
They live apart after their marriage, and the young man comes
often to see the captain and look after him, saving his life at
least twice. He and the old man enter into partnership and
make money. But suddenly the captain disappears: he has
gone West and gotten a divorce from his wife for desertion.
Both she and the young man are furious, but the captain explains to the latter that he is apparently meant to live long.
The young man and Mrs. Slopper meet: they are swept into
each other's arms. They marry, *she* won't forgive the captain,
but he does, and cherishes his memory when he is gone. *A
Landsman's Tale*, finally, is told by a mysterious man who comes
to visit a little town full of retired captains. The town is getting up a Public Library, and the captains make speeches: then
call on the landsman. He tells them a wild story of a shipwreck
and two boxes, one containing food, the other books, and the
choice that had to be made of taking one or the other into the
single boat left after the storm. By unanimous vote they decide
on the books. The stranger then leaves a bank-note for the new
Library and departs.

The Stories of the Three Burglars relates how a householder
puts drugged wine out every night and at last catches three
burglars. Two of them put up plausible stories of how they
drifted into crime, one of them claiming to be a realist out for
copy. The third admits he is a professional cracksman. All
three are handed over to the police; but first they afford the
householder, his wife and Aunt Martha an interesting session.

John Gayther's Garden and the Stories Told Therein consists of eleven tales, three of them told by John Gayther himself. Among these is the first—*What I Found in the Sea*—a
yarn laid in tropic waters. John goes down in diving
clothes and explores two sunken ships, one full of empty

barrels which afford him oxygen, the other a Spanish galleon well loaded with coin. But he has an enemy aboard, a stockbroker, who cuts his line and then later, when he comes up anyhow, tries to get the sailors to kill him. The captain and John leave a buoy and return with a salvaging ship, but can never again locate the treasure. But near at hand cruises the stockbroker with *his* ship, also searching. *The Bushwhacker Nurse* is told by the Daughter of the House, and is a story she has made up and wants John to hear. Almia is a young woman of independent turn of mind who aspires to do big and noble things, but finds everything, including nursing, under irksome control. So she becomes a free-lance, or bushwhacker nurse, captures two soldiers who are engaged in single combat, picks up a third man who is more interested in science and social science than in fighting, and a general who is directing the carnage before her horrified eyes. His side loses, but at least the bloodshed ceases. The story ends without a marriage, but John tells his young mistress that it really ends with Almia's wedding the dark young man who worsted his opponent in the single combat. *The Lady in the Box* is related by John Gayther to the Mistress and the Daughter of the House, the former interrupting often. The story is laid in Florence and concerns a beautiful young wife whom her husband, a physician, puts into trances, the longest of them intended to be forty years. Meantime, the wife is left in the possession of others; but finally the doctor reappears and wakens her. She is shocked to see him an old man; he departs; she is wooed by two younger men; she waxes older; they depart; she becomes old; and she and her aged husband are reunited. The Mistress of the House tells *The Cot and the Rill*, interrupted often by her husband, a naval captain. It concerns a rich man and his wife who buy a thousand acres with a cot and a rill in the midst of it. *She* longs for a simple life, and is determined to cook, wash and sweep. But her husband smuggles in Isadore, a famous chef, and Isadore makes himself tactfully useful in all ways. But the wife must have visitors, first Mr. Rounders, whom Isadore hates for criticizing some of his fine dishes in New York, then some ladies. Isadore serves Mr. Rounds his food raw; the ladies show the whole place up as artificial simplicity. They are all glad to return to town and give the place away. The Master of the House gets his chance next in *The Gilded Fool and the King Conch-Shell*. A returned sea captain builds him a little house and prepares half of it for a bride, then sets out with his friend Sam to find her. Arriving at a toll-gate, they find they haven't the right change and the toll-gate keeper can't break their five-dollar bill. So they wait about and a young woman drives up. Later our friends go on to Thompsontown; when along came the young woman and the toll-gate lady. The captain won't have either of them, but Sam bullies and persuades the latter to have him. The captain marries an old friend of his, Susan, and not the young lady— to the disappointment of the Daughter of the House. The story, by the way, has been heard by the whole family, and a newcomer, a Frenchman, who now tells *My Balloon Hunt*. John doesn't want to hear it at first, but is glad he did, for it relieves his mind of one growing burden: his fear that the Frenchman is not married. It seems that the Frenchman and his wife Irene went hunting in a balloon for tigers. Natives guide them along with a drag rope. Suddenly a tiger looks out, the natives scatter and our hunters fire. Irene wounds him in a toe. The tiger roars, leaps to the side of the car, drives out the Frenchman and draws up inside with Irene. The Frenchman guides the craft over a stream and Irene leaps to safety and to him, while off into space floats the tiger.

Then one day Pomona and Jonas appear, with a story they'd like to publish. It is called *The Foreign Prince and the Hermit's Daughter*. The Prince has lost his realm, so a Hermit advises that he rent one. He does, sends for the Hermit and the Hermit's daughter, marries the latter, on the advice of the former, wins the kingdom (for she is the heir to it, as soon as a bothersome Dowager dies), and lives happy ever after. The Daughter of the House next tells of the *Unconscious Amanda*, who loses consciousness for fifty years, returns to learn the devotion of a nephew who adores her and a lover who has never declared his love, and sees a young relative meeting her true love.—An old professor then offers *My Translatophone*—an instrument he has invented to translate any foreign language into English. The girl he loved had just returned from Burma, so he asked her to speak Burmese into his translatophone. She complies, and in perfect English her voice informs him that she loves him and went to Burma because he appeared to love inventing rather than herself. Of course in the end he wins her, but first, through the meddlesomeness of another girl, he destroys his precious machine, which might even have translated the language of birds and beasts. The Next Neighbor, who is by this time an important part of John Gayther's Garden, now relates the story of *The Vice-Consort*. This is the name given by the narrator to a rather plain woman whom five wives have already asked to marry their husbands, if they—the wives—do not survive them. The narrator gets scared over a possible early demise and is the sixth to ask help. The Vice-consort consents, but the wife gets so jealous that she tries to marry her off. She fails, but learns that she is engaged anyway.—John Gayther concludes with *Blackgum Ag'in' Thunder*, the story of a farmer who thinks he'll begin over, tries being a librarian for a part of a day, schemes with a neighbor to obtain and market auks' eggs, and ends up back in his corn-row. For his wife is Thunder, against himself as Blackgum.—The winter now comes on apace, the family depart, the red thrush ceases its song "and John Gayther walks alone in his garden."

To turn, finally, to the several novels we have not yet considered:

The Hundredth Man has a complicated plot, usually far off from the title: but to begin with the latter, Horace Stratford,

a well-to-do New York bachelor and man of ideas, is looking for
a "hundredth man." Every hundredth book, crime, circumstance or man, he had observed in his reading, was outstanding:
his "immediate occupation was the discovering of a hundredth
man among his present friends and associates." In the course
of the long and somewhat complicated story that follows, Mr.
Stratford breaks off the engagement of Gay Armatt and a Mr.
Crisman, but not for the purpose of marrying her himself.
Indeed, he is glad when his young friend Thorne marries her.
Mrs. Justin, Gay's patron, is skeptical of Mr. Stratford's unselfish motives throughout, wants him to marry Gay himself,
and when he doesn't, hails him as his own hundredth man.

Meantime more humorous and dramatic sides to the novel
emerge from "Vatoldi's," a restaurant owned by Mr. Stull, a
banker, and conducted for him, on the quiet, by the overworked
and underpaid John People, whose mother, Mrs. People, and
uncle, Enoch Bulripple, want him off for a rest. His uncle does
get him on shipboard for a time and then handles a waiters'
strike (they insist on "dress suits"); discovers the identity of
the owner of the place, gets a vacation and a partnership for
his nephew, and thwarts a plan of revenge on Mr. Stull's part
against his and Mrs. People's farm. Meantime, nephew John
finds that Miss Stull is not for him: she takes Mr. Crisman
instead: and John marries Miss Burns.

In *The Late Mrs. Null* (1886) we have a pair of older folks,
Colonel Brandon and Mrs. Keswick, once sweethearts, now
"enemies"; Roberta, the Colonel's niece, and Junius, Mrs. Keswick's nephew, who want and get each other; and Mr. Croft
(suitor to Roberta) and Annie, another niece of Mrs. Keswick,
brought south by her to marry Junius: for business reasons up
North she has gone under the name of Mrs. Null. In due time
Croft switches from Roberta to her, and Mrs. Keswick, furious,
calls her "The late Mrs. Null." Mrs. Keswick accepts the inevitable for the young folks: but there is still Colonel Brandon.
She informs him she is now accepting his proposal of many

years since: he accepts his doom: only to be jilted at the altar.

The Merry Chanter (1890) is a ship that Doris and Charles buy, intending to carry flour in it from Boston to other New England ports. They obtain an all-captain crew, ballast with stones and get covered with barnacles. For they don't sail at all, and at the end a butcher, who has shipped as passenger, buys the boat and presents its former owners with the wooden figure of the Merry Chanter itself. Meantime Lord Crabstairs and the butcher both love Dolor Tripp and devote themselves assiduously to her. She marries Crabstairs; he almost has to go to jail for debt, but is rescued by a buyer who takes over enough of his "old junk" to free him.

Ardis Claverden (1890) is loved by many, by Dr. Lester, Mr. Surrey, Egbert Dalrymple and Roger Cunworth, for example. Roger wins her. Dr. Lester toasts her in her father's rarest wine and Egbert walks into the water and is heard of no more.—The comedy is afforded by a group of Englishmen studying agriculture in Virginia. *Ardis Claverden* is a fairly serious story. Mr. Surrey is a peppery lover and Roger has some fire. In Stockton's longer stories there is usually much rivalry among several men over one girl. Meanwhile, the girl is quietly choosing someone whose success is seemingly scarcely at stake at any time. Yet all this striving among the unsuccessful makes a story rather amusing to author and reader, if not to the young men.

The Squirrel Inn, 1891 (as summarized by a student) tells of "Walter Lodloe, a young writer who is on his way to a country inn to spend the summer. On the boat, before its departure, he offers to watch a baby while the mother goes in search of someone who has failed to appear. The boat leaves before she returns and naturally Lodloe believes that she did it to rid herself of the baby. He decides to keep the child and have a nurse-maid for it. He really seems to enjoy the prospect.

"But at the next port his hopes are dashed when the mother appears. She is quite frantic about the baby. It seems she left the boat to look for the child's nurse, who at the last minute refused to go to the country.

"Mrs. Christie, the young widow, and Mr. Lodloe soon discover that they are bound for the same place, The Squirrel Inn. Having arrived at Lethbury, the village near the inn, Lodloe tells Mrs. Christie to go on to the inn while he looks for a nurse for her baby. He finds a much educated young lady who has studied at Bryn Mawr.

"At the inn there is a Greek scholar, Mr. Tippengray, who seems to be about to fall into the clutches of a spinster from Lethbury, Calthea Rose.

"The plot becomes quite complicated at this place, when Mr. Tippengray falls in love with Ida Mayberry, the nurse. Calthea Rose becomes very jealous and decides to have Ida marry a Mr. Beam who has just returned from South America and who is an old *fiancé* of hers. Things seem to go along fine excepting that Ida appears to monopolize both Mr. Beam and Mr. Tippengray. At last she decides to take the Greek scholar. Calthea now sees that she must marry Mr. Beam or remain an old maid. Mr. Lodloe and Mrs. Christie become engaged, thus leaving Mr. and Mrs. Petter, the owners of the inn, alone.

"A word or two should have been said before about the Squirrel Inn. It was somewhat of a rambling structure; each section was built in a different style of architecture. An Elizabethan window might open on a Moorish balcony, or a French chateau tower might rise out of an old English gable. Mr. Petter, the proprieter, refused all guests who were not acquainted with the Rockmores of Germantown."

In the House of Martha (1891) a man has gone to Europe, but when he returns nobody will listen to his accounts of what he saw; so he hires a young man, but the poor fellow falls asleep and he discharges him. His next listener, Chester Walkirk, was better, but he suggested that our friend make a book out of his travels and hire an amanuensis. After refusing several, our author-to-be gets a nun from The House of Martha. This young

woman may not look from beneath her bonnet, nor sit in the same
room with him, so he dictates through a grating. But one day
a wasp attacks her; she beats him off with her bonnet and discloses her beautiful countenance. Our author now reluctantly
gets his travels done, and in order to hold the nun begins to
"fictionize." That is well enough until he launches a love story;
whereupon the nun informs him hearing love stories is against
the rule. However, Walkirk interviews her Mother Superior
and gets her permission. But another sister is determined to
stop such actions and takes Sylvia (for that is her reason)
away from our author. He and Walkirk go on vacation, there
are further complications, the author is ready to become a
brother of the House of Martha, etc. But fortunately the
House is dissolved and our young people are married; but first,
they finish the love story.

The Girl at Cobhurst (1898) offers us one man and several
women. Two older ones, one with a Will and the other a Cook,
are backing Dora and Cicely, respectively, for the hand óf
Ralph Haverley, who has charge of Cobhurst. Later he is made
heir to it by Mrs. Panney, the old lady with the will, and
marries Cicely.

In *The Associate Hermits* (1899) a young woman who
doesn't believe in wedding trips sends her father and mother off
on one instead. They are joined by Margery, eighteen-year-old
daughter of friends. They all go to Peter Sadler's place, which
provides special camps for special tastes. Next to our new-
comers' is a smaller one with several young men in it. The
young men like Margery, and Margery likes and marries Clyde,
one of them. The "Bishop" marries Corona. Peter and the
guide are well drawn. Margery, like Olivia, in *The Captain's
Toll-Gate*, is a capable young American girl. Stockton's young
men set off his independent young women.

A Bicycle of Cathay has unity—and interest. A young
schoolmaster goes on a bicycle vacation. The doctor's daughter
gives him pills for malaria. He meets several charming girls and

falls in love with them, and takes the pills, but not for malaria. Then he returns and marries the doctor's daughter. Her name turns out to be Europa. "Better fifty years of Europa than a cycle of Cathay" is her hope for him. Incidentally, said an *Athenaeum* reviewer (1901) "the reader learns that an American village schoolmaster gets delightfully long holidays and that casual hospitality is given to strangers in America after a manner which was to be found in England only by the shores of old romance." The book is a Stockton triumph, human, amusing, with numerous incidents like that of the bear to enliven the course of love.

The Captain's Toll-Gate (1903) contains a vixen in Maria Port, a disagreeable village gossip who sets her cap unsuccessfully for the Captain, and Olivia, the Captain's niece, a strong-minded young person who rejects three lovers, saves her uncle and the President of the United States by killing, yes, *killing*, a "socialist," and marries a young professor. What more would you? to say nothing of the friendly Easterfields and the Dorcas Society and the old restful houses. The noise of motor cars enters not into Stockton. The suspicion, which one has in *Kate Bonnet*, that Stockton is doing a Max Beerbohm job with some of his late stories recurs in this: he marshals his people like James, he has the scholar win, as in Meredith, his girls have a distinct air of Howells, with a sense of humor added. Probably he was borrowing a bit here and there and a desire is present in him to make his people more than just "humours." Could he have lived longer he would have essayed full length portraits, perhaps.

Stockton is remembered offhand for *The Lady or the Tiger?* and for *Rudder Grange*. The Pomona of the latter is a creation: but so are the Mrs. Lecks and Mrs. Aleshine of *The Casting Away of Mrs. Lecks and Mrs. Aleshine*. But his types are really very numerous and very varied—old New England ladies, boys and girls, ghosts, fairies, giants, inventors, painters, authors, Southerners, darkies, inn-keepers, burglars, old salts and other sailors, and gardeners. Age or middle-age yielded him the most humor: yet one gets greatly attached to his engaged young men and women and to his young married folks—people who have flowed inevitably and peacefully together, know their minds thoroughly, have no problems, and so can enjoy life sanely and soberly. Why not? In his longer stories he complicates matters, and then one gets a bit bored with his American girl: enough of her is enough, and we turn with a certain relief, as did Stockton, to her elders, who, if not so freshly charming, are, at least, though often pickled in brine, salty but not acrid. And the brightness and gayety of this rare spirit in our noisy world that some say has no more place for him! Read him, read him: skip all these summaries and read him!

IN PRAISE OF "THE EARLY AMERICAN NOVEL"

THOUGH I haven't perused—for that is the word—the earliest American novels themselves, I have read Miss Loshe's account of them with profit and delight. For her *Early American Novel* is lively reading. Scorn not a doctor's thesis, when a good one, and an interesting.

Miss Loshe's first chapter, *The Didactic and Sentimental*, is the most entertaining part of her book. It shows how the Reverend Enos Hitchcock and Royall Tyler both advocated home-made novels, deploring the necessity for English substitutes; and how, when Americans did begin supplying such a need, Puritanism and Colonialism had still to be coped with. Mrs. Morton's *The Power of Sympathy* attempted the moral regeneration of youth. "Of the many passages of attempted poetical style," says Miss Loshe, "the most elaborate are a Dante-inspired vision of the lower world shown to the guilty father, and the history of Fidelia, a pink-ribboned New England Ophelia, whose morbid interest in the brook is justified by the fact that her lover once drowned himself in it." "Poems" are injected. "One extract from Harrington's epitaph, composed by himself, may illustrate the gift of the American Sappho:

'When on their urn celestial care descends,
Two lovers come, whom fair success attends,
O'er the pale marble shall they join their heads,
And drink the falling tears each other sheds,
Then sadly say, with mutual pity mov'd,
O! may we never love as they have loved.' "

Mrs. Rowson's *Charlotte Temple* contains "two of the very blackest villains obtainable." Mrs. Foster's *Coquette* is shown to display some advance in skill; but Caroline Matilda Warren's *The Gamesters; or Ruins of Innocence*, is truly moral again, being written against gambling. Helena Wells contributed two novels to "counteract the pernicious tendency of modern philosophy." Besides, many ladies, Lavinia, Sabina, *et al.*, wrote for *The Massachusetts Magazine* and received the guerdon of high editorial praise.

To return to the novel: "Death, my dear Maria, is a serious event," says Caroline in *The Hapless Orphan, or the Innocent Victim of Revenge*, "By an American lady" (1793). A monument of wonderful proportions and decorations is projected by Helen for her lover. "But at length the malevolent Eliza triumphs. Caroline is carried off by villains in Eliza's pay, and the devoted Helen, flying in pursuit, only arrives in time to save her body from a company of medical students. Nothing happens to Eliza."

The Art of Courting must be edifying reading, seven brands of wooing being set forth. Meanwhile in Tyler's *The Algerine Captive*, a touch of new realism appears, the author insisting on seeing captives as they are. Lastly Hugh Henry Brackenridge, in his *Modern Chivalry*, a satirical account of American politics of the time, sprinkles the saving salt of humor on all these extravagances. He modeled himself on Cervantes and Butler and yet produced something very American.

But he was the exception. Puritanism and provincial colonialism—the dependence of America on Richardson, Sterne, Mackenzie and the lachrymose school generally in England,— kept our earliest novel tearful and instructive. "Weep and be good," it bade our forefathers, or perhaps, "Weep and ye shall be good."

CHARLES BROCKDEN BROWN AND THE GODWIN CIRCLE

WHO has not read Mary Wollstonecraft's love-letters to the American, Gilbert Imlay; and who has not pitied her and disliked him? while realizing all the time, that, according to the easy theories of both, either was justified in taking leave of the other at short notice. Unhappy Mary Wollstonecraft,—later to marry William Godwin, and to die in giving birth to the future Lady Shelley. Poor Godwin, too, with his own daughter and Imlay's, married again presently to Mrs. Clairmont, thereby annexing to the family Claire Clairmont, later to be the mistress of Byron.

Yet how interesting the Godwins were in themselves, and how important, for a time, in their relations to America. Miss Loshe mentions, for instance (p. 68), *The Emigrants*, "by Gilbert Imlay, whose name is remembered only for its association with that of Mary Wollstonecraft. The aim of the tale is to call attention to the political questions then occupying Europe, and particularly to the effects of laws concerning marriage and divorce, and emphasis is laid on the imbecility of such institutions as are incompatible with reason and nature."

But of real importance are the relations between Charles Brockden Brown and Godwin and Shelley. When Miss Loshe speaks of Brown's intention to make his heroines "women of a newer type, to let them speak and act and love for themselves, relying on their own judgment, and not on the conventions of society, or on the divinely inspired wisdom of a father or husband," she puts her finger on the good there was in this movement, that greater independence for women, which, in its saner aspects, is a real contribution, in America, especially, towards Progress, say what we will.

The influence of Godwin's *Caleb Williams* on Brown's earlier books is noticed by all.[1] He says himself in his unfinished romance *Jessica*, "When I revolve the transcendental merits of Caleb Williams, my pleasure is diminished and is preserved from a total extinction only by the reflection that this performance is the first." Later Brown—as also Shelley—seems to have drawn away from Godwin. But Godwin loved his pupils to the end. When Godwin published *Mandeville* he said in his preface, "The impression which first led me to look with an eye of favor upon the subject here treated was derived from a story-book called *Wieland*, written by a person certainly of distinguished genius, who, I believe, was born and died in the province of Pennsylvania, in the United States of North America, and who called himself C. B. Brown."

But if Godwin made this bland admission of indebtedness, Shelley's enthusiasm for both Godwin and Brown was more unqualified. Shelley's affinity for the Gothic tale of Walpole, Mrs. Radcliffe and "Monk" Lewis early showed itself in his high-flown romances *Zastrozzi* and *St. Irvyne, or the Rosicrucian.* Then, as his later manner was influenced by Greek and Peacock, whose steadying effect is rightly pointed out by Mark Twain, who, in his *Defence of Harriet Shelley*, thinks him and Harriet Shelley the decent members of the group—so his second period was naturally given over to the teachings of Godwin and to the art of his disciple, Brown. *The Assassins* and *The Coliseum* show an advance in literary quality, due in part, perhaps, to the example of *Caleb Williams.*

"Nothing so blended itself with the structure of his interior mind as the creations of Brown," says Peacock in his *Memoirs*

[1] "His specific indebtedness to Godwin appears chiefly in a fondness for the central situation of *Caleb Williams*: an innocent and somewhat helpless youth in the grasp of a patron turned enemy," says Carl Van Doren in *The American Novel*, p. 10. He then shows that in *Ormond* Brown made a young woman the victim, as he had already done in his now lost *Sky-Walk.*

of Shelley.   Dr. A. Droop's *Die Belesenheit Shelley's*, 1906, discloses acquaintance on Shelley's part with Brown's *Wieland, Ormond, Edgar Huntley, Arthur Merwyn* and *Jane Talbot.*

Interesting, too, is the fact that of the whole set and their stories, Godwin's, Brown's, Shelley's, Mrs. Shelley's,—only Mrs. Shelley's *Frankenstein* remains really something of a masterpiece, something often read, a book which has added a word to the language.   So Godwin influenced Brown, Brown and Godwin influenced Shelley, and Shelley influenced Mrs. Shelley, and one good story came out of reams and floods of words—and, incidentally, reasserted the spiritual kinship of America and England.

COOPER'S PREFACES

WHETHER you agree with Mark Twain that Cooper's defects overshadow his virtues, or with Mr. Brownell that his virtues highly transcend his faults, or whether, best of all, you just like Cooper because you read him when you were a boy or girl, you will at any rate agree with me, I think, who have read him all too little, that some of his prefaces are characteristic and interesting.

Of his first novel, *Precaution* (1820), Cooper could write, "When it was finally put into a publisher's hands, 'with all its imperfections on its head,' the last thought of the writer was any expectation that it would be followed by a series of similar tales from the same pen." Yet by the next year *The Spy* was out. "The dispute between England and the United States," says the author, "though not strictly a family quarrel, had many of the features of a civil war.—There is now no enemy to fear, but the one that resides within. By accustoming ourselves to regard even the people as erring beings, and by using the restraints that wisdom has adduced from experience, there is much reason to hope that the same Providence which has so well aided us in our infancy may continue to smile on our manhood." Prophetical, this, of his later manner of helping Providence along in America.

In introducing *The Pioneers* (1823), which was a result of his own early life on the then frontier, Cooper is careful to disclaim any correspondence between his romance and real life. How odd it sounds to-day, nurtured as we all are on Reality, to have Cooper say of himself: "There was a constant temptation to delineate that which he had known, rather than that which he had imagined. This rigid adhesion to truth, an indispensable requisite in history and travels, destroys the charm of fiction." Then how he winces to think that any persons should have

103

accused him of "converting" his own sister "into the heroine of a work of fiction." Meredith was less fastidious in *Evan Harrington.*

In *The Pilot,* published in 1824, Cooper explains the well-known genesis of the tale, inspired as it was by the inadequacy of Scott's *Pirate:* adding that the work is not intended primarily for females, and declaring further that a little use of the rod is good for sailors and landsmen alike,—until, as we should say to-day, its use is rendered unnecessary by education.

Lionel Lincoln (1825), best known for its Battle of Bunker Hill, disclaims sources, historical or contemporary. No Irving, no grandfather, no black-letter book has or have been used. Moreover the author's "presumption has not even imagined the vivacity of the Eastern States; he has not analyzed the homogeneous character of the Middle; and he has left the South in the undisturbed possession of all their saturnine wit."

The Last of the Mohicans preface (1826) is very temperate indeed, the nearest approach·to "ginger" appearing when the author speaks of "the seemingly inevitable fate of all these people who disappear before the advances, or it might be termed the inroads, of civilization." Compare the indignation of a Joaquin Miller and a C. F. Lummis! *The Prairie* (1827), too, is mild enough, closing, as it does "the career of Leatherstocking,—driven from his beloved forests to such a refuge" on the plain, "dying as he had lived, a philosopher of the wilderness, with few of the failings, none of the vices and all the nature and truth of his position."

In *The Red Rover* (1828), Cooper admits that Smollett has set a high standard for nautical tales and declares "the history of this country has very little to aid the writer of fiction, whether the scene be laid on the land or on the water;—doubtless owing to the staid character of the people."

Cooper's next book, *The Wept of Wish-ton-Wish* (1829), was written, he says, to convey, if possible, "something of the dangers and privations our ancestors encountered in preparing the land we enjoy for its present state of security and abundance." As for his *The Water-Witch* (1830), while admitting it a comparative failure, Cooper at the same time declares it his most imaginative book, its fault lying in "blending too much the real with the purely ideal."

The years 1831–3 saw the publication of *The Bravo*, laid in Venice, *The Heidenmauer*, on the Rhine, and the *Headsman*, in Switzerland. They are dull books intended to show Europe the superiority of democracy to aristocracy. But the Introduction to the *Bravo* contains some sound political philosophy; those to *The Heidenmauer* and *The Headsman* some delightful mountain and river scenery.

Since Cooper's day his next novel *The Monikins* (1835), has, it seems, been read by only two persons. Professor Lounsbury (*James Fenimore Cooper*, p. 134) says he is the only one. The other person is not the present writer but a student of his. It is only fair to add that he did not force this student to read the book. She chose it herself, unwitting.—The Introduction has it that the author has saved a lady's life in Switzerland, and tells how *The Monikins* itself (a satire, by the way, on English and American society and politics) was sent him in manuscript (accompanied by a diamond ring) by the lady's husband; with the stipulation that the manuscript be published in America. The difference in tone with that of *Lionel Lincoln* is marked.

By the time Cooper published his next two novels, *Homeward Bound* (1838) and *Home as Found* (1838), he was *persona non grata* to Americans, owing to his *A Letter to his Countrymen*, his *Sketches of Switzerland* and his *Gleanings in Europe*. In his Preface to *Homeward Bound* he gives the Press and Politics a dig; in that to *Home as Found* he attacks American society more generally. America is a "barren field," he declares ,"for writers of fiction and drama. We believe that no attempt to delineate ordinary American life, either on the stage, or in the pages of a novel, has been rewarded with success." Mrs. Stowe and Howells were yet to be.

In a Preface to *The Pathfinder* (1840), Cooper speaks of the malignity with which certain individuals assailed his book on its first appearance. He then asserts that an author is not the worst judge of his productions, as the world always holds. In introducing *Mercedes of Castile* (1840), his story of Columbus and his companions, he says that he "states truth with a profession of fiction, while the great moral caterers of the age state fiction with the profession of truth." In *The Deerslayer* (1841) he defends his Indians on the ground that "it is the privilege of all writers of fiction, more particularly when their works aspire to the elevation of romance, to present the *beau-ideal* of their characters to the reader."

"It is a strong proof of the diffuse tendency of everything in this country that America has never collected a fleet," he remarks in his Preface to *The Two Admirals* (1842). "One of the misfortunes of a nation is to hear little beside its own praises," he observes in *Wyandotte* (1843). "Perhaps the greater portion of all our peculiar opinions have their foundation in prejudices," is his contribution in *Afloat and Ashore* (1844). *Miles Wallingsford* (1844) expresses Cooper's indignation over the "anti-rent combination." "We conceive that true patriotism consists in laying bare anything like public vice," he continues in reference to the same subject in *Satanstoe* (1845). There is still more of a like sort in *The Chainbearer* (1846) and in *The Red-Skins* (1846). In *Jack Tier* (1848) he expresses friendly feelings towards the Mexicans. "Good appears to rise out of evil," he says in *Oak Openings* (1848), "and the inscrutable ways of Providence are vindicated by general results, rather than by instances of particular care." In *The Sea Lions* (1849) he speaks of the "laudable desire" of explorers "to enlarge the circle of human knowledge"; and in *The Ways of the Hour* (1850), finally, he complains of our jury-system.

So we see the man in his prefaces: the romancer, the conservative democrat, the critic of society, English and American, the fighter, the patriot; and now, with the lapse of time, the man as he was, strong, opinionated, but a good man and a well-meaning one.

A HENRY JAMES PARAGRAPH ON HAWTHORNE

WHEN, in his interesting little book, *Great Spiritual Writers of America*, George Hamlin Fitch shows a deep affection for what he calls *Hawthorne's Sombre Romances*, I can feel with him to the full, except for the following sentences. "Endowed with one of the vivid creative minds, Hawthorne's rare gifts have failed to impress many critics, who, like Henry James, in that unhappy sketch in which he revealed his own limitations, bewailed the fact that the author of *The Scarlet Letter* had no real historical background for his tales. Fine literary artificer as he is, I would give all of Henry James's work for one of Hawthorne's tales like *Roger Malvin's Burial*, or *Young Goodman Brown*." Now I wouldn't. I want all of both. And much as I love Hawthorne, and slowly as I have come to a like appreciation of Henry James, I am yet constrained to believe James our greatest writer of fiction.

True, James's book on Hawthorne is a volume for English readers; it is one of the English Men of Letters Series, in fact; as Woodberry's two are for New Englanders and other Americans. We are fortunate, again, to possess each. And how good, too, for the student of James, to have James's views on his one American rival in fiction (Poe excepted) for fame. "He was not a man with a theory," says he of Hawthorne, "he was guiltless of a system, and I am not sure that he had ever heard of Realism."

Now James had; nor do I find that his amused glance at Hawthorne making simple entries in his Note-books about peat-smoke, a dog and a bird shows him unappreciative of the Master's real service to literature in, say, *The Scarlet Letter*,— "something that might at last be sent to Europe as exquisite in

quality as anything that had been received"; the best of it being
"that the thing was absolutely American." James remarks
that Hawthorne's entries argue a thinly-composed society, and
they do, but he does not fail to see how Hawthorne's genius
transcended it. He thinks Hawthorne's characters not living
enough, his preoccupation with conscience too intense, his
allegorizing tendency too pronounced. He enjoys Hawthorne's
English Note-books more than his Italian—or American. He
smiles a little, but so did Hawthorne, at the Brook Farm en-
thusiasts, with their "dish-washing and aesthetics," their "wood-
chopping and philosophy." But after all, who has surpassed
James's concluding sentences on Hawthorne, whom he really
revered and understood?

"He was," says James, "a beautiful, natural, refined genius,
and his life had been singularly exempt from worldly preoccu-
pations and vulgar efforts. It had been as pure, as simple, as
unsophisticated, as his work. He had lived primarily in his
domestic affections, which were of the tenderest kind; and then
—without eagerness, without pretension, but with a great deal
of quiet devotion—in his charming art. His work will remain;
it is too original and exquisite to pass away; among the men
of imagination he will always have his niche. No one has had
just that vision of life, and no one has had a literary form that
more successfully expressed his vision. He was not a moralist,
and he was not simply a poet. The moralists are weightier,
denser, richer, in a sense; the poets are more purely inconclusive
and irresponsible. He combined in a singular degree the spontaneity of the imagination with a haunting care for moral problems. Man's conscience was his theme, but he saw it in the light
of a creative fancy which added, out of its own substance, an
interest, and, I may almost say, an importance."

A WORD ON FRANK NORRIS AND JACK LONDON

OF our novelists Frank Norris made the nearest approach to setting down accurately that America we heard of in his day as "complex," flowing about us, "mutable as the sea," the America that had not found itself, the America that knows itself better since the War. True, Norris was provincial, but he was something more. His "epic strength," his clear flash of words down a page, exciting the eye to fly over it at speed, the rush up to the climax, the bits of descriptions set like jewels, the devotion and conscience of the man and the artist everywhere—all these things were more than sectional, partaking, in a measure, of the universal. And then, he was the novelist of the young. And why should they not have their novelists? American life, in his time, seemed essentially the life of the young, the young business man, the young president, the young college professor, the young lawyer, physician and politician—and the young girl. He seized upon the spirit of those times —he wrote of their guiding forces, youth and energy, and he kept (with Jack London) the youthful record of that boyish Western time.

Professor Fred Lewis Pattee, whose *American Literature Since 1870* is an eloquent plea for Americanism in American Literature, is singularly out of sympathy with that very American writer, Jack London. Why does he do him so much less justice than those other favorites in Europe and America, Walt Whitman and Joaquin Miller?

At any rate he makes some very disparaging remarks about him in the second volume of *The Cambridge History of American*

Literature.[1] "London," says he, "gave the mass what it demanded, every sensation which the brutal underworld he knew had afforded him, and he sold his work well. Of the graces demanded in the earlier periods, finish, elegance of style, melody, elevation in tone, he knew nothing. He had immediacy—he told vivid stories of physical prowess in the world of the present moment; he had the note of authority—he wrote only of wild epic things of which he had himself been a large part; he had sensation—the appeal of the crude physical horror, the strange and unheard-of in hitherto unknown regions; and he had a barbaric style—a lurid wealth of adjectives, a melodramatic intensity, and a headlong rush of incident that sweeps the reader along as in a stampede. Force undoubtedly he had and freshness of material, but, lacking poise and moral background and beauty of style, he must be passed as an ephemeral sensation."

Strong words these! "I believe that spiritual sweetness and unselfishness will conquer the gross gluttony of to-day," said London in *What Life Means to Me.*[2] Everyone who knows anything of the man or his work is aware that he not only liked brute strength but at the same time sympathized with the weak. Yet he believed that our best service to the latter is to rouse them. "My final word," said he when he resigned from the Socialist party, "is that liberty, freedom and independence are royal things that cannot be presented to, nor thrust upon, races or classes." And how is a man's influence negligible when he gave a push, however slight, to tyrant-ridden Russia, serving as a tonic to its pessimism and despair?[3] As for his writing, occasionally a man writes because he can't help it. "So," says Oliver Madox Hueffer,[4] "so it was with Jack London; so one hopes it may be with the future writers of the Pacific Slope, where, if anywhere, we must look for the 'great American school,'

[1] Since this note was written Professor Pattee has published a long and generous study of London called *The Prophet of the Last Frontier,* in *Sidelights on American Literature.*
[2] *Cosmopolitan,* 40, 530.
[3] *Jack London as Titan* (*Dial,* Jan. 25, 1917, Vol. 62, p. 49).
[4] *Living Age,* 292, 124–6.

which can never find birth until its upholders have finally cast off the shackles of European 'literature.' " That is overstated, of course, for London, for one, didn't just write, nor cast off Europe, as any reader of *Martin Eden* knows. He labored at his writing and he acquired as much of the world's knowledge in a few years as many do in many. And if he was not exactly cultured himself, he acknowledged culture in others. That is one of his glories.

And the other is that this lover of "red blood" was in some measure a psychologist! And what other Far Western writer (except possibly Bierce, Norris and Gertrude Atherton, in their degrees) was that? That he was more drawn to psychological themes than to adventure stories is the statement of his friend John D. Barry.[5] But the public would not buy his psychology. Even so, Wilfred Lay[6] shows how much psychology went into one book that the public did and can still buy, a book never more interesting and romantic than in the Era of Prohibition.

But I could not be a good Californian, I admit, without being a little prepossessed in London's favor. And that "prejudice" was intensified, for me, by something very human, a talk on his life, a little, but on his books, more, that his daughter, Joan, delivered to a class of mine in the American Novel at the University of California. She was herself a member of the course and that afternoon, at least, the young West hearkened. I shall see her long, ticking off the forty or more of her father's books and commenting on her favorites. And then another day she and another student and the latter's brother and his car came for me, and we had dinner with Mrs. London and her two daughters and the rest on the heights above Oakland— and Jack London's spirit that evening was not wholly over the Bay in The Valley of the Moon.

[5] *Overland Monthly*, N. S., 69, 43.
[6] *John Barleycorn Under Psycho-Analysis* (*Bookman*, 45, pp. 47–54).

SOME CRITICS OF WILLIAM DEAN HOWELLS

"THE task of interpreting Mr. Howells still awaits American criticism," said *The New Republic*[1] in its review of Alexander Harvey's amazing book on Howells.[2] "So faithful and interested an artist as himself has stored up treasures of national consciousness which will gain in value as time goes on." Yet despite Howells' delicacy of apprehension of others, his reliable democracy and scrupulous virtue, the writer finds in him a "retardation of impulse." Harry Thurston Peck, in a long essay on Howells, wonders if after all Howells is not a better critic than novelist. Yet "all great novels are a criticism of life," Howells told Joyce Kilmer.[3] A reviewer in *The Westminster Review*,[4] thinks those works of Howells wherein he sings of his early love, Italy, much to be preferred to the "string of pretty trivialities which he calls novels." He says Howells reflects a soulless society instead of satirizing it. Yet Elizabeth Luther Cary[5] hails Howells as the poet of common things, and says truly of his characters that "they represent the easy, unpedantic intelligence, the somewhat lazy culture, the ready humor, the touch of bravado in turning a joke with fate, the curious mingling of poetry and practicality, with which the American spirit, when it is raised quite above the commercialism by which it is never utterly submerged, is so distractingly endowed." As for the Folletts, they say further that "Mr. Howells is quite the most American thing we have

[1] Vol. 10, April 21, 1917.
[2] *William Dean Howells, A Study of the Achievement of a Literary Artist*, 1917.
[3] *Literature in the Making.*
[4] Vol. 178, 1912, pp. 597–608.
[5] *The Lamp*, 29, 1904–05.

produced; that is, the most broadly and soundly representative." [6]

"Girls with white dresses and virginal looks, languid manners, mild witticisms, here, there and everywhere; a couple of young men, one a little cynical, the other a little overshadowed by his love," murmurs the author of *The Confessions of a Young Man.*

Yet Mr. Harvey calls Howells as great a literary artist as Mr. Moore's god, Balzac, "greater from that point of view than Thackeray, or George Eliot, or Tolstoy, or Kipling." He exalts his style and his technique and writes eloquently of his portraits of good women. He flays the women writers of the New England group, though, the "sissy" school, he calls them, concludes with an index unparalleled for originality, and shouts throughout the book at American Philistinism, our inheritance, he declares, from England. Any defects in Howells' picture of American life he lays not at the door of Howells but at that of America. Howells' picture of America is perfect; it is America as she is. If you don't like Howells, you don't like America. Kindred views, naturally, are held by Mr. Mencken in *A Book of Prefaces* and *Prejudices.*[7] If you don't deplore Puritanism throughout its devastating course from Hawthorne to Anthony Comstock, if you won't or can't read Theodore Dreiser you haven't a better America at heart. These books are thrillers: "criticism," according to Mr. Mencken, "should first find out what an author is trying to do, and beat a drum for him when it is worth doing and he does it well": yet how interesting, in a quieter way, is Pattee's *A History of American Literature Since 1870,* the only history of literature (with the possible exception of Moody's) that "reads like a novel," as they used to say before the novel got difficult. James, as we have seen, is an American whom Professor Pattee cannot stomach. Naturally so: for

[6] *Some Modern Novelists,* p. 100.
[7] In *Prejudices, First Series,* he says: "What remains of Howells is his style. He loosened the tightness of English, and let a blast of Elizabethan air into it."

James didn't go West (to stay), or from the West to the East,
as Howells did; but "flew de coop" altogether. "Howells' Silas
Lapham is a living personality; James's Christopher Newman
is a lay figure in Yankee costume," says he. But that false note
apart, how harmoniously *he* beats the drum for Howells, for
Mark Twain, Whitman, Joaquin Miller and other good Americans. With what extraordinary sympathy and insight—despite
his chapter heading, *The Recorders of the New England Decline!*—he studies Mrs. Stowe, Rose Terry Cooke, Elizabeth
Stuart Phelps Ward, Harriet Prescott Spofford, Sarah Orne
Jewett, Mary E. Wilkins Freeman, and Alice Brown. And his
twenty pages on Howells: how fair, how illuminating!

He sees the three manners of Howells, for example, the early
poetical, the middle realistic, and the later ethical. Yet he
loves the earliest stories best. "These are the creations of a
young poet, a romancer, a dreamer," says he; "the later manner
was an artificial acquirement like the taste of olives." "In
America every art ends at last in a sermon," he says without
bitterness.

Yet unlike Mr. Harvey, whose chapter on *The Howells Philosophy of Woman* is a panegyric, Pattee cannot abide Howells'
females. "The Richardson feminine," says he, "is a trembling,
innocent, helpless creature pursued by men; the Howells type
is the same woman transplanted into the nineteenth century,
inconsequent, temperamental, often birdlike and charming, elec-
tric at repartee, pursued by men and fleeing flutteringly from
them, yet dependent upon them for her very existence. In all
of these fictions there is scarcely a feminine figure, at least in a
leading role, of whom her sex may be proud." Compare with
this the whole chapter which Mr. Harvey devotes to praise of
Marcia. Then by way of compensation read again Mr. Harvey's graceless attack on the New England women writers and
follow it with Pattee's sound, exhilarating, courteous treatment
of them. So do critics strike fire from one another and temper

each other's ardor.   Long may they battle over American literature.

Meanwhile, two whole books (by no means controversial)
have been added to the Howells criticism.   Delmar Gross Cooke
(*William Dean Howells*, 1922) after much painstaking exposition, concludes that Howells was a great novelist who was also
a great dramatist, and praises Mark Twain for signalizing once
and for all Howells' chief virtue—his love of human beings.
Then "Howells never relinquished his faith in the effectiveness
of the novel as a socializing instrument.   He thought of literature as already out of the palace and the cloister and perhaps
as far as the forum, and cherished what will seem to many of
his friends the optimistic delusion that it must one day reach the
market place."

Mr. Firkins' *William Dean Howells*, 1924, Mr. Herrick objects to as too much like a doctor's thesis.   Yet chapter after
chapter of exposition again accomplished, Mr. Firkins is con-
vinced of the vitality of Howells' fiction, of the good quality of
his later poems and of the very real value of his appreciative
criticism.   And his simplicity he finds above praise.   That, says
he finely, "is ultimate, not obvious; and it requires a dash of
subtlety in the reader to grasp the fact of his normality."

FRANK NORRIS AND OTHERS ON THE ART OF FICTION

IN 1884 Sir Walter Besant and Henry James discussed the art of fiction, or, as Stevenson preferred to call it in his *Humble Remonstrance*, "the art of fictitious narrative in prose." Besant believed good novels have purpose and ideas; and he declared the art of fiction in general required "power of description, truth and fidelity, observation, selection, clearness of conception and of outline, dramatic grouping, directness of purpose, a profound belief on the part of the story-teller in the reality of his story, and beauty of workmanship." Henry James showed with much charm of manner and diction—"in the tone and for the ear of good society," says Stevenson—that a novel should be interesting, should produce the illusion of life, and should be sincere. As for a moral purpose,—"No good novel will ever proceed from a superficial mind; that seems to me an axiom which, for the artist in fiction, will cover all needful moral ground." Stevenson divided the novel into three types, adventure, character and dramatic, the last of which he said is calculated to appeal to our emotional and moral natures. Moreover, he gave specific advice to young writers. Choose your motive, says he, and make setting, incident, character and dialogue subserve it. Dispense with sub-plots, as a rule, and all else extraneous. As for beginning and end, that only matters in a short story. "The *dénouement* of a long story is nothing," he says in his *Letters*, "it is just a 'full close' which you may approach and accompany as you please—it is a coda, not an essential member in the rhythm; but the body and end of a short story is bone of the bone and blood of the blood of the beginning." Poe held like views and expressed them in his much-quoted notice of Hawthorne's *Twice-Told Tales* (1842) and in his *Marginalia* (*The Works of Edgar Allan Poe*, Crowell, New York, 1902, Vol. xvi, pp. 18, 170 and 171).

F. Marion Crawford, too, in *The Novel, What It Is* (1908), and George Meredith in *Diana of the Crossways* and elsewhere have a suggestion or two to offer. The novelist, according to Crawford, should appeal primarily to the heart, and by the heart he means the self "roused to emotional activity." Meredith on the other hand, says hard thinking should precede novel-writing; and that the pen should "rouse the inward vision, instead of labouring with a drop-scene brush, as it were, to the eye."

So, characteristically, Besant advises purpose and keen observation in its behalf, James, interest resulting from sincerity and a well-stocked mind, Stevenson, a well-defined motive set forth with an economy of means, Crawford an insistent appeal to the heart, and Meredith the consistent arousing of mind and spirit.

Meanwhile in America Frank Norris published in 1903 a volume on the subject, calling it *The Responsibilities of the Novelist and Other Literary Essays*. At the possible expense of proportion, let us note more fully what he has to say.

In one place he observes truly that no novelist's handbook of any value has ever been compiled, but that life all about us takes its place. "For the novelist," he writes, "where is there of cut-and-dried science that he can learn that will help him? . . . Some day the handbook may be compiled—it is quite possible—but meanwhile, and *faute de mieux*, there is that you may study better than all handbooks,"—Life. "From the study of your fellows you shall learn more than from the study of all the text-books that ever will be written."

He lays much stress on the novelist's attitude toward his work and especially towards life. "Impressionableness, emotionality and communicativeness are three very important qualities of mind that make for novel writing," says he. And "an

attitude of sympathy and generosity and toleration is the firs
requisite of the really great novelist." Then he believes i
Biblical simplicity. Elaborate, decorative phrases may be per
missible during unimportant portions of the story; but whe
the crisis arrives the simplest and the fewest words are sufficient
The reader's time and attention, he points out, must be econo
mized. All good novels have a pivotal point. All must lead t
that, and from that on the rest of the piece is decline. Th
approach must be slow. The poor writer hurries over tha
stage, that he may hasten to show his real power. The goo
writer is purposely somewhat dull to begin with. Persons, lo
calities, neighborhoods must be fully represented, insisted upon
impressed upon the reader's mind. Meantime there is a page,
few sentences, a chapter, that are baffling, that seem to hav
no connection with the course of the story. The reader i
puzzled: but he is supposed to be; his best course is to proceed
and trust to developments. Again the story moves; again th
exasperating note sounds, grown clearer now. Meantime th
characters have become living persons, grouping themselves
probably, about the hero and heroine. There may be a lov
scene or two. Still nothing has happened by way of action.

Then the story stirs, very much impeded, at first, with mor
locality, more love scenes, more opportunity for close acquain
tance with the characters. Gradually they themselves grow
less and less prominent as ends: they now assume their place
as means for developing the action. And the complicatior
tightens. Some happening or other chronicled in earlier chapters collides with the development of the plot and sends it i
another direction. Then another incident, probably also al
ready prepared for, meets with *that* and turns it in another
The action, meantime, is ever increasing in speed: suddenly th
motif of the piece, a note faintly heard from the first, sound
clearly, and "the complication is solved in an instant with al
the violence of an explosion, and the catastrophe, the climax, th
pivotal event fairly leaps from the pages with a rush of actio

that leaves you stunned, breathless and overwhelmed with the sheer power of its presentation."

Thus the great moment of the novel, the effect, is set down in a few wonderfully telling words, quite unimpressive read apart, but tremendous in its proper context.

The unskilful writer, says Norris, who has not prepared properly for his climax, will strive for effect by the opposite method of elaboration, length, words and noise. The reader is annoyed, unprepared, unenlightened. The writer has not had the patience to plod, to systematize, to drudge. He has neglected method for "inspiration" and "genius."

So Norris really applies the principles of the short story to the novel. The result, as Pattee points out, is too headlong, too breathless, too journalistic for comfort. One gets out of breath reading Norris, as one does with Jack London. Yet the concentration, the passionate energy of both are unforgettable and are as characteristically American as the more slowly-moving English novels are eminently English.

Or if not natively American, they are French-American. Norris's master was Zola, whom he considered a romanticist, not a realist! Nor does he stand alone as an American influenced by French fiction. "Owen Wister has revealed a not uncommon experience of our younger writing men in confessing that the impulse towards writing his Western stories came to him after reading the delightful pages of a French romancer," says Bliss Perry in *The American Mind*, p. 41. Robert Herrick has admitted that while at Harvard and for some time later he was also under the Gallic spell. He changed later to the longer English and Russian forms. In this connection his comment on Mrs. Wharton's technique may be quoted.

He says in the *New Republic*, Vol. 2: "The ground for according such distinction (i.e., as Henry James accorded) to Mrs. Wharton is plain to one acquainted with the craftsman's side of the novelist's business. Mrs. Wharton writes well—perhaps too consciously well. Technically she has formed her method on the approved tradition of French fiction, the tradition of refinements and exclusions, of subtleties and intentions, the tradition of Flaubert and Turgenieff, on which Mr. James admiringly formed himself a generation ago, rather than on the richer if less æsthetically satisfying tradition of English and Russian fiction, of Fielding and Thackeray, of Tolstoy and Dostoëvsky. (To Herrick, Turgenieff is more French than Russian). In this approved school triumphs are more easily won, at least more enthusiastically recognized by the expert who has served his term there, than in the other looser tradition." —Whether Norris, finally, would in time have deserted the French technique for the older, leisurely English, he did not live to show.

ON THE TREND OF THE AMERICAN NOVEL

O UR most characteristic American writing, as must be pointed out again and again, is not the self-conscious literary performance of a Poe or a Hawthorne," says Bliss Perry.[1] "It is civic writing; a citizen literature, produced like *The Federalist*, and Garrison's editorials and Grant's *Memoirs*, without any stylistic consciousness whatever; a sort of writing which has been incidental to the accomplishment of some political, social or moral purpose, and which scarcely regards itself as literature at all. The supreme example of it is the 'Gettysburg Address.' " Yet he adds two pages later, in reference to Howells and James, "The analysis of the mingled racial, psychological, social and professional traits in these masters of contemporary American fiction presents to the critic a problem as fascinating as, and I think, more complex than, a corresponding study of Meredith or Hardy, of Daudet or D'Annunzio."

In fact "there is only one expert," said Mark Twain in *What Paul Bourget Thinks of Us*, "who is qualified to examine the souls and the life of a people and make a valuable report —the native novelist. This expert is so rare that the most populous country can never have fifteen confessedly competent ones in stock at one time. . . . Does the native novelist try to generalize the nation? No, he lays plainly before you the ways and speech and life of a few people grouped in a certain place —his own place—and that is one book, and when a thousand able novels have been written, *there* you have the soul of the people; and not anywhere else can these be had. And the

[1] *The American Mind*, p. 43.

121

shadings of character, manners, feelings, ambitions, will be infinite."

In his *Provincial Types in American Fiction* (1907), Horace Spencer Fiske foresees a fusion of these provincial elements. "American Literature may, in fact," says he, "be said to be made up of an aggregation of sectional literatures, the literature of New England, the South, the Middle West and the Far West. This aggregation naturally lacks unity, but it is all American; and perhaps at some time these diverse characteristics may be fused by some masterly writer of fiction into a harmonious whole which shall, by its vast variety, yet unifying American spirit, be recognized as the great American novel."

In January, 1912, *The North American Review*[2] printed a paper written by Arnold Bennett in 1903 on *The Future of the American Novel*. "The great novels of the future will spring from the action and reaction of place on place and activity on activity," says he. "There can be small doubt that they will run on the lines of *The Octopus*, though one may venture to prophesy that they will contain a little less sentimentality. . . . The American novelist of the future will do well to bear in mind that life unadulterated is the best possible material for art." He, too, looks for something national in American fiction. Mr. Howells, on the contrary,[3] thinks the American novel will and should continue to be local but should emphasize character above all else. As for Henry James, when he visited us in 1904–5 he noted possibilities for a Meredithian comic pen in the matter of the relations of American men and women,—"high sport," says he in *New England, an Autumn Impression*, "for the ironic poet—who has surely hitherto neglected one of his greatest current opportunities."

Mr. Robert Herrick, meantime, has already availed himself in novels like *To-gether*, *One Woman's Life*, *Clark's Field*, *Waste* and *Chimes* of these possibilities. And in 1913–14, in

[2] Vol. 1, p. 195.
[3] *Harper's Magazine*, Vol. 124, 1912, p. 636.

he *Yale Review*, he foresaw that we must first develop a truly
ational spirit before we can have a distinctive literature. We
ck solidarity, says he, and our novels are sentimental, weakly
eligious, prudish, and undemocratic. Mr. Herrick sees in the
Var a unifying force, but he does not expect it to bear vig-
rous fruit at once. Indeed in the *Nation* of December 7, 1921,
e finds the world after three years of peace in a state of coma.
n this condition of paralysis we wait for its possible cure.
Until men and women," he declares, "have ceased to debate
nd speculate upon the fundamental issues and react to life
nconsciously and forcibly, with a real conviction about the
usiness of living, a new literature is not to be expected." Mean-
hile we report and record in our *Main Streets* and *Domesday
Books*. Finally, contributing to *The New Republic's* symposium
April 12, 1922) on the novel of to-morrow, Mr. Herrick finds
hat America is ready to be "done" and ready or nearly ready
o be re-appraised and re-stated. But he hungers for the spirit.
For we must not forget," he concludes, "that men and women,
owever much at times they may seem to ignore or even repudi-
te the fact, are more interested in the inner truth buried some-
here within their souls, than with all the outer adjustments
nd mechanics of their lives—and the two are only incidentally
elated."

In his *Contemporary American Novelists* (1922), Mr. Van
Doren writes in like strain. He criticizes "the now moribund
ult of local color," saying of it (p. 2), "The defects of local
olor inhere in the constitution of the cult itself, which, as its
ame suggests, thought first of color and then of form, first of
he piquant surfaces and then—if at all—of the stubborn deeps
f human life." And Mr. Lewisohn, in some penetrating pas-
ages on the Novel in *The Creative Life* (1924), observes that
with the expressionism of Dorothy Richardson, Evelyn Scott,
James Joyce, Waldo Frank, *et al.*, and the creative vision of
Jacob Wassermen before him, "the novelist of to-day, at all
events, has his choice among several very different but equally

fascinating methods, and the immediate future of the novel should by virtue of these varieties of expression be both lively and fruitful." After praise of *The Way of All Flesh*, *The Forsyte Saga* and *Of Human Bondage*, Mr. Lewisohn continues, "We could go to the Continent and add the sovereign lucidity and depth of Thomas Mann, the valiant creative speech of Romain Rolland and the exquisite glowing patterns of Ricarda Huch." To get to the real and away from the endlessly superficial, even though the result be painful, is what he yearns for, —finding something of this in Dreiser and Sherwood Anderson, in Hergesheimer and Sinclair Lewis. Indeed, were a Charles Lamb to make a selection of best specimens from American novels, says he, he would have a collection larger and more important than any conceivable anthology from the Elizabethan or Jacobean playwrights. But he has yet to see any one whole novel among us that equals one of the great novels of Europe.

Mrs. Wharton, meanwhile, in *The Great American Novel* (*Yale Review*, July, 1927) raises a protest against limiting the American novel to endless reduplications of Main Street. She thinks we have Americanized America and the whole globe, "to the deep detriment" of their picturesqueness. We have a few great American novels: another will suddenly, probably very quietly, appear. When it does, "its scenes may be laid in an American small town or in a European capital; it may deal with the present or the past, with great events or trivial happenings; but in the latter case it will certainly contrive to relate them to something greater than themselves."

ON THE AMERICAN NOVEL TO-DAY

CHARLES C. BALDWIN'S *The Men Who Make Our Novels* (1925), is a book indeed for persons interested in the American novel to-day, or puzzled by it, or in doubt as to its vigor and variety. Even to have inspired its writing is almost excuse enough for the eighty-eight novelists who call forth Mr. Baldwin's witty, admiring, penetrating or impatient remarks on them. How many more should be added to his list one hesitates to say. Ernest Hemingway and John Erskine, for instance, are coming along! Robert Morse Lovett came twice and departed. And Will Payne, Abraham Cahan, "Henry G. Aikman" and Edwin Lefevre have written good novels. And there are Du Bose Heyward and his superb *Porgy*, and Glenway Wescott and his *The Apple of the Eye* and *The Grandmothers;* and Frank Harris and *The Bomb*, etc., Will Harben and Georgia, Frank H. Spearman and railroading, and Harry Kemp and his two interesting autobiographical novels, *Tramping on Life* and *More Miles*. As far as that goes, the versatile Alvin Johnson's *The Professor and the Petticoat* isn't to be winked at, in any sense. And there's Thornton Wilder.

But to return. So vivid is David Graham Phillips to Mr. Baldwin that he includes him among his many living novelists. Then he deals with such established reputations as James Lane Allen (alive at the time), Howells, Thomas Nelson Page and Newton Fuessle (not long dead), Sherwood Anderson, Cabell, Dreiser, Hergesheimer, Robert Herrick (whom he admires), Sinclair Lewis and Booth Tarkington. There is room, too, for Henry B. Fuller, E. W. Howe (whom he greatly likes), William Allen White, Meredith Nicholson, Edward Lucas White, Owen Wister and Winston Churchill. Rex Beach, Robert Chambers,

James Oliver Curwood, Thomas Dixon, Zane Grey, Emerson Hough, George Barr McCutcheon, Harold McGrath, Samuel Merwin, Henry Kitchell Webster, and Harold Bell Wright get what's coming to them. Upton Sinclair is in for a nice little puff. Rupert Hughes, as Major Hughes, is a target, chiefly, for Mr. Baldwin's wit. Stewart Edward White is commended, and so is Samuel Hopkins Adams, sometimes.

But the pleasantest part of the ride on the Baldwin locomotive (forgive me) is traveling along with certain new or near new writers: Bill Adams, with his short stories of the sea; Joseph Anthony, with *Rekindled Fires*, "that Cranford of the emigrant" (see also his *The Golden Village*); Louis Bromfield (pretty much all of him); Heywood Broun, with his novel, *Sun Field*, about Babe Ruth; John Cournos and his life of the young Russian in America, and, in *The New Candide*, a young American abroad, seeing the freaks there, for a change; John Dos Passos and his *Three Soldiers*, his travel book *Rosinante to the Road Again*, and, I assume now, *Manhattan Transfer*; Harvey Fergusson and his *The Blood of the Conquerors*, *Capitol Hill*, *Women and Wives*, and now *Hot Saturday* and *The Wolf Song*; F. Scott Fitzgerald, from whom Baldwin expects more, while praising his portraits of the young; Ben Hecht, who is himself, and a worthy self, in *Eric Dorn*; Robert Nathan, with his whimsical and poetical stories; Jay William Hudson, a college professor who is also author of *Nowhere Else in the World*, a story of a dreamer in Chicago (but first he is long in Europe, then suffers as an instructor in a middle-West machine shop, miscalled a University); T. S. Stribling, author both of *Birthright* and *Teeftallow*, about the new negro and the hill folk of the South; and *Fombombo*, about Venezuela; Elias Tobenkin, novelist, especially, of the Russian Jew and the German in America; Allan Updegraff, both fanciful and realistic; Carl Van Vechten, amusing, clever, finished and strange; Waldo Frank, original and experimental; Webb Waldron, destined to be taken up by the discriminating, and Ben Ames Williams, a Hergesheimer to-be.

The other authors in the book are Thomas Beer, Arthur
Bullard, Struthers Burt, Donn Byrne, Octavus Roy Cohen,
Coningsby Dawson, Garet Garrett, George Gibbs, Hermann
Hagedorn, Henry Sydnor Harrison, George F. Hummel, Wal-
lace Irwin, Owen Johnson, Peter B. Kyne, Joseph C. Lincoln,
Hugh Lofting, Peter Clark Macfarlane, Percy Marks, Edgar
Lee Masters, William McFee, Christopher Morley, Charles G.
Norris, Grant Overton, Elliott H. Paul, Ernest Poole, Edwin
Meade Robinson, Robert Simpson, Freeman Tilden, Arthur
Train, Louis Joseph Vance, Brand Whitlock, John Wiley and
Harry Leon Wilson.

Here is a variety of novelists and a diversity of settings and
subjects. East, West, North, South; white man, black man,
yellow man; American, European, South American; fact and
fancy; school, college, factory, mine, slum, Wall Street, Main
Street, mansion and hovel, all manner of men and women, children and animals; Hollywood, New Mexico; art, religion, business, law, medicine, teaching; traveling, sitting still; prejudice,
humanitarianism, selfishness, altruism; shallow optimism and
reasoned; despair and hope; motors and noise and peace and
life and death, crime and justice and war and peace, country
and city, small town and large; the American at home and
abroad; youth and age, fine things and "raw"; finished writing
and crude; scene and interpretation: in short, America.

And the women likewise. Here we have as guide Mr. Grant
Overton, self-styled literary reporter, who includes in his *The
Women Who Make Our Novels* (1918), women who are artistically fine, or widely popular, or both. He begins with Edith Wharton, whose work, needless to say, he praises without stint; and
ends with Mary Heaton Vorse, whose *The Prestons* (a nice
family story), has his high regard. Alice Brown and Ellen
Glasgow, Mary Roberts Rinehart, Margaret Deland, Kate
Douglas Wiggin, Mary E. Wilkins Freeman, Willa Cather,
Edna Ferber and Dorothy Canfield Fisher are of course included. Gertrude Atherton and Mary Austin are extremely

well understood and interpreted by him, and Kathleen Norris is
admirably if somewhat flatteringly presented. He has the kindest of feelings for Mary Johnston, Amelia E. Barr, Cora Harris
and Helen R. Martin. Mary S. Watts is exalted. The two
Porters get their dues. Marjorie B. Cooke's *Bambi*, Mary E.
Waller's *Wood-Carver of 'Lympus*, Eleanor Hallowell Abbott's
fancies, Honoré Willsie's Western stories, Clara Louise Burn-
ham's Christian Science, Grace S. Richmond's stories of emotion,
are pointed out, approved or excused. Demetra Vaka, Anna
Katherine Green, Sophie Kerr, Harriet F. Comstock, Frances
Hodgson Burnett, Alice Hegan Rice, Alice Duer Miller and
Zona Gale complete Mr. Overton's list. Of course Elizabeth
Madox Roberts' notable *The Time of Man* and *My Heart and
My Flesh* are not present. And one trembles to think of the
dozens of others the people at large are reading—trembles if
he tries to list them all ("B. M. Bower," for example, and W.
M. Raine and H. H. Knibbs and Margaret Pedler, and Temple
Bailey). But by turning to *The Book Review Digest* he will
find scores of them already set down. Among the most read,
of course, are Ethel M. Dell and Elinor Glyn—if they *are* English. One lives in Hollywood anyway and surely the other cannot long resist it. And we might add to Mr. Overton's list of
artistically fine, Evelyn Scott and Elinor Wylie, Isabel Paterson,
Margaret Ashmun, Martha Ostenso, Edna Bryner, Julia Peter-
kin and Mary Borden, who, though transplanted to England, is
now author of *Flamingo*, a novel of New York. And Sarah
Comstock has written two good novels in *The Daughter of Helen
Kent* and *Speak to the Earth*.

Altogether, the current American novel, like the American
life that it describes and interprets, is flourishing.

G. B. S., OR FROM BASHVILLE TO METHUSELAH

IN *Heretics* Mr. G. K. Chesterton declares that "no man has any right whatever merely to enjoy the work of Mr. Bernard Shaw"; for "Mr. Shaw writes either to convince or to enrage us." Now Mr. Chesterton not being at hand to stand me on my head, I can say with a certain sense of security that I *have* the right to enjoy Mr. Shaw, and do; and to assert at the same time that whereas Shaw sometimes enrages me, he less often convinces me.

Wherefore (being enraged for a paragraph or so) I find myself asking Mr. Shaw *why* there is next to nothing in English education? why there are next to no ideas in Shakespeare? why divorce should be so confounded easy? why children should not be made to learn their lessons and to respect authority? why rudeness is such a virtue? why a nation at death throes with an enemy is comic? why modern women are all cave women? why most business men, professional men and politicians are "crooks"? And the answer comes over the waters, Why not, yea, why not?

And then groaning anew I turn from the Atlantic and remark over the Pacific to Lenin (via Shaw Wireless) that I am tired of hearing that it is the serious and not the comic that counts in Shaw. Lenin, who has heard Shaw address the Fabians and has presumably read the Revolutionists' Handbook, waves a busy hand and smiles a futurist smile. (I wrote this prior to Lenin's demise and haven't the courage to bury it with him: let both lie in state).

Then I remember that I teach. So I turn to my students. They will have to listen. Shaw, I pronounce crisply, is a man

who fills me with admiration for his talents as a wit and humorist, but who leaves me colder on the side of his ideas, except
of course, when he is belaboring Poverty and War. Yet he has
a passage on Bunyan that "couldn't be beat." He has done
Butler, Ibsen and Wagner, and done them well. In his novel
Love Among the Artists he praises truly creative music and
painting, in contrast to art that is conventional and academic.
His frank handling of Christianity, though irreverent in places,
is predominantly sincere. He is against capital punishment,
and in a brilliant preface to the Webbs' *English Prisons Under
Local Government* denounces Vengeance. Society should not
reduce the criminal to the minimum privilege of breathing. "A
criminal," says he humanely, "must be treated not as a man
who has forfeited all rights and liberties by the breaking of a
single law, but as one who, through some specific weakness or
weaknesses, is incapable of exercising some specific liberty or liberties." Again, his Preface to *Heartbreak House* will live long
as the record of war mania in England and America. He has
given the sentimentalists a run for their lives. And assuredly
his assiduous creation and dissemination of the Shaw legend
is the unique thing of its sort in Literature.

But there is something incomplete about him even so. He
doesn't praise God or Nature or Woman. God is too dependent
on Man, Nature hardly figures at all, and woman is a primitive
and a hoyden.

Shaw might admit these charges (except, perhaps, the last)
and still observe that his treatment of *Man* has not been surpassed (least of all by Shakespeare). Does he not propose com-
munism for him and remind him that he is by nature rational?
And has he not shown him the way in countless speeches and
writings to be more rational? Has he not denounced soldiers
and churchmen, doctors and landlords, teachers and politicians,
flesh-eaters, wine-bibbers and tobacco-users, censors and
æsthetes, and defended prizefighters, phoneticians, rude young
persons, live old ones, servants and revolutionists? Yet who

takes all this seriously? Well, Mr. Chesterton, so as to combat it, and many others, for Shaw or against him; Messrs. McCabe and Mencken, for instance.

Kind readers (I am addressing you now), like what you like in Shaw: I like the comic in him, and the impudent because it is comic. ("You suit me well, for you can make me laugh," quoth she: that's Marianne Moore to Shaw). He says we must get rid of reputations, even our own. He says he writes prefaces, as Dryden did, because he can, and wishes Shakespeare had sacrificed a few plays and done the same. He says the school-boy makes good use of Homer when he throws him at another boy's head. He makes Caesar bald-headed, Cleopatra a flapper, Napoleon the dupe of a clever girl, Patiomkin a "simp," Shakespeare a glorified reporter. He hears that the Crown Prince left the theatre when *Androcles* was performed in Berlin and regrets that in London no English Imperialist was intelligent and earnest enough to do the same. He makes Tarleton say in *Misalliance*, "Good thing, the empire. Educates us. Opens our minds. Knocks the Bible out of us. And civilizes the other chaps"; and later of Poland, "Oh, yes. Interesting nation. Lucky people, to get the government of their country taken off their hands. Nothing to do but cultivate themselves. Same as we took Gibraltar off the hands of the Spaniards. Saves the Spanish taxpayer. Jolly good thing for us if the Germans took Portsmouth." He says we should never strike a child except in anger; that sex infatuation is only effective in the comic spirit; that the universal regard for money is the one hopeful fact of our civilization; that it is a mistake to get married, a bigger one not to,—but that argument on the subject should be postponed till after the ceremony. Finally, he almost died once because he would eat no meat. So he wrote: "My situation is a solemn one. Life is offered to me on condition of eating beefsteaks. My weeping family crowd about me with Bovril and Brand's Essence. But death is better than cannibalism. My will contains directions for my funeral, which will be followed not by mourning coaches, but by herds of oxen, sheep, swine, flocks of poultry, and a small travelling aquarium of live fish, all wearing white scarves in honor of the man who perished rather than eat his fellow-creatures. It will be, with the exception of Noah's Ark, the most remarkable thing of the kind ever seen."

And now let us be serious and observe the humor of Shaw's plays. *Widowers' Houses*, the first of them, is funny because Blanche Sartorius just *makes* Harry Trench marry her. Papa wants him, too, for his connections, and is willing to treat his tenants better to placate Harry's silly scruples. *The Philanderer* is Shaw's burlesque on the Ibsenites. Julia and Grace are emancipated females; but both suddenly fall in love—with the same man. In the end the man gets rid of one of the girls and the other gets rid of him. The whole piece dances and sparkles with absurdity. Not so *Mrs. Warren's Profession*. Vivie's struggle against the conventionality of her unconventional parent is Ibsenite, not Ibsenistic. It is not quite cold, but it is logical. It is therefore better drama than it is life. It needs more Shaw in it. Of that, though, there is a-plenty in *Arms and the Man*. There are two heroines, mistress and maid, the one looking for a real man, the other for one who will make of her a real lady. Both bag their game. But the "feature" of the piece is its satire of women's hero-worship of soldiers. Quite the opposite may be said of *The Man of Destiny*. This brilliant one-act skit gives the real victory (and over Napoleon at that) to a young girl. Yet Napoleon comes out of it all a rather delightful, human, clever, honorable young fellow, less caricatured, for some reason, than most of Shaw's "great" men. The aristocratic and foppish General Burgoyne figures in the next play, *The Devil's Disciple*, but Old Nick's adherent himself is Dick Dudgeon, a rebel against the Puritan excesses of New England. Dick presents himself a vicarious sacrifice for the patriotic Reverend Anthony Anderson; who in turn becomes Captain Anderson and rescues his rescuer. "A wary builder of scenes is this man Shaw," cries Mr. Mencken, "a Sardou peeping from behind Ibsen's whiskers." In his melodramatic scenes Shaw has a grand time. He enjoys them too much to burlesque them in the usual manner of humorists. Meanwhile, in this same prolific period, he wrote *Candida* and *You Never Can Tell*. He likes Candida the play (and we do, too, for it is brilliant), but not Candida the woman. In a word, Candida is a perfectly respectable vampire, and he doesn't care for half-way people. *You Never Can Tell* might as well be called (borrowing from George Ade in the *American Magazine*) *Our Amazing Young People*. Mr. Mencken gently designates these two grown-up terrors as "unconscionable egoists, disrespectful to their elders, self-willed and obstinate, and nuisances in general." But "they got fun!" In a hotel dining-room they are priceless. And William, the perfect waiter, father of a successful barrister whom he has supported "until he was thirty-seven, sir," is one of the truest, bluest (I mean whitest) figures of modern letters, more real, more human, surely, than anything else in Shaw. Shakespeare, who is true, might have made him. It is William, too, who says "You never can tell, sir, you never can tell." That is profound, it is so simple, and is again worthy of Shakespeare: for a moment our rationalist admits irrationality. The tragedy of the play is the unhappy disagreement between the advanced wife and the morose, tyrannical father—very Modern Drama people these—whom Meredith would project as sinners against the Comic Muse.

Captain Brassbound's Conversion, the next play, has been called "a satirical melodrama disguised as a farce." Brassbound, a sort of Mediæval Revenge pirate, grapples with a modern woman of beauty and brains and she outwits him and makes a lamb of him, rescues her brother-in-law and returns to England, leaving Brassbound, much shaken in his piratic faith, to continue preying (spelled *ey*) on the coast of Morocco. But we are forgetting *Caesar and Cleopatra*. Caesar would appear to fare hardly at the hands of dramatists. Even

Shakespeare in *his* portrait, reduced the proportions Plutarch gave his hero. Shaw goes further and makes him bald, resigned, worldly, weary, presenting Cleopatra with Antony so he won't have to be bothered making love to her himself. Cleopatra is sixteen and Caesar is as careful as if he were a professor in a female college. *Man and Superman* contains the famous pursuit of John Tanner by Ann Whitefield, the equally noted scene in Hell, the pointed Revolutionist's Handbook, and the Life Force. Humor, wit and burlesque tumble over each other. Much, and more, of all this, appeared earlier in Shaw's novel *An Unsocial Socialist* where a woman pursues a man, marries him and is deserted by him. Here already woman is the agent of that ruthless Life Force that will have its way with hapless man, unless he resists. In his *plays* man resists too—but no use! —Another victory for man, in novel form, is found in *The Irrational Knot*. Connolly is rational: he admires his wife for running away from him, and asks her back when her lover deserts her. He admires her for doing what she wanted to do— for asserting her will. But she finds him too reasonable, too cool, too intellectual, and declines his offer. As for that little skit, *The Admirable Bashville, or Constancy Unrewarded* (a hasty dramatization in blank verse of his novel *Cashel Byron's Profession*), the very title, combining as it does Barrie and Richardson, is a stroke of genius. And the play is an improvement on the novel in the sense that in it the tone of burlesque is better sustained. Butler Bashville, you remember, falls in love with his mistress, but she marries a pugilist,—who, however, is really noble and heir to an estate! In another playlet, *How He Lied to Her Husband*, Shaw has fun with the Shavians. Aurora Bumpus and Henry Upjohn have seen *Candida* and decide on an intrigue of their own. But Mr. Bumpus interferes and Henry lies to him. Then Bumpus gets angry, but is mollified by Henry's sonnets to Mrs. Bumpus and plans to print them privately. *John Bull's Other Island* is another masterpiece of denomination. In it an English reformer, rather than his Irish

friend, wins an Irish bride and in time Irish hearts politically.
With all its fun the piece would seem to teach that sympathetic
Englishmen may do Ireland more good than patriotic Irishmen.
Major Barbara advocates feeding people well first and saving
their souls afterwards. It laughs at the Salvation Army one
moment and the tainted capitalist the next. An earl's daughter,
a Major in the Army and her scholar-lover beating the bass
drum are only exceeded in interest by the wealthy maker of
explosives trumpeting forth his barefaced philosophy. *The
Doctor's Dilemma* is a rather uncalled-for attack on the ethics
of the medical profession. It is arresting in idea, but being
questionable and presented seriously, the theme is harmful:
unless, of course, we say, "It's only a play and presents a possible situation." Here we have three famous physicians sacrificing a man because all three love his wife! But I too am
getting serious over Shaw. *Getting Married* is comical again.
The play reaches no conclusion on marriage: Shaw never does:
in fact, he is married himself and never talks about his wife
in print; there are restraints even in Shaw. But *Getting Married* babbles a-plenty through its several characters: *they* say
many of the things that are generally inhibited—if felt at all.
But wouldn't we be fine birds if we felt all the feelings of the
modern drama? *The Shewing-Up of Blanco Posnet*, banned in
1909 and produced in London in 1921, is laid in our own beloved wilds, but has hardly the verisimilitude of Bret Harte.
Blanco is a good-for-nothing with some of the imaginative qualities of the hard-drinking man. He fears God literally, who, he
declares, is always after him. He marries a harlot in the end,
after handing over a stolen horse to another woman to save
her child. The humor is grim, when not rather silly. And one
good sentiment is now presumably a trifle out of date (?), to wit:
"I tell you, Blanco, what keeps America to-day the purest of
the nations is that when she's not working she is too drunk to
hear the voice of the tempter." *Press Cuttings* is good burlesque again. The Prime Minister, Mr. Balsquith, disguised as

a suffragette, chains himself to the scraper of General Mitchiner and talks politics and war with him very amusingly. *The Dark Lady of the Sonnets* features Shakespeare, Queen Elizabeth and Mary Fitton. The two ladies (especially the Queen, who enters sleep-walking) afford Shakespeare, who dances about, tablets in hand, much material for his dramas—words, scenes and phrases. In *Misalliance* we have a good satirical portrait of a colonial administrator, Lord Summerhays; also an amusing alliance between the latter's babyish son and a strong-minded young Polish woman who drops in in an aeroplane. Hypatia, to whom the Big Baby was engaged, institutes a clever and successful pursuit of Percival, handsome aviator. Johnny, her keen-tongued "Rotarian" brother, her practical mother, her middle-class father (full of reading and ideas), and Gunner, a clerk who comes in to kill Lord Summerhays, complete the fun. *Fanny's First Play* (supposed to be written by a young lady just out of Cambridge) is a mad thing. Bobby and Margaret both get into jail. Bobby, and Dora, who isn't much conventionally, but is drawn with good English realism, pair off, while Margaret and Jergins, a Duke masquerading as a butler, do the same. The epilogue contains Shaw's famous discussion by the critics of who wrote the play. In great contrast is *Androcles and the Lion*. Androcles is, like William, a living character. His simplicity and humility are really Christian. And the several other types of primitive Christian presented—the soldier who is trying to turn the other cheek, the clever girl who is both Christian and woman, and the cowardly rascal who joins the new faith because he thinks he can sin at will and be forgiven—are extremely well done. And the meeting of Androcles and the lion in the arena, and the terror of the Emperor and all that, are marvellously diverting. In the short piece *Overruled*, says Mr. McCabe, "two married couples exchange partners and discuss the muddle which ensues, until the dinner-gong puts an end to the discussion . . . Shaw's mind is poised between the untruth of monogamy and the inconvenience of polygamy." *Pygmalion* is the amusing account of a phonetician's transformation of a flower-girl into a lady. Her father is another conversion: Mr. Wannafellar, American millionaire, raises him up from poverty, to his victim's great discomfort. Shaw explains in a delightful epilogue that Liza doesn't marry her benefactor; he is preoccupied with his brilliant mother and phonetics: she takes the obedient and adoring Freddy. In discussing Eliza, Shaw for once says something almost sensible about a young woman's reasons for marrying or not marrying a man. "When a bachelor interests and dominates and teaches and becomes important to a spinster, as Higgins with Eliza," says he, "she always, if she has character enough to be capable of it, considers very seriously indeed whether she will play for becoming that bachelor's wife, especially if he is so little interested in marriage that a determined and devoted woman might capture him if she set herself resolutely to it. . . . Eliza's instinct tells her not to marry Higgins. It does not tell her to give him up. It is not in the slightest doubt as to his remaining one of the strongest personal interests in her life."

In *The Great Catherine* (to turn to it next) Catherine takes a strong fancy to a handsome young Englishman. His efforts to escape, his several discomfitures and his triumphant rescue by his English sweetheart are ludicrous—in a strain of boisterous Anglo-Irish humor. Patiomkin and the other Russians, too, are a whole show in themselves. *The Inca of Perusalem* is the Kaiser, who comes to treat with a princess who is slated to marry some one of his sons. A young *ci-devant* millionairess who is acting as the princess's maid (her father the archdeacon having advised it) receives the Inca, who talks in a very Hohenzollern strain. The comedy is excellent. Twice or more Shaw is with the Kaiser. He makes him say that as long as he gave his people the arts they laughed; that when he gave them war they applauded and adored him. Shaw also reminds us that the piece was written before the Kaiser's fall, lest he appear to be kicking a man when he is down. Finally he hits America when he has the Inca praying that he may be President of a Republic like ours, the only form of government, he says, that yields its rulers unquestioned power. As for *O'Flaherty, V.C.*, it is a little masterpiece. It is Lady Gregory with the sting of Shaw added. There is a lovely family jar near the end and O'Flaherty concludes that for peace he prefers the front. O'Flaherty, who is in the English Army fighting "Boshes," tells his mother (who insists Shakespeare was born in Cork) that he is in the French and Russian armies; "and sure," he asks, "who ever heard of the French or the Russians doing anything to the English but fighting them?" O'Flaherty encounters Father Quinlan. "He says, 'You know, don't you,' he says, 'that it's your duty, as a Christian and a good son of the Holy Church to love your enemies?' he says. 'I know it's my duty as a soldier to kill them,' I says. 'That's right, Dinny,' he says, 'quite right. But,' says he, 'you can kill them and do them a good turn afterwards to show your love for them,' he says; 'and it's your duty to have a mass said for the souls of the hundreds of Germans you say you killed,' says he; 'for many and many of them were Bavarians and good Catholics,' he says. 'Is it we that must pay for masses for the souls of the Boshes?' I says. 'Let the King of England pay for them,' I says; 'for it was his quarrel and not mine.'" Later Mrs. O'Flaherty is angry with her son for shaking hands with King George. "You would take the hand of a tyrant red with the blood of Ireland," says she. "Arra, mother," interrupts her honest son, "he's not half the tyrant you are, God help him. His hand was cleaner than mine, that had the blood of his own relatives on it, maybe. In *Augustus Does His Bit* "a distinguished member of the governing class," as Shaw denominates him, is inveigled out of a valuable military document by a brilliantly attired lady who does it all to amuse the town and the soldiers home on leave. Augustus's clerk, who occupies many war-time offices at Little Pifflington, is amusing, especially when he at last gets accepted for service. *"Heartbreak House,"* says Shaw in his wonderful preface to that dreary piece, "is not merely the name of the play which follows. . . . Heartbreak House did not know how to live, at which point all that was left to it was the boast at least it knew how to die. . . . Thus were the firstborn of Heartbreak House smitten; and the young, the innocent, the hopeful expiated the folly and worthlessness of their elders. . . . In the meantime there is, for him (President Wilson), another history to write; for me, another comedy to stage. Perhaps, after all, that is what wars are for, and what historians and playwrights are for. If men will not learn until their lessons are written in blood, why blood they must have, their own for preference." The play itself aims to present the "over-heated drawing room" that was Europe before the war. But Shaw doesn't succeed any too well. Henry James did it much better, and Chekhov. The second and third acts are "awful"; the first is lightened by a few passages. For instance Ellie says of Hector, "He saved the life of a tiger from a hunting party: one of King Edward's hunting parties in India. The king was furious: that was why he never had his military services properly recognized"; or when Mrs. Hushabye says to a new arrival, "What business had you to kiss me?" to which he promptly replies, "I thought I would like to"; and there is almost a human cry in Mrs. Hushabye's words later, "What do men want? They have their food, their firesides, their clothes mended, and our love at the end of the day. Why are they not satisfied? Why do they envy us the pain with which we bring them into the world, and make strange dangers and torments for themselves to be even with us?" His other 1917 play, *Annajanska, the Bolshevik Empress*, Shaw wrote for the Coliseum variety house as an escape, says he, "from the awful legitimacy of the highbrow theatre." He adds that a friend commended it as being the only one of his plays that is not too long. "So I have made it a page or two longer," says he. Annajanska is a grand-duchess who has joined the Bolsheviks, to the great grief of General Strammfest. "Are you," says the latter, "the daughter of a Panjandrum, a Bolshevist?" To which the Duchess (and Shaw with her) replies, "I am anything that will make the world less like a prison and more like a circus."

And now for *Back to Methuselah*, with its one hundred pages of preface and its three hundred pages of play. 'Tis time, says Shaw, to continue our study of that Life Force already introduced to Shavians in *Man and Superman*. Shaw is against the Neo-Darwinians and their fetich of Natural Selection and is for the Neo-Lamarckians, who hold, says he, that "living organisms changed because they wanted to." In a political way the Russians want to change while the other nations want to leave things to Nature. "The Western Powers," says he, "are drifting and colliding and running on the rocks, in the hope that if they continue to do their worst they will get Naturally Selected for survival without the trouble of thinking about it." He declares one-half of Europe is letting itself be kicked around in very sound Neo-Darwinian fashion. "And the good-natured majority," he continues, "are looking on in helpless horror, or allowing themselves to be persuaded by the newspapers of their exploiters that the kicking is not only a sound commercial investment, but an act of divine justice of which they are the ardent instruments." Meanwhile, as usual, he despairs of education. Our teachers, for one thing (and here Shaw almost verges on saying something useful about our educational tyrannies) don't care to teach political science. "Our schools," says he, "teach the morality of feudalism corrupted by commercialism, and hold up the military conqueror, the robber baron and the profiteer as models of the illustrious and the successful." Having abandoned education, therefore—as we in America have not, nor the Herbert Fishers in England,—he turns to Religion, the religion, he adds, that "God helps him who helps himself." If man is to be saved, he must save himself. In short, his Evolution must be Creative.

Hence follow five plays, *In the Beginning, The Gospel of*

the Brothers Barnabas, *The Thing Happens, The Tragedy of an Elderly Gentleman* and *As Far as Thought Can Reach.*   In the first, Lilith has created Adam and Eve; the Serpent bids them create Cain and Abel! and Cain turns killer.   Adam is the average man, Eve the ever-hopeful mother of the race; the Serpent the knowledge of good and evil, the lover of chance and the upholder of free will.   In the second, *The Gospel of the Brothers Barnabas,* Conrad and Franklyn have a scheme for living three hundred years and Lloyd George and Mr. Asquith enter and hear of it.   "How do you do, Mr. Barnabas?" says the latter (whose play name is Lubin).   "I had the pleasure of meeting you once at the Mansion House.   I think it was to celebrate the conclusion of the hundred years peace with America."   "It was long before that," answers Franklyn: "a meeting about Venezuela, when we were on the point of going to war with America."   "Yes, you are quite right," answers the dreamy Premier, "I knew it was something about America."   As for Lloyd George, he is all interest in the new Methuselah gospel and wants to incorporate it at once into his party platform.   "The church is all right essentially," he remarks conciliatingly in one place.   "Get rid of the establishment; get rid of the bishops; get rid of the candlesticks; get rid of the thirty-nine articles; and the Church of England is as good as any other Church; and I don't care who hears me say so."   The piece concludes with Shaw's usual attack on the War and the Church for supporting it; but meanwhile Creative Evolution, Life, goes on.—The third play, *The Thing Happens,* is laid in A.D. 2170. The British Isles are under a President who calls often upon Confucius and other Chinese sages and officials.   The political tenet of that day is, "govern your country with impartial foreigners."   The President, who is a cross between Asquith and Lloyd George, is what is known as a short-liver, which is still, in the 22nd Century, the more popular of the two possibilities. The long-livers, however, are well represented by the Archbishop (the young clergyman of the former play) and Mrs. Lute-

string. Both are over two hundred and marry in the end, to
the distress of the conservatives, who can't bear to contemplate
persons destined to three hundred years. The fourth play, *The
Tragedy of an Elderly Gentleman*, is the most unfailingly comical of the cycle. The old gentleman, his chief and some ladies
have come to Ireland from the new center of the British domains
at Bagdad (Napoleon is along, too, from his kingdom of Tu-
rania) to consult the oracle. The old gentleman is always trying to explain himself and weeping when he can't. He dies at
the end, being a short-liver. The inhabitants don't understand
anything. They don't know what "blush" means, or "decencies,"
or "marriage," or anything. These ancient Irish are long-
livers. They still condescend, though, to dress up and be
oracles, since it is expected of them. But they expose the whole
process. They know people will go off and lie about them anyway, just for prestige. And they are always tapping the air
and communicating with one another with tuning-forks. A
statue to Sir John Falstaff, prince of cowards and liars, is a
prized keepsake from the past, when seven capital cities of
Europe were blown up, and most of the inhabitants killed with
poison gases. At last cowardice became a public virtue: hence
Sir John. Meantime the Elderly Gentleman gives us some infor-
mation about the contest between the white and the other races.
It seems when the Mahometan Reformation came to pass the
awakening was easy: for there were no bishops and priests to
get rid of. As for Napoleon, he at last knows fear, when he
makes the oracle uncover her face.—The last part is called *As
Far as Thought Can Reach*, and at moments Shaw almost at-
tains to mysticism and poetry. The year is A.D. 31,920 and
the ancients have things their way. They are divided into pri-
mary, secondary and tertiary, according to their century. We
are present at the birth of a new child who kicks and swears
inside his big egg till some one saws it open. The child is a
charming lovable thing who likes to throw her arms about her
new comrades. But they either repulse her or get tired of her

in a short time. They are good Shavians, suspicious of emotion, lovers of mind. We learn many things,—that art is false, and life alone is true; that the name of God has come down to these people in many forms, Jove and Voltaire, for instance; that the process of creating man by man was no simple task, despite Creative Evolution; that when a thing is funny we should search it for a hidden truth; that the deepest truth of all is that we can create nothing but ourselves; that we *can* add a cubit to our stature, a muscle to our arm. "The day will come when there will be no people, only thought," says the She-ancient; "and that will be life eternal," adds the He-ancient. "I trust I shall meet my fatal accident before that day dawns," says the child Ecrasia. At the end the dehumanized creatures go off into the temple and leave the newly-Born to shift for herself. Then the spirits of Adam, Eve, Cain, the Serpent and Lilith enter. Adam and Cain don't see much to the Life Experiment after these many moons, but the Serpent is hopeful and the women more so. "All's well," cries Eve as she fades away with the others and leaves Lilith alone. And ere Lilith vanishes she, too, can say: "Of Life only there is no end; and though of its million starry mansions many are empty and many still unbuilt, and though its vast domain is as yet unbearably desert, my seed shall one day fill it and master its matter to the uttermost confines. And for what may be beyond, the eyesight of Lilith is too short. Enough that there is a Beyond."

And with that, proud Ireland's son, England's gadfly, Germany's playwright and America's critic and entertainer should lay his pen orderly away, compose his limbs and fold his arms over his breast. Far from it. Have we not since sat for three hours and thirty minutes beholding French Catholics and English statesmen fighting for the life of the Maid? And when the play is done and church and state shaken, and England belabored again with Irish cudgels, lo, don't we receive "an extra," an epilogue of supernal irony—Joan being canonized in the presence of all her converted foes? But hark, more still: "Shall

I return among you?" asks St. Joan. Whereupon king and
soldier and priest rise from repentant knees and bowing depart,
gravely excusing themselves. A dead saint, yes; but a live rebel,
no. They go to help the same old world wag on.

And now? Well, Shaw's learned the tango—and received
the Nobel prize, because, he says, he wrote nothing that year;
and issued *Translations and Tomfooleries,* and supplied a preface to the catalogue of Colonel Lawrence's illustrations to
the *Seven Pillars of Wisdom.* Lawrence made up his mind
to lose money by his book and its pictures, says Shaw,
and he admires him for it, and for his efforts to obliterate himself by retiring as a private into the Royal Air Force.
So does one great self-advertiser pay tribute to another
—both geniuses, though just why the pacifist Shaw should
be so enthusiastic over this rather ruthless killer—
But to return to *Translations and Tomfooleries.* The
"translation" is Trebisch's *Frau Gitta's Sühne* into Shaw's
Jitta's Atonement. "In real life the consequences of conjugal
infidelity are seldom either so serious as they are assumed to be
in romantic tragedy, or so trivial as in farcical comedy," says
Shaw in his Preface. So he has the "ill-assorted pair" settle
down and find life bearable, instead of Jitta's living unhappily
and her husband's bearing malice, as in Trebisch. The next two
pieces, *The Admirable Bashville* and *Press Cuttings,* are reprints; the other tomfooleries are *The Glimpse of Reality, a
Tragedietta,* in which an Italian Count (time 15th century)
nearly meets his death at the hands of a girl, her lover and her
father, but whom they hesitate to kill because he has things to
say of the Soul; *Passion, Poison and Petrifaction, a Brief Tragedy for Barns and Booths,* in which a husband eats some ceiling
to counteract poison and is petrified; *The Fascinating Foun-
dling, a Disgrace to the Author,* in which Brabazon and Anasta-
sia come successively to the Lord Chancellor, each looking for
a mate, and fall at the end into each other's arms; and *The
Music Cure, a Piece of Utter Nonsense,* which brings pretty

Lord Reginald Fitzambey and mighty Strega Thundridge together: presumably to beat the piano ever after as one.

And now: "Life is ever changing," he tells George Sylvester
Viereck (*Liberty*, August 13, 1927). "However, my chief task
is done."

"You mean your plays?"

"No, my prefaces."

And now? Now he publishes a preface to another man's
plays—to William Archer's, and a sincere and heartfelt preface
it is. "When I returned to an Archerless London it seemed
to me that the place had entered on a new age in which I was
lagging superfluous," says he. We cannot think so: instead,
we beg for another play.

CELT AND SAXON IN SHAKESPEARE'S HENRY IV

IT is not without interest in the days of Meredith's *Celt and Saxon* and of the Celtic Renaissance generally, to note anew Shakespeare's Welsh and English portraits of Glendower and Hotspur, both admirable men.

The two nearly come to blows as to whether or not the heavens were filled with fiery shapes in acknowledgment of Glendower's birth. Glendower stands stoutly by the tale, and Hotspur scoffs at it. Later, in answer to a taunt from Hotspur regarding his accent, Glendower declares,

> "I can speak English, lord, as well as you;
> For I was train'd up in the English court;
> Where, being but young, I framed to the harp
> Many an English ditty lovely well,
> And gave the tongue a helpful ornament,
> A virtue that was never seen in you."

To which Hotspur replies,

> "Marry,
> And I am glad of it with all my heart:
> I had rather be a kitten and cry mew
> Than one of these same metre ballad-mongers;
> I had rather hear a brazen canstick turn'd,
> Or a dry wheel grate on the axle-tree;
> And that would set my teeth nothing on edge,
> Nothing so much as mincing poetry:
> 'Tis like the forced gait of a shuffling nag."

Whereupon Mortimer, who is kin to both, expostulates with Hotspur, who answers peevishly:

"I cannot choose: sometimes he angers me
With telling me of the moldwarp and the ant,
Of the dreamer Merlin and his prophecies,
And of a dragon and a finless fish,
A clip-wing'd griffin and a moulten raven,
A couching lion and a ramping cat,
And such a deal of skimble-skamble stuff
As puts me from my faith."

Mortimer listens patiently to more of the same sort, then answers calmly,

"In faith, he is a worthy gentleman,
Exceedingly well read, and profited
In strange concealments; valiant as a lion,
And wondrous affable, and as bountiful
As mines of India."

In comparison with which we can only include Worcester's charge to Hotspur,—a warning still good for Saxons dealing with Celts:

"In faith, my lord, you are too wilful-blame;
And since your coming here have done enough
To put him quite beside his patience.
You must needs learn, lord, to amend this fault:
Though sometimes it shows greatness, courage, blood,—
And that's the dearest grace it renders you,—
Yet oftentimes it doth present harsh rage,
Defect of manners, want of government,
Pride, haughtiness, opinion and disdain:
The least of which haunting a nobleman
Loseth men's hearts, and leaves behind a stain
Upon the beauty of all parts besides,
Beguiling them of commendation."

LIONEL JOHNSON: THE CLASSICIST AS CELT

IN his Introduction to *The Poetical Works of Lionel Johnson*, 1915, Ezra Pound thinks that Johnson "would have been content always writing Latin, but failing that, he set himself to the task of bringing into English all that he could of the fineness of Latinity. He wrote an English that had grown out of Latin." That his poems *in* Latin are good was apparent to Mr. Yeats, who included two of them, *Satanas* and *Iesu Cor*, in his *Twenty-One Poems Written by Lionel Johnson*, 1898. In *The Classics* Johnson celebrates his favorite Greeks and Latins. *Plato in London* is a fine appreciation of Plato. *Propheta Gentium*, *Sortes Virgilianae* and *A Friend* praise Virgil. *Romans* eulogizes both Caesar and Cicero:

"You were no friends: but you are brothers now!"

Sertorius tells the story of the Roman leader in Spain and the white hind worshiped by his soldiers. *Julian at Eleusis* catches the spirit of revived paganism. Three poems to Lucretius show the same enthusiasm for the great Roman Epicurean that Johnson discloses for him in a passage in his chief study in comparative literature, *The Art of Thomas Hardy*. *Lucretius and Omar*, again, is one of the essays of his principal prose volume,[1] *Post Liminium*, 1911. *The Inimitable Lucian* (whom he did not quite like), *Santo Virgilio* and even *Erasmus My Darling* are other prose contributions to things Greek and Latin.

With such a strong prepossession for the classical, what

[1] *Some Winchester Letters of Lionel Johnson*, 1919, and *Reviews and Critical Papers of Lionel Johnson*, edited by Robert Shafer, 1921, display enthusiasm for Browning, Whitman, Meredith, Emerson, Stevenson, Kipling and other moderns.

was this Englishman's relation to his ancestral Celtic?   In
Renan Truly Shown (a review of Mme. Darmesteter's *Renan*)
he writes,[2] "Take the pages with which this distinguished work
opens; and you will meet the truth about the poetic and un-
satisfactory Celt and his rain-deluged, misted corners of the
earth.   How vividly, if quietly, Mme. Darmesteter interprets
both land and race!"   Of Parnell he observes in a review of
O'Brien's *Life of Charles Stewart Parnell*, "By the side of most
Irishmen, in whom versatility is a charm and instability a danger, he appears the incarnation of set and sworn endeavour."
Of Mangan's poetry he says in his essay on Mangan, "In its
marvellous moments of entire success, it is greater than anything that Ireland has yet produced in English verse, from
Goldsmith to Mr. Yeats."   Earlier he gives a vivid picture of
the poet in Dublin: "He wanders about the rotting alleys and
foul streets, a wasted ghost, with the 'Dark Rosaleen' on his
lips, and a strange light in those mystical blue eyes, which burn
for us yet in the reminiscences of all who ever saw him and wrote
of the unforgettable sight."

In *The Poets of the Nineteenth Century* he observes that
"Ireland has, almost for the first time, added an admirable
contribution to the sum of English verse."   *Poetry and Patriotism in Ireland*, to which Mr. Boyd pays his tribute in *Ireland's Literary Renaissance*, is a plea for a national literature
in the broadest sense,—a literature open to all influences, Irish,
English, Continental, Oriental. "Considering," says he, "to what
magnificent uses Rome turned the forms and metres of Greece,
and England those of France and Italy, without ceasing to be
Roman and English, we need not fear lest an Irish poet should
cease to be Irish, if he study and borrow and adapt the best
achievements of foreign art to the service of the Irish Muses."
The classicist and the Celt speak again in the following: "Melancholy, and sorrow, and the cry of pain, it has been said by
some, are more poetical than serenity and ardour: for my part,

2 *Post Liminium.*

I do not believe it.   Rather, I believe that the Irish poetry of
free and triumphant Ireland will have the wonderful joyousness
and happy splendour of the old heroic and romantic Ireland,
chastened and tempered by the seriousness inseparable from
Christianity.   Meanwhile let us encourage all excellence; there
is room for all. . . After all, who is to decide what is, absolutely and definitely, the Celtic and Irish note?. . . The passion for perfection seems to me as truly Celtic a thing as the
ready indulgence of sentiment: our illuminations, our penman-
ship, our work in stone and metal, all our arts of design, show
an infinite love of taking pains. . . . Many of us, at present,
are somewhat agitated and nervous; we ask hasty and suspicious
questions: 'Is that quite Celtic?   Is this book typically Irish?'
. . . A living literature cannot help being national: it may
feed upon the literature of the past, and of other nations; but,
if it be good literature, it must bear the seal and sign of its
own nationality, and of its own age. . . . If we are to foster,
encourage and develop Irish literature, and not least of all,
Irish poetry, it must be with a wise generosity; in a finely national, not in a pettily provincial spirit. . . . Unquestionably,
we would rather have our poets choose Irish themes, and sing
of Tara sooner than of Troy; of Ossian sooner than of Orpheus;
but if they went to China or Peru for their inspirations, the
result would be neither Chinese nor Peruvian, but 'kindly Irish
of the Irish' still."   Again and again Johnson reiterates his
plea for manysidedness, clarity, color, mind, emotion.   He points
out that it is not the scholars who are "busy in preserving, eluci-
dating, translating, and transmitting to posterity the Gaelic
literature of every age and kind" who attempt to fetter Ireland's literary catholicity, but rather patriots more enthusiastic
than well-balanced or well-read.   His concluding sentence is
characteristic.   "We want a silence," says he, "to fall upon
Ireland, a silence from lamentation and from conflict: and then,
in that happy dawn, the only voices will be voices of the Irish
Muses, reigning in their old home; and the voices of the Irish

people, speaking peace and good will through all our loved and holy Ireland."

These quotations are long; but with the exception of Mr. Boyd, I don't find critics giving the essay from which they are drawn its important place in Johnson's work and in the history of Irish literary criticism.   Turning, meantime, to Johnson's poetry, in how far has the poet practiced what the critic preached?   In his *Shelburne Essays*, First Series, Mr. More quotes Johnson's *Sertorius* entire, as a poem "in which the vague longing of these Irish dreamers is told in a parable of the Roman leaders in Spain."   Johnson's classicism of course commends him strongly to Mr. More; so when the latter writes in *The Drift of Romanticism*, "The light in the old (Celtic) tales is hard and sharp and brilliant, whereas our modern writers rather like to merge the outlines of nature in an all-obliterating grey," he does not have Johnson in mind.   Indeed he declares in his earlier volume, "If I were asked to name the ode written in recent years which exhibits the whitest heat of poetical emotion expressed in language of the most perfect and classical restraint, which conforms most nearly to the great models of old, I should without hesitation name Mr. Johnson's *Ireland*." Here, to use Johnson's own terms, are "passion, ardor, serenity, perfection."

Yet say what he will in theory, in practice Johnson sees more of the melancholy and the pensive in Ireland than the joyous and the radiant.   *Ireland, The Red Wind, Christmas and Ireland, Celtic Speech, Desideria* are passionately sorrowful.   Yet which of these is without praise, patience and hope? And *Parnell, To Weep Irish, Ireland's Dead, Saint Columba, Ways of War, Ninety-Eight, To the Dead of '98, Right and Might* rise to more triumphant strains; till the poet can sing in *The Faith,*

> "When the storm-winds flee
> Gone the gale:
> Peace shall thee
> Heal, O Inisfail!

"Then by hill and vale,
    Lough and sea,
    Inisfail!
Joy shall sing of thee.

"Glory, and what glee,
    Then shall hail
    Thee, ah! thee,
Mournful Inisfail!"

But all Celtdom is not Irish, and Johnson's one perfect lyric comes out of Wales. *Sylvan Morfydd* and *To Morfydd Dead* are good, but *To Morfydd* is wonderful. I should quote it entire, if Katharine Tynan had not anticipated me in her essay on Johnson in *The Dublin Review*. Mr. Yeats and Miss Guiney too have it in their respective selections: I shall never forget the thrill of it when I first read it in Miss Guiney's book. Some of the same ecstasy is in the Cornish poems,—*A Cornish Night*, *Cornwall* and *Hawker of Morwenstow*. And for beauty still, let the reader go to *Gwynedd, Cadgwith, Moel Fammau, Wales, Cyhiraeth, Heddon's Mouth* and *Evening in Wales*. And let him close, if he will, with *Dead*, whose title alone is ominous; for

"In Merioneth, over the sad moor
    Drives the rain, the cold wind blows:
    Past the ruinous church door,
The poor procession without music goes.

"Lonely she wandered out her hour, and died.
    Now the mournful curlew cries
    Over her, laid down beside
Death's lonely people: lightly down she lies.

"In Merioneth, the wind lives and wails,
    On from hill to lonely hill:
    Down the loud, triumphant gales,
A spirit cries *Be strong!* and cries: *Be still!*"

So wrote a classicist breathed upon and made lyrical by the Celtic spirit.

WILLIAM SHARP ON THE CELTIC REVIVAL

I CANNOT at all agree with Mr. Sharp's estimates of the works of Fiona Macleod," writes Mr. Paul Elmer More in *The Drift of Romanticism*. "He apparently valued most the later writings in which the human motives disappear in a haze of disorganized symbolism, whereas the normal reader is likely to find his interest centering, with some minor exceptions, in the tales of *Pharais* and *The Mountain Lovers*. In these the discipline Sharp had acquired from long apprenticeship to the press kept him within the bounds of reason, while the new freedom and the Celtic imagery added a note of strange and fascinating beauty." [1] To Mr. More, Fiona Macleod's symbolism is not impressive; his form and verse are often empty mouthings; he puts emotion above reason; he exalts revery; in a word, he is a Romanticist, which, to Mr. More, with all respect to his critical distinction, is enough said.

William Sharp was not a genius of the first water either as critic or creative artist; but many have liked his work, and some have "adored" it. Even Mr. More praises some of his things. On the whole, however, he prefers Lady Gregory and Synge, whose feet are on solid ground. We have seen that he also admires Lionel Johnson; but all schools find something to praise in that fine spirit.

I cannot write an impassioned defense of Fiona Macleod; but I am interested to note what he thought and said of the Celtic Renaissance and what he considered his own relation to it to be.

In *The Shadowy Waters* Sharp seems to speak directly to

[1] Mr. More also likes *Where the Forest Murmurs*.

153

Mr. More. "To ignore now," he writes, "the Anglo-Celtic school—I prefer to say the Anglo-Celtic group—would be too parochial even for a London critic trained in the narrowest academical and literary conventions. One may ignore this or that writer; all cannot be ignored, for they are now many, and some have that distinction which rebukes the sullen." This is instructive when set beside Mr. More's contention that "in his inability to distinguish between an idea or even a genuine emotion and the fluttering of tired nerves Fiona Macleod fell again and again into meaningless rhetoric that makes the loosest vapourings of 'A. E.' or Mr. W. B. Yeats seem solid and compact of reason." [2] How much truer criticism, really, is the following from Sharp's review of *The Four Winds of Eirinn*: "Ethna Carbery's poems are the poems of the Irish heart, and Miss Hull's and Lady Gregory's re-told saga-tales are the mirror of the ancient Irish genius, as Mr. Yeats's poetry is preëminently the poetry of the Irish spirit: but the poems of 'A. E.' are the poems of a strayed visionary, of a visionary strayed into Ireland, and in love with that imagination and with that dream, but obviously in himself of no country set within known frontiers, of no land withheld by familiar shores. Surcharged with the intensest spirit of Ireland in the less mystical and poetic sense, is the slim volume of a handful of prose papers by Miss Ethel Goddard, entitled *Dreams for Ireland*. This book is uplifted with a radiant hope and with an ecstasy of spiritual conviction that make the heart young to contemplate: would God that its glad faith and untroubled prophecies could be fulfilled in our time, or that in our time even the shadows of the great things to come could lighten the twilight road."

Mr. More admits that Sharp did not "unite himself unreservedly with the so-called Celtic movement, and deprecated its too common hostility to prosaic sense and to everything Saxon."

---

[2] "But reality has more than one way of speaking," says George Meredith in his defence of Celtic poets. (See his Introduction to The Poems of Dora Sigerson Shorter, 1907.)

Yet, as we have seen, Mr. More believes he "frothed" more than the avowed adherents of the present Renaissance. But what Sharp really believed in was not Celticism but Anglo-Celticism, of which school he declares (*For the Beauty of an Idea: Prelude*) both Yeats and AE to be shining examples. In *Celtic* he shows that he himself is not so much seeking old Celtic enchantment as new enchantment comparable to the old. "The ideal of art," says he, "should be to represent beautiful life. . . . So far as I understand the 'Celtic movement,' it is a natural outcome, the natural expression of a freshly inspired spiritual and artistic energy. . . . There is no set law upon beauty. It has no geography. It is the domain of the spirit. . . . As for literature, there is, for us all, only English literature. All else is provincial or dialect."

In his Prologue to *The Sin-Eater*, however, he confesses to a closer relation to the movement. "The beauty of the World, the pathos of Life, the gloom, the fatalism, the spiritual glamour—it is out of these, the inheritance of the Gael, that I have wrought these tales. Well do I know that they do not give 'a rounded and complete portrait of the Celt.' . . . Elsewhere I may give such delineation as I can, and is within my own knowledge of the manysidedness of the Celt, and even of the insular Gael. But in this book, as in *Pharais* and *The Mountain Lovers*, I give the life of the Gael in what is, to me, in accord with my own observation and experience, its most poignant characteristics—that is, of course, in certain circumstances, in a particular environment. . . . Some of my critics, heedless of the complex conditions which differentiate the Irish and the Scottish Celt, complain of the Celtic gloom that dusks the life of the men and women I have tried to draw. That may be just. I wish merely to say that I have not striven to depict the blither Irish Celt. I have sought mainly to express something of the 'Celtic Gloom,' which, to many Gaels if not to all, is so distinctive in the remote life of a doomed and passing race. . . . The Celt falls, but his spirit rises in the heart and the brain

of the Anglo-Celtic peoples, with whom are the destinies of
the generations to come."

Lionel Johnson wanted all literatures to come to Ireland
and be made part of it; William Sharp desired Irish literature,
and all other forms of the Celtic, to ally themselves with England and be content to be British. In this he resembled a whole
group of writers; among them George Meredith, whom, by the
way, he called "The Prince of Celtdom."

THE IRISH NOTE IN J. M. SYNGE'S TRANSLATIONS

SYNGE'S plays, travel books and verses have been ably and appreciatively treated by numerous critics. But a note may be added regarding his translations.

Next to Lionel Johnson, Synge was the scholar of the Celtic group. It is well known that when Yeats found him in Paris and persuaded him to take an active part in the Irish Revival, Synge was working at French criticism, which he hoped to master with a view to becoming a French critic himself. "He thought M. Loti the best living writer of prose," says Mr. Masefield in *John M. Synge; A Few Personal Recollections*, 1915. "There are marks of M. Loti's influence in the Aran book." He won prizes in Hebrew and Irish at Trinity College, Dublin, and graduated B. A. in 1892. "He had read considerably in some six languages (Hebrew, Irish, German, Italian, French and English)," says Masefield, "and widely in at least four of these, besides his scholarship in the universal language of music. Among his early plans for books were schemes for a translation from some of the prose of St. Francis of Assisi (which he abandoned, because an English translation was published at the time), and for a critical study of Racine, whose pure and noble art always meant much to him. Some critical and other writings of this period exist in manuscript. They are said to be carefully written, but wanting in inner impulse." Mr. Masefield adds that as a craftsman Synge respected the skill of the French Decadents, but disliked their vision. "From what I can remember," Mr. Masefield concludes, "I should say that his favourite author, during the greater part of his life, was Racine."

In the *Nation* for Dec. 26, 1912, Stuart P. Sherman held
that Anatole France, not Racine, was a more likely favorite of
Synge, and declared that only a close study of Synge's literary
sources could explain the remarkable style of his plays.   He
does not agree with Yeats that Synge's manner is all Irish.   He
says that "the orthodox way of 'explaining' Synge is to ignore
the poems and translations and point to the volume on the Aran
Islands."   He admits, though, that while the poems are partly
imitative, the translations are unmistakably Synge's.   "Here,"
says he, "are all the peculiar marks of Synge himself,—the irre-
sistibly quaint idiom, the drifting rhythm, the loose sentence
structure, thought thrown after thought, as it were, without pre-
meditation, and blossoming from phrase to phrase, the window
opened upon a mist of vague and limitless emotion, the poignant
and adorable Celtic wistfulness—we are here in the presence
of a pure miracle of that style which is Synge's special creation,
and which distinguishes him not merely from Leopardi, but also
from all his Anglo-Irish contemporaries.   With all its apparent spontaneity, his style is as patiently and cunningly wrought
out as the style of Walter Pater,—wrought out of a scrupu-
lously select vocabulary, idiom and images, with an exacting ear
controlling the cadence and shepherding the roving and dreamy
phrases.   With the aid of this perfected instrument he is able to
appropriate, and seal as his own, poems from authors as diverse
as Petrarch and Walter von der Vogelweide, Leopardi and Villon.   This fact, taken together with his dependence in the original poems, tends to justify a search beneath the surface of his
other work for alien forces secretly shaping his emotions and
determining his forms."

Yet granting for argument that the poems are imitative,
and that the plays are only apparently pure Irish, how do the
translations, which are obviously nothing more than Irish tran-
scriptions, prove that Synge's style is not wholly Irish, but
builded out of innumerable foreign sources?   The truth about
Synge seems to be simply that he read and studied other litera-

tures than his own as Yeats read and interpreted Blake, but
that he made almost as little use of them in his creative writing
as Yeats has of Blake in his poetry. Blake's influence on Yeats'
ideas is another matter, and on *Where There Is Nothing*.

Hardly a paragraph in Synge's translations fails to yield
an Irish turn of Speech. He is more Irish than Father Prout,
whose translations from Horace have been ably discussed by
Mr. Monahan in *Nova Hibernia*. As one reads one hears in
every accent an Irishman, not an Italian, a German or a Frenchman. In these paraphrases Synge is not really translating;
rather is he obeying Lionel Johnson, and bringing the world's
literature to Ireland, to be minted anew as Irish coin. Reading
Synge's translations is like gazing on Italian, German or Flem-
ish conceptions of the Virgin,—conceptions not drawn from
women of Galilee, but from the painters' own countries and
times. Synge's Laura is not an Italian but an Irish Laura;
Synge's Old Women are not Villon's but Irish old women; and
Synge's Silvia, again, is not an Italian but an Irish Silvia. No
lack of scholarship was responsible for these transformations;
Synge was conscious in the matter; he was deliberately making
over some famous foreign figures into Irish. "The translations," he says himself in his Preface, "are sometimes free, sometimes literal, *according as seemed most fitting with the form of
language I have used*,"—the language and idiom, namely, of
Ireland.

IDEAS OF GOOD AND EVIL IN THE POETRY OF AE

THE metaphysical nature of AE's work is as marked as its exquisite poetical expression. "To comprehend his view of life," says Mr. Morris,[1] "one must return by way of Blake and Jacob Boehme, by way of Swedenborg and Crashaw and Santa Teresa to the neo-Platonists of Alexandria, to Plato himself, and to the sacred books of the east." He seeks the Absolute, to which he goes for revelation, manifested as it is everywhere, alike in Mother Earth, the stars and Infinity.

Yet if men, the earth, the stars and dreams are phases of the Spirit of Good, what of Evil in us, in Nature and the Universe? Here is a fitting theme for a seer; and here is a poet with an angel's sight and a pen dipped in moonbeams.

His poem *Duality* has for its motto, "From me spring good and evil." In it we see man fated to be at war with himself:

"Whose passionate peace is still to be at strife,
O'erthrown but in the unconflicting spheres."

Yet in *The Vestiture of the Soul* he applies his idealism to earthly things. A pauper's tattered dress saddens but does not quench his spirit; for the world's evil is but a patched garment; the soul in Earth and man and the stars cannot be crushed by it. In *Inheritance* he asks men why they still cry out with pain? for their forebears

"Each before he passed away
Gave clear articulate cries of woe;
Your pain is theirs of long ago:"

[1] *The Celtic Dawn*, 1917, p. 26.

a fact which moves him to an apology in his Foreword to his *Collected Poems*, for a strain of the doleful in himself. "When I first discovered for myself," he writes, "how near was the King in His Beauty I thought I would be the singer of the happiest songs. Forgive me, Spirit of my Spirit, for this, that I have found it easier to read the mystery told in tears and understood Thee better in sorrow than in joy; that, though I would not, I have made the way seem thorny, and have wandered in too many byways, imagining myself into moods which held Thee not. I should have parted the true from the false, but I have not yet passed from myself who am in the words of this book. Time is a swift winnower, and that he will do quickly for me."

> "Could you and I but of each other say
> From what a lordly House we took our way,
> And to what Hostel of the Gods we wend,
> Oh would we not anticipate the end?
> Oh would we not have paradise to-day?"

he cries in *Kinship*, with a sincerity only slightly sweetened by the Omar Khayyám rhythm.

Earth in his philosophy is something to worship, to rise from to stars, to return to for strength, for combat, pity, salvation. In the *Earth Breath* he sings,

> "One of all thy generations,
>   Mother, hails to thee.
> Hail, and hail, and hail for ever,
>   Though I turn again
> From thy joy unto the human
>   Vesticture of pain.
> I thy child who went forth radiant
>   In the golden prime,
> Find thee still the mother-hearted
>   Through my night in time;
> Find in thee the old enchantment
>   There behind the veil
> Where the gods, my brothers, linger,
>   Hail, forever, hail!"

Earth to him remains pure and holy, though men suffer; and he turns from them to her.

In *Love*, however, he prays that ere he lose himself in the spaces he may yet taste of earth's sorrow:

"I would still hear the cry of the fallen recalling me back from
      above,
To go down to the side of the people who weep in the shadow
      of death."

In *The man to the Angel*, he celebrates the "blows of fortune":

"I have wept a million tears:
   Pure and proud one, where are thine,
   What the gain though all thy years
   In unbroken beauty shine?

All your beauty cannot win
   Truth we learn in pain and sighs:
   You can never enter in
   To the circle of the wise."

In *Pain*, indeed, he makes a god of Suffering:

"Of my god I know this much,
   And in singing I repeat,
   Though there's anguish in his touch,
   Yet his soul within is sweet."

Comfort from the stars is a constantly recurring note. In *Tragedy* a king is put to shame by them. In *The Black Age* the shadowy hosts of woe suffer because they are lost children of the stars. As for the poet, he arises and finds God in the heavens. Yet in *The Dawn of Darkness* the stars no longer soothe him, and he sees and feels only the sorrows of Time. But stoic defiance of suffering comes out in the inscription to *The Earth Breath and Other Poems*: for

"Of my night I give to you the stars,
   And of my sorrow here the sweetest gains,
   And out of Hell, beyond its iron bars,
      My scorn of all its pains."

In *Immortality*, stars are lights of Pity:

> "Lights of infinite pity star the grey dusk of our days:
> Surely here is soul: with it we have eternal breath."

Evil is in the world, then, and in Man, and is conquered both by going forth to meet it and by escaping from it into the Infinite. In *The Hour of Twilight* comfort is found in conversing with ancestral souls that "beckon the wounded spirit." *Shadow and Glory* is a dialogue: Shadow is corporeal man, Glory, eternal. Glory calls Shadow back to contemplation of the Infinite whence both sprang. *Endurance* teaches that even the death of man's beloved is a finite thing: again the poet seeks the stars. The *Mid-World* shows that joy and pain ebb and flow:

> "Rejoice to-day: to-morrow
> A turning tide shall flow
> Through infinite tones of sorrow
> To reach an equal woe."

Joy and pain, with pain now in the ascendant, infuse *The Tide of Sorrow*. But comfort is strong again in *In the Womb*:

> "And day by day the dawn or dark enfolds
> And feeds with beauty eyes that cannot see
> How in her womb the mighty mother moulds
> The infant spirit for eternity."

The Divine Vision (the title poem of AE's third volume) calls pity "only seer." Freedom embodies liberty in a bird which flies into that light which the poet also seeks. *The Nuts of Knowledge* is Irish, but also how Blakean! Instead of "eating of the tree of good and evil," AE takes food from the Sacred Hazel, the Celtic tree of life.

> I think when night towers up aloft and shakes the trembling
>   dew,
> How every high and lonely thought that thrills my being
>   through
> Is but a ruddy berry dropped down through the purple air,
> And from the magic tree of life the fruit falls everywhere."

In the *Twilight of Earth*, though, he finds the nuts of knowledge insufficient; instead of eating them idly, he would wage war along "the starry track." *The Burning Glass* and the *Morning Star* disclose AE worshipping woman mystically, as a star. In a *Farewell* he hears "a whisper of battle afar in the world" and passes "from a council of the stars and of the hills to a life that is new." He would conquer the earth and the skies. The theme is suggested earlier in *A Woman's Voice.*

The heavenly and earthly mingle in AE's equisite *A New Being:*

> "I know myself no more, my child,
>   Since thou art come to me,
> Pity so tender and so wild
>   Hath wrapped my thoughts of thee."

And *The Secret Love* gets the better of Time in human-wise: for

> "You and I can mock his fabled wing,
> For a kiss is an immortal thing.
> And the throb wherein those old lips met
> Is a living music in us yet."

Hope in Failure sings the chastening power of trouble and shows how pity is born of it. *The Everlasting Battle* is the eternal strife of man feeling himself both human and divine. In *A Midnight Meditation,* AE relates how ages ago men and angels fell into revolt: concluding

> "And now my grief I see
> Was but the ancient shadow part of me,
> Not yet attuned to good."

ON THE INFLUENCE OF LADY GREGORY ON
WILLIAM BUTLER YEATS

IN that curious fantasy, *The Unicorn from the Stars*," says Katherine Brógy in *Lady Gregory and the Lore of Ireland* (*Forum*, vol. 48, p. 465, 1912), "one gets the impression that it is Lady Gregory's realism alone which holds back Mr. Yeats' mysticism from a glory of spontaneous combustion!" Whether Lady Gregory's *The Unicorn from the Stars* is an improvement on Yeats' *Where There Is Nothing*, is very questionable; whether the realism of Yeats' later manner is preferable to his early poetical one, is scarcely that: it isn't. But the backbone of the Irish Theatre, after all, is Lady Gregory, and her indomitable will and purpose can no more be discounted by Yeats there than the fairies could in his more mystical youth.

The direct influence of Lady Gregory's plays on Yeats is slight, though her important share in the composition of *The Pot of Broth* is pointed out by Mr. Boyd in Chapter VII of his *Ireland's Literary Renaissance*. Of her translations, on the other hand, and their relation to himself, Yeats writes in Appendix I to his *Dramatic Poems*.

"Almost every story I have used, or person I have spoken of," says he, "is in one or other of Lady Gregory's *Gods and Fighting Men* and *Cuchulain of Muirthemne*. If my present small Dublin audience for poetical drama grows and spreads beyond Dublin, I shall owe it to these two books, masterpieces of prose, which can but make the old stories as familiar to Irishmen everywhere as the stories of Arthur and his knights to all the readers of books. I cannot believe that it is from friendship that I weigh these books with Malory and feel no discontent at the tally, or that it is the wish to make the circumstantial origin of my own art familiar that would make me give them before all other books to Irish girls and boys." He then shows that while not taking his stories from her, he yet has most of those she has treated: he would have her books read along with his. Indeed, in her *Our Irish Theatre*, Lady Gregory states that she gathered folk-lore under Yates' direction. As a result, however, Yeats writes in his Dedication to her of his *Where There Is Nothing*, "You taught me to understand again, and much more perfectly than before, the true countenance of country life." The teacher, in short, learned from the taught. In his Preface to *The Unicorn from the Stars* he adds that Lady Gregory's knowledge of rural life and speech kept *Cathleen ni Houlihan* from the clouds. In fact they wrote the piece together. After attributing most of *The Unicorn from the Stars* to her, finally, he concludes that his part of it consists in trying to bring together the rough life of the road and the frenzy of the poet,—"a prophecy, as it were, of the time when it will be once again possible for a Dickens and a Shelley to be born in the same body." Lady Gregory is responsible for the rest.

How strongly Lady Gregory, or Time, or the Muse,[1] have influenced Yeats away from romanticism to realism is finally everywhere apparent in *The Green Helmet* and in *Responsibilities*. Unhappily so! for when Yeats needs romantic realism he might get it better from Synge, to whose *Tinker's Wedding* Mr. Morris (*The Celtic Dawn*, 1917) thinks he probably owed the suggestion of *Where There Is Nothing*. In it, at any rate, Yeats shares in the genius of Synge; in *The Unicorn from the Stars* he surrenders his peculiar genius to the lesser talent of a sincere but unlike artist. Yet perhaps *Cathleen ni Houlihan* was worth giving up something to write. And the gratitude he

---

[1] Indeed Llewellyn Jones, in *First Impressions*, 1925, writes an interesting defence of *The Later Poetry of W. B. Yeats*, in which he praises him for his sincerity and for "not repeating his old tunes."

expresses to his friend in *The Trembling of the Veil* for her watchful care over him when he was long ill is our gratitude, too. Meanwhile in one of his *Later Poems*, in *To a Friend Whose Work Has Come to Nothing*, he bids her take courage for the failure of some good she has striven to bring to pass: "Turn away

> "And like a laughing string
> Whereon mad fingers play
> Amid a place of stone,
> Be secret and exult,
> Because of all things known
> That is most difficult."

Indeed the bitter note, in crabbed verse, is not seldom present in his later poetry; but meantime his haunting prose still echoes down the spheres. And in *Four Plays for Dancers* he is fascinated by Noh drama, mask plays and plays with little scenery. Meanwhile his fictitious friends Robartes and Asperne, of his earlier stories, *The Tables of the Law; The Adoration of the Magi* (1914), still accompany him and hold out promises for our future delectation—and instruction. "They take their place in a phantasmagoria in which I endeavour to explain my philosophy of life and death," says this dreamer of dreams.

A NOTE ON LIONEL JOHNSON, KATHARINE TYNAN HINKSON AND LOUISE IMOGEN GUINEY

IN *The Dublin Review* for October, 1907, Katharine Tynan Hinkson wrote an admirable essay on Lionel Johnson, and printed those notes on several contemporary poets which Ezra Pound includes in his Introduction to Johnson's *Poetical Works* (1915). To Mrs. Hinkson, Johnson's "intellect and his knowledge in a sense overdominated his poetry. It smacks so much of scholarship at times as to be over-deliberate, over-informed. Except at its very best it lacks the passion, the impulse, the rush of inspired poetry. I recall only one poem which has throughout the white light of poetry, the movement and the energy. That is the poem *To Morfydd*, in which for once Lionel Johnson stood side by side with the Celtic poets he admired so passionately."

While a friend of Lionel Johnson, then, and an appreciative one, Mrs. Hinkson is by no means essentially of the Johnsonian school. Though her first book, *Louise de la Vallière*, went far afield, she has not since gleaned from all the world, as Johnson proposed, to lay its spoils at Ireland's feet. Rather she gathers the simple and radiant things at home. In *Cuckoo Songs* (1894),

> "A small monotonous song I sing,
>   My notes are faint and few
> Like his, whose coming wakes the Spring,
>   Cuckoo!   Cuckoo!"

And *Innocencies* (1905), continues the strain:

> "I sing of children and of folk on wings,
>   Of faith, of love, of quiet country things;

168

> Of death that is but lying down at night
> And waking with the birds at morning light;
> And of the Love of God encompassing;
> And of the seasons round from Spring to Spring;
> I sing of gardens, fields, and flowers and trees:
> Therefore I call my love-songs Innocencies."

Ballads and Lyrics (1891), even opens with an *Apologia:*

> "So in my book there will be found
> No gleanings from a foreign ground.
> If such you seek, go buy, go buy
> Of some more travelled folk than I.
> Kind Master Critic, say not, please,
> How that her world so narrow is,
> Since here she warns expectant eyes
> That homely is her merchandise!"

Homely, to be sure, but sweet, and acceptable to many on both sides of the Water.

So Lionel Johnson's foremost "appreciator" after all is not Katharine Tynan, but our American poet and critic, Louise Imogen Guiney, to whom Johnson's *Post Liminium* is fittingly dedicated. Her poems on Winchester and Oxford at once show kinship with Johnson, who has written so passionately of both. The classical temper of his poetry and prose appeal to one herself in the classical tradition. "The real short-coming of his verse lies in its Latin strictness and asceticism," she writes in *On Lionel Johnson* (*Atlantic Monthly,* December, 1902); "somewhat repellent to any readers but those of his own temper." Yet she admits no rhetoric in him, and while acknowledging him, as he was, a remarkable critic, declares that he was all poet. Why Johnson meant so much to Miss Guiney is apparent at once when one turns to Jessie B. Rittenhouse's *The Younger American Poets.* "She is a classic by temperament," says Miss Rittenhouse, "and has drawn to herself, as by chemical affinity, such things as are rare and choice in the world of books and life.—Miss Guiney hives in many fields and lands the quaint, the picturesque, the beautiful, to which her temperament calls her unerringly." She was an American much in love with England, as Johnson was an Englishman smitten with Ireland. But she can write of Greece too, of Rome, of France, of Italy, of Japan. She is of the "more travelled folk" to whom Mrs. Hinkson directs us. Yet she can sing a simple *Irish Peasant Song* too:

"I try to knead and spin, but my life is low the while,
 Oh, I long to be alone, and walk abroad a mile;
 Yet if I walk alone, and think of naught at all,
 Why from me that's young should the wild tears fall?

"The shower-sodden earth, the earth-coloured streams,
 May breathe on me awake, and moan to me in dreams,
 And yonder ivy fondling the broke castle-wall,
 It pulls upon my heart till the wild tears fall.

"The cabin-door looks down a furze-lighted hill,
 And far as Leighlin Cross the fields are green and still;
 But once I hear the blackbird in Leighlin hedges call,
 The foolishness is on me, and the wild tears fall."

NEW GODS FOR OLD

As one reads the concluding sentence of Miss Harriet Manning Blake's *Classic Myth in the Poetic Drama of the Age of Elizabeth*, a sentence in which she expresses the hope that the great drama on classic myth may yet be written, one may recall with concern Thomas Hardy's dismissal of all ancient mythologies from his *Dynasts*. "The wide prevalence of the monistic theory of the universe," says he in his Preface, 1904, "forbade, in this twentieth century, the importation of divine personages from any antique mythology as ready-made sources or channels of Causation, even in verse, and excluded the celestial machinery of, say, *Paradise Lost*, as peremptorily as that of the *Iliad* or the *Eddas*." In their stead he employs "phantasmal Intelligences," chosen, he puts it, "with a single view to the modern expression of a modern outlook, and in frank divergence from classical and other dramatic precedent which ruled the ancient voicings of ancient themes."

In the late eighteenth century and early nineteenth a lonelier figure than Mr. Hardy's was also banishing old gods, only to substitute new. Mr. Hardy has dispensed with the old gods, or any gods, save only the Will, as unscientific; William Blake parted with the old because, to him, they were scientific. To him ancient Greeks and modern rationalists were of like breed: both put reason before feeling, memory before inspiration. "We do not want either Greek or Roman models if we are but just and true to our own Imaginations, those Worlds of Eternity in which we shall live forever, in Jesus our Lord," he cries in one place.[1] "The Classics! it is the classics, and not Goths nor monks that desolate Europe with wars," he adds in another.[2] "Grecian is

[1] Preface to *Milton*.
[2] *On Homer's Poetry*.

171

Mathematic Form: Gothic is Living Form. Mathematic Form
is eternal in the Reasoning Memory: Living Form is Eternal
Existence," he declares in a third.[3]

For all that mattered to Blake was spirit. A great inner
drama unfolded forever before him. He gazed with wonder, and
came to regard poetical imagination, his own genius, as superb,
supreme, identical with Christ and with God. He wrote down and
painted his visions. At least some of them took definite form;
others remained, except to him (who saw all of them so clearly!),
undefined. Scores of beings, all vivid to him, are names only to
us. In ten years of "seeing" Blake had framed a mythology of
his own, "as tangled and interdependent a system of theology,"
says Mr. Chesterton,[4] "as the Catholic Church has accumulated
in two thousand." "Trembling," says Blake himself,[5]

"Trembling I sit day and night; my friends are astonish'd at me,
Yet they forgive my wanderings, I rest not from my great task,
To open the Eternal Worlds, to open the immortal Eyes
Of man inwards into the Worlds of Thought, into Eternity,
Ever expanding in the Bosom of God the Human Imagination.

True, his friends forgive him! Yet the influence of his
mythology of the "brain of man" [6] on even such friends as Swinburne, Yeats, and Symons is slight. Commentators armed with
inspiration *and* reason cannot completely unravel his system.
Yet with the example he sets of a new mythology; with devil
plays, witch plays, Arthurian legends, Norse tales, ghost stories,
and Christian dogma behind and around him; with Yeats and the
Celtic school and their mythology; with Wells and Dreiser and
their supernatural science; with Butler's mythology of the un-
born; with Ezra Pond pursuing things Chinese, with Tagore
popularizing Hindoo story, with the anthropologists featuring
primitive literatures, with Foote and Cadman putting American

[3] *On Virgil.*
[4] *William Blake,* p. 156.
[5] *Jerusalem.*
[6] F. E. Pierce. *Selections from the Symbolical Poems of William Blake,*
1915, p. viii.

folk-lore into music, and with Whiteman, Gershwin and others defending that form of American music brought to us by our African forebears, one wonders, at times, what the fate of classical mythology will be.

And speaking of Yeats, one must pause long enough to note what he says, as only he can, of Blake and his mythology. Blake, he observes in his *Ideas of Good and Evil*, Blake "was a man crying out for a new mythology, and trying to make one because he could not find one to his hand. Had he been a Catholic of Dante's time he would have been content with Mary and the angels; or had he been a scholar of our time he would have taken his symbols where Wagner took his, from Norse mythology; or have followed, with the help of Professor Rhys, that pathway into Welsh mythology which he found in *Jerusalem*, or have gone to Ireland—and he was probably an Irishman—and chosen for his symbols the sacred mountains, along whose sides the peasant still sees enchanted fires, and the divinities which have not faded from the belief, if they have faded from the prayers, of simple hearts."

For this passage—though long in quotation—is pertinent to our purposes here, its only errors being that, as Mr. Symons has sufficiently shown in his book, Blake was not an Irishman, and second, that, when an Irishman did arise, an Irishman likewise seeking a new mythology, he did not find it on the sacred slopes of Celtdom, but beyond the sands of Nineveh; except, of course, that that Irishman is not a scholar, but an aristocrat, a soldier, and an author who disapproves of commercialized drama and hard, plodding art. "Genius," says he, "is the infinite capacity for not taking pains."

And therewith Lord Dunsany, the greatest myth-maker of our time, is at once at one with Blake and Yeats. "Dunsany's two greatest analogies are perhaps Maeterlinck and William Blake—that strange, half-mad Blake who wandered in heaven and hell, writing prophetic books, picturing them marvelously; like Dunsany, creating new gods, naming them strange names,"

writes Edna Garrett Boyd.[7] There is, indeed, in all these men
the same conviction, and its repeated assertion, of the immense
superiority of instinct over reason. "Instinct is swift and unconscious," says Dunsany, "while Reason is plodding and slow.
. . . An artist's message is from instinct to sympathy. . . .
This age has become a schoolroom, and nasty exact little facts
hem us round, leaving no room for wonder. . . . Our slow per-
ceptions and toilsome reasoning can never keep pace with any
work of art, and if I could tell you for certain the exact sources
of *The Gods of the Mountain* I could tell you from what storms
and out of what countries comes every drop of the spring that
is laughing out of the hill." "Yet take my *Gods of the Mountain*," he says of this favorite play—"Some beggars, being hard
up, pretend to be gods. Then they get all they want. But
Destiny, Nemesis, the Gods, punish them by turning them into
the very idols they desired to be."[8]

But "I am not trying to teach anybody anything," he has-
tens to add. If so, how different his purpose from Blake's,
whose prophetical books are a new Christianity! Yet "I want,"
says Dunsany elsewhere, "I want to write about men and women
and the great forces that have been with them from their cradles
up, ("to know mankind as others know men," as he says of the
poet's mission in another place)—forces that the ages have
neither aged nor weakened." After this declaration how extraordinary that Mr. Bierstadt should say, "His place is that
of pure abstract thought, devoid of emotion, and so neither in
his gods nor in the world they rule do we find a trace of passion, human or divine. It is this that sets his work apart from
the lives of men, and it is this that is his greatest limitation."
Yet one need only refer the critic to Chu-Bu and Sheemish, in
The Book of Wonder, for about as funny human gods as the
world has had since Lucian and Disraeli. And Miss Boyd,

[7] *Lord Dunsany, Dreamer, The Forum,* Vol. 57, 1917, p. 501.
[8] See Dunsany's letters to Stuart Walker in Bierstadt's *Dunsany the
Dramatist.*

though appreciating Dunsany greatly, and writing of him eloquently, feels the infinite littleness of man in his scheme, the impotency of his gods, his sophistication, his lack of sunny humor, his sardonic irony. Mr. Vale is nearer when he writes,[9] "Lord Dunsany has a predilection for the gods. . . . No man is more competent to take these Elder Brothers by the hand and establish them in a new mythology, in which shall be symbolized the strivings, the passions, the illusions and disillusionments of the human race, now consciously growing old and a little world-weary. . . . He is at once a poet, playwright, philosopher, satirist and symbolist." And Mr. Morris [10] is nearer still when he finds that "Dunsany portrays the combat of man with the gods, the creations of his own ignorance, for the gods are merely the symbolic expression of man's lack of control over his experience, and with time the destroyer, the illustrations of man's ultimate futility."

But why ultimate futility? Dunsany's chief purpose in living and writing is not to destroy man's faith, but to dream in peace, to fight in war, and to evoke beauty always. "The River of Myth," he wrote in 1908, "which becomes one with the Waters of Fable in the desert outside the city, floats under a gate of pure gold, rejoicing, and under many arches fantastically carven that are one with either bank." [11] "I don't know that my fellow-officers know that I write, and all European soils are so harassed by war that nothing grows there but death," he observed in 1916 to Stuart Walker. And in the Preface to *The Last Book of Wonder* of the same year, he says the war "comes to this, that though we are all killed there will be song again, but if we were to submit and so survive there could be neither songs nor dreams, nor any joyous free things any more." Futility here would seem to be only futility if the enemy won. And Dunsany is earnest enough about war to compose a war poem. Here it is: [12]

[9] *Lord Dunsany's Gods, The Forum*, Vol. 51, 1914, p. 790.
[10] *The Celtic Dawn*, p. 143.
[11] *The Sword of Welleran*, p. 55.
[12] *The Living Age*, Vol. 293, 1917, p. 258.

"The great guns of England, they listen mile on mile
To the boasts of a broken War-Lord; they lift their throats
    and smile;
        But the old woods are fallen
        For a while.

"The old woods are fallen; yet they will come again,
They will come back some springtime with the warm winds and
    the rain,
        For Nature guardeth her children,
            Never in vain.

"They will come back some season; it may be a hundred years;
It is all one to Nature with the centuries that are hers;
        She shall bring back her children
            And dry their tears.

"But the tears of a would-be War-Lord shall never cease to flow.
He shall weep for the poisoned armies whenever the gas-winds
    blow,
        He shall always weep for his widows,
            And all Hell shall know.

"The tears of a pitiless Kaiser, shallow they'll flow and wide,
Wide as the desolation made by his silly pride
        When he slaughtered a little people
            To stab France in her side.

"Over the ragged cinders they shall flow on and on
With the listless falling of streams that find not oblivion,
        For ages and ages of years
            Till the last star is gone."

But to return from war to dreams, here uprises on our ken
another artist for wonder's sake. And that he may play at
will with his fancies he dreams his dreams at the edge of Time.
"Of pure poetry," says Dunsany in his Introduction to *Songs
of the Fields* by Francis Ledwidge, "Of pure poetry there are
two kinds, that which mirrors the beauty of the world in which
our bodies are, and that which builds the more mysterious king-

doms where geography ends and fairyland begins, with gods
and heroes at war, and sirens singing still and Alph going down
to the darkness of Xanadu.   Mr. Ledwidge gives us the first
kind."   Needless to add, Dunsany himself joins Coleridge in
affording us the second—in prose, it is true, but in prose of the
most poetical beauty.

Dunsany's is a land of dreams on the edge of Time.   Mine
is a world, thinks he, neither the Restoration's land of cuckoldry
nor Oscar Wilde's London drawing-rooms, but a land in which
I can wander at will, with no sex, politics, Christians or heathens
to distract me or to scandalize others.   Good, in theory; but in
practice, with none of these human bones of contention, he must
substitute other passions, if, as is inevitable with him, Imagination is to reign.   The new gods being dead, he revives some old!
"Before there stood gods upon Olympus, or ever Allah was
Allah," says he in *The Gods of Pegana*, "had wrought and rested
Mana-Yood Sushai."   How very recent Greece and Rome seem
when Dunsany and Blake dream!   Men are but specks far down
in an unrealized present.   It is as when Professor Breasted
speaks of Egypt.   And with a whole new pantheon out of the
Void, Dunsany becomes, in spite of himself, moral, and contributes to men, in spite of himself, his reading of life.

To all men, that is to say, who plod slowly after reason—to
all men, let us add, but to Mr. Yeats, to whom Dunsany's appeal
by instinct is swift and unconscious.   "So strange," says Yeats
dreamily, in his *Selections from the Writings of Dunsany*, "so
strange is the pleasure they give, so hard to analyze and de-
scribe, I do not know why these stories and plays delight me.
Now they set me to thinking of some old Irish jewel covered
with Indian arabesques that hangs in a friend's hall, now of
St. Mark's at Venice, now of cloud palaces in the sundown; but
more often still of a strange country or state of the soul that
once for a few weeks I entered in deep sleep and after lost and
have ever mourned and desired."

But what does Dunsany mean to persons not mystics or

dreamers? I have known such to debate the question with zeal. *The Lonely Idol* (in *Fifty-one Tales*) affords an answer, I fancy. Dunsany has a little outlandish god to whom no one longer prays, so *he* prays to him, pitying his fallen state; yet earnestly beseeching him no longer to be the friend of Time, that enemy of Beauty, but to "let lovely things live on for the sake of our tears." Throughout his work he insinuates this paradox, that the gods are not, yet that all the gods are, and if not prayed to, or if found out to be powerless and futile in the face of the greater gods, or Space and Time, will ruthlessly destroy us. When Uldoon (in *Time and the Gods*) learned the secret of the gods he returned to his people, and they said:

" 'Hast thou found the secret of the gods?'

"And he answered:

" 'I have found it, and the secret of the gods is this:—

" 'Zyni Moë, the small snake, seeing the figure and the shadow of a man between him and the cool river, raised his head and struck once. And the gods are pleased with Zyni Moë, and have called him the Protector of the Secret of the gods.' "

So too with the prophet Ord. Ord discovers that Fate and Chance are above the gods, so is deprived of all his earthly goods and turned into the South Wind. Some day, though, he may penetrate the ice of the north and enter the gods' last dwelling-place, whereupon Fate and Chance will sweep the gods away.[13]

But what of Mana-Yood-Sushai, who created lesser gods, then slept while they made worlds for play? Answers Dunsany, "But at the Last will Mana-Yood-Sushai forget to rest, and will make again new gods and new worlds, and will destroy the gods whom he hath made.

"And the gods and the worlds shall depart, and then shall be only Mana-Yood-Sushai. . . . Then shall Mana-Yood-Sushai be all alone, with neither Death nor Time, and never the

---

13 " 'Then Time shall never slay the gods,' I said. And he answered, 'They shall die by the bedside of the last man.' " (From *A Shop in Go-By Street* in *Tales of Three Hemispheres*.)

hours, singing in his ears, nor the swish of passing lives." Then, but then only, shall Destiny move him to create anew.

But what of us who live before that End, and what of the gods? That Destiny and God are; but that the little gods are Evil and Good, and that Evil must be most often besought, lest it destroy Good, which is Beauty. Once make a god of anything, ugly or beautiful, you make an idol of it soon and turn it into stone. Identify yourself with it and you become a stone. Make no god of Beauty: woo it instead and behold it: render it indestructible!

But what of the effect of Dunsany's new mythology, and Blake's and Hardy's and others', on classical mythology? The answer is too obvious to write a paper about, if the real purpose of the present were not something else,—namely an excuse for enthusiasm for Dunsany. The answer to our question, however, is no more than that there is room for both, and that classical mythology goes on as of yore, restricted, it is true, in a realistic age, as it was tempered before in the age of Donne.

For if Bridges and Watson, with their classical bias, be called survivals of the Victorian age, if Stephen Phillips and Hewlett be dead, at least Abercrombie and Phillpotts are much alive, and making their respective uses of classic myth. In America, Cawein was full of it, and Woodberry, Ledoux, and Robinson are yet, while Carman and Bynner by no means exclude it.

Or to bring matters closer to date, let any reader turn to the anthologies of Georgian Poetry, or to Braithwaite's yearly selections, and find, amidst imagism and *vers libre* and all else modern, such poems as T. Sturge Moore's *A Sicilian Idyl*, De la Mare's *Alexander*, Sara Teasdale's *Sappho*, George Sterling's *The Hunting of Dian*, Amelia Burr's *Ulysses in Ithaca*, and Lewis Parke Chamberlayne's *Leaves from the Anthology*.

New mythologies have arisen, and more will conceivably fol-

low, but the gods of Greece and Rome endure.[14] Our expanding
literatures have room for all, and the battles of the classicists,
the romanticists, the realists, the retrogressives and the modern-
ists will end in a catholicity of taste that will continue to appear
anarchy to conservatives and democracy to liberals.   Indi-
vidualists will form new mythologies; moderates and classicists
will follow the old.   And I have yet to see an individualist, even,
quite free of our common literary heritage.   Blake wasn't, nor
are Hardy and Dunsany.

[14] The reader is referred to Professor Henry Rushton Fairclough's distinguished study, *The Classics and Our Twentieth Century Poets* (Stanford
University Press, 1927).

LORD DUNSANY: AMATEUR AND ARTIST

EDWARD JOHN MORETON DRAX PLUNKETT, 18th Baron Dunsany, was born a lord and reared a soldier. After Eton he was sent, not to Oxford or Cambridge, but to Sandhurst, England's West Point. At such places, he has remarked to someone (Clayton Hamilton, I think), one is trained; at Universities one is educated. It is futile to speculate as to what effect Sandhurst had on him, or what difference Oxford or Cambridge might have made. Cambridge might have killed the *amateur* in him. Oxford might have confirmed it. As it is he is both *amateur* and artist. He says he prefers idealistic drama to realistic. That may be due to Sandhurst or to his South African campaign, or to the Great War. The last happily spared him to produce *If* in London. *If* ran for weeks! He has been at least twice in America and likes us because we like him. At home, he reminds us (as I have already the reader), he is a soldier and a lord; with us he is a dramatist, a poet and a teller of tales. Besides his estate in County Meath, Ireland, and Dunstall Priory, at Shoreham, Kent, he owns countless castles in Spain, in the clouds, and on the edge of Time. To all of these, I fancy, Americans are welcome,— unless, of course, we come quoting Josh Billings to the effect that "building air castles is a harmless business as long as you don't attempt to live in them!"

Dunsany's *amateur* talent is suggested in *If Shakespeare Lived To-day*, a conversation between two members of a London club who are perturbed because one William Shakespeare is putting up with them. An editor is asked if he knows the man and he admits he doesn't. But better far is *Fame and the*

Poet. The speakers are Harry de Reves, a poet who keeps an altar to Fame and Lieutenant-Major Dick Prattle, who has dropped in from the ends of the earth, he says, to get a decent tie or two. To continue—

PRATTLE (seeing paper and ink)

But what are you doing?

DE REVES

Writing.

PRATTLE

Writing? I didn't know you wrote.

DE REVES

Yes, I've taken to it rather.

PRATTLE

I say—writing's no good. What do you write?

DE REVES

Oh, poetry.

PRATTLE

Poetry? Good Lord!

DE REVES

Yes, that sort of thing, you know.

PRATTLE

Good Lord, do you make any money by it?

DE REVES

No. Hardly any.

PRATTLE

I say—why don't you chuck it?

DE REVES

Oh, I don't know. Some people seem to like my stuff, rather. That's why I go on.

PRATTLE

I'd chuck it, if there's no money in it.

DE REVES

Oh, but then it's hardly in your line, is it? You'd hardly approve of poetry if there was money in it.

PRATTLE

Oh, I don't say that. If I could make as much money by poetry as I can by betting I don't say I wouldn't try the poetry touch, only—

DE REVES

Only what?

PRATTLE

Oh, I don't know. Only there seems more sense in betting, somehow.

DE REVES

Well, yes. I suppose it's easier to tell what an earthly horse is going to do than to tell what Pegasus—

PRATTLE

What's Pegasus?

DE REVES

Oh, the winged horse of poetry.

PRATTLE

I say! You don't believe in a winged horse, do you?

DE REVES

In our trade we believe in all fabulous things. They all represent some large truth to us. An emblem like Pegasus is as real a thing to a poet as a Derby winner would be to you.

PRATTLE

I say. (Give me a cigarette. Thanks.) What? Then you'd believe in nymphs and fauns and Pan, and all those kind of birds?

DE REVES

Yes, yes, in all of them.

PRATTLE

Good Lord!

De Reves, (to finish the story), is almost shamed into taking Prattle's advice to chuck his poems, when Fame descends from her pedestal and bawls his name noisily from the housetops.

But if he is a charming *amateur* here, Dunsany is a "dull boy" in his war stories. Deliver us from these! They are all work and no play. They are tamer than Alfred Noyes'. Yet who has written finer war *verses* than some from *The Great Guns of England?* And his lines *Victory*, as he recites them, are superb. But lovelier are his poems on red-rose-crumpled mountains of North Africa and on our own Monadnock. May he journey into New Mexico next and paint its paintings in words.

In the preceding essay I have supplied a brief study (so why repeat?) of Dunsany's New Mythology, that strange theogony, half Celtic, half Oriental, half Dunsany's own, as his countrymen might say. Perhaps of all his works bits of his Wonder Books will live longest—

In these, like those other inspired *amateurs*, Wilde and Whistler, Dunsany is really a genius and an artist. Yet, when all is said, who shall say less of him as a playwright? Recall the two burglars in *The Glittering Gate*, prying open Heaven's door, only to face laughter and the Void; or *King Argimenes* gnawing his bone and leading his proud revolt; or the citizens worshipping the stone beggars in *The Gods of the Mountain*, till the true gods come to slay; or the King and his Court (in *The Golden Doom*) bowing to the supposed mystic writing a boy and a girl have placed on his door; or the unhappy suitor unwilling to go back for *The Lost Silk Hat* and unable to go on without it; or the gods calling out the toff and his companions to death one by one: truly *A Night at an Inn!* or the Queen in *The Queen's Enemies* turning the Nile on those who do not love her, unable as she is to bear to be unloved; or the King of *The Tents of the Arabs* using strategy to be rid of his throne that he may go out forever into the desert of his Beloved; or the gods in *The Laughter of the Gods*, fulfilling a prophecy forced upon them by their prophet, in order that men may know that gods are gods?

Slight, are they not? but the little things may be the perfect things. More ambitious than these, Dunsany's long play, *If*, delighted many in London one summer. The critics preferred *A Bill of Divorcement*, the long-delayed *Shewing-up of Blanco Posnet* and *The Playboy of the Western World*. These are good plays. One of them is great. But so is *If*—great in its cleverness of idea and in its power to transport and enchant. Who can forget John Beal, prevented by a guard and a gate from catching a train, or his wife at home at "The Acacias," with her bad taste in furnishings and her dread of "foreigners"? Or the arrival of the old Oriental to repay John for a service he has done him, enabling him, by means of a crystal, to go back some years, begin some event differently and live on accordingly? I leave to the reader (for the play is by now long published) the scenes in Persia, or thereabouts,—where Beal becomes a great potentate, is plotted against by the girl he has met and befriended on the train, reaches home at last, and awakens in his chair—there to be found by his wife, none the wiser, unless he tells her, for his long journey in the lands of wonder.

May the gods be praised for Dunsany and *If;* even for the Envoi to *A Ballade of the Last Night* of it, furnished the *Spectator,* Oct. 29, 1921:

> "Trotsky! or whosoe'er to-day
>   Usurps the place of princes, hear!
> For good and all no man shall say
>   The Pass is closed on Shaldomir."

Indeed, the Pass not being closed, we have since received (1923) a whole volume of *Plays of Near and Far.* Two little pieces in it, *A Good Bargain* and *Cheezo,* are funny—and—Near. In the first Satan gives a monk youth in exchange for the monk's bothersome halo. In the second, "great new foods," of which Cheezo is the latest, are held up to laughter. Here, says Dunsany, "is a play of Right and Wrong, and Wrong triumphs." The two other plays in the book are Far, but of real moment artistically. In *The Flight of the Queen* the royal Princes follow the Queen to Aether Mountain, but only Zoon reaches the summit with her. The others are slain by the workers of the golden hoard, the Princes having broken with their Destiny, which was Idleness. As for Zoon, who persists in holding the royal hand, Zoon the Queen slaps and tips over the mountain, her Fate being that she shall be Queen, not Woman.—The other play, *The Compromise of the King of the Golden Isles,* returns to the jealous gods. A politician advises the King to defy the Emperor, who has sent for a fugitive refugee. The King compromises by turning the man out of sanctuary and allowing him to escape. The Emperor thereupon sends two cups, one poisoned, for the King to choose between. The King consults his priests; is told which to drink; suspects it is the poisoned one, as indeed it is; drinks the other; has the priests examined, who say it was the gods' will he should drink the poisoned one; drinks from it and dies.

Meanwhile, in *The Prince of Stamboul* (it's in Webber and Webster's *Short Plays for Young People*, 1925) a child who is ill must sleep, but cannot and will not till she hears Tommy Toddler play "Home, Sweet Home." Her mother calls in the Prince of Stamboul, who is a Frenchman made a prince by the Czar for his violin playing. The Prince sends his car for Tommy, and in a few minutes the little flutist is performing for the child Marian.

The Murderers and *Lord Adrian* come in about here; *Who's Who* says so, but where in *Vanity Fair* or elsewhere are they? [1] However, *Alexander and Three Small Plays* appeared in book form in 1926. In the first, Thaïs gets Clitus to persuade Alexander to send away Apollo, who has been his adviser. He does so, kills Clitus, dies and is mourned by the Amazon Queen Rhododactilos. The first of the Small Plays, *The Old King's Tale*, tells of Youth egged on by Age to defy the gods; the second, *The Evil Kettle*, has James Watt, inspired by the Devil, invent the steam-engine: only to have a modern city shown him as its result; while the third, *The Amusements of Khan Kharuda*, shows a Khan pleasant with men in the town, but on occasion quick at summoning the thunder.

Four long stories add to the joy of nations. *The King of Elfland's Daughter* is sought and won by a king's son. She comes with him to earth and they have a son; then the mother departs, but returns; and the earth is changed; and the fields "are no longer the fields we know." In *Don Rodriguez* an old lord gives his older son his sword and mandolin: for they win all things of those arbiters, women. His younger son is dull and clever, "on whom those traits that women love have not been bestowed by God." So *he* wins fame, fortune, a hold on fairy-

---

[1] I have just asked Dunsany of these, at the conclusion of one of his New York lectures (April 27, 1928). He tells me neither is yet printed, but that the first has been produced. As for *Lord Adrian*, that is a long play, not yet put on; but his best, he declares.

land and friendship of the King of Spain.   No so bad, what?
In *The Charwoman's Shadow* a youth is sent by his father to
seek gold by magic for his sister's dowry: the boy gives his
shadow to an old magician as pay for it.   But the lad's sister
persuades him to procure a love potion instead of gold: with it
she wins her Duke.   Then the youth learns the secret of the
shadow box, opens it and get his shadow and the old charwoman's, too, as he has promised.   She, on its recovery, is restored to beauty, and the kindly Duke gets his King to declare
her noble.   The magician, cheated of a promising pupil, betakes
himself, his secrets and all his elfs and sprites to the Country
Towards Moon's Rising, and the Golden Age closes.   Finally.
at this writing, *The Blessing of Pan* is a nature song played
into the ears of British complacency by an inspired farmer's
boy.

In *Etcetera* (1924), Vincent Starrett reprints from *The
Plaindealer* Dunsany's *Request:*

"When I am out of fashion,
  Like hats that once they wore,
Or some long opened ration,
  And no one reads me more,
Then give me some compassion
  Who loved my books before.

"When new young men write verses
  That I don't understand,
And thick gray mist immerses
  My mind-seen glittering land,
And only weary hearses
  Travel its golden sand,

"Say to that jeunesse doree,
  Though it be trite to say,
That I too found a glory
  Far eastward of Cathay,
And wrote a golden story
  That's had its golden day."

ANDREW LANG, SCHOLAR-CRITIC

IF Robert Louis Stevenson was complacent over anything it was that he had kept himself free of journalism. Yet in England, as the saying goes, even a journalist is somebody. Mr. John Cowper Powys said as much one day when speaking of Mr. Gosse, a man whom in this country many regard, I fancy, as a first-rate man of letters. And that master journalist, William Ernest Henley, was a poet, too. But what has become of Andrew Lang, on either side of the waters?

Students of Homer at one well-known University in our far West hear much of Andrew Lang on the Homeric question. Anthropologists number him among them. Children know his fairy books. His *History of English Literature from Beowulf to Swinburne* is occasionally used, his *A History of Scotland* oftener. He wrote *The Mystery of Mary Stuart, John Knox and the Reformation* and *Prince Charles Edward*. In 1903 he published *The Valet's Tragedy and Other Studies*, about some of the Mysteries of history. His translations from Homer and Theocritus, and his *Aucassin and Nicolette*, are well regarded. Dr. Helen Louise Cohen gives him space in her fine book, *The Ballade*. His *Letters to Dead Authors* still live. Some of his verse is good.[1] Then why is he neglected? Why are there next to no esays on him? Because he was a journalist, as the distinguished author of a Life of Poe which Lang called cold, once said? Nay, rather that the trouble is not taken to appraise him. No one collects his writings. No one writes a biography of him.

I have always thought of Lang as a witty critic of scholar-

[1] See reviews of *The Poetical Works of Andrew Lang*, edited by Mrs. Lang, 1923, in *The Quarterly Review*, Vol. 240, pp. 263–275, and in *The Edinburgh Review*, Vols. 238–9, pp. 270–286.

ship—of real scholarship, sometimes; of pretense, at others, but a critic for all that, and that, too, despite his flippant air and his disclaimer of scholarship himself. He was the Comic Spirit hovering over the fads, fancies and convictions of learned men. Would he had entered the Piers Plowman controversy and broken a lance with those manly exponents of Piers' multiple authorship—who would merely have remarked, probably, that Lang's procedure was not strictly argument. Suffice it that he did make war on President Butler, the "Molièristes," the Baconians, the multiple Homerites and the Max Müllerites. The first of these was too delicately waged to penetrate a citdal of academic officialdom impervious to heavier guns. "Poor Lang," says Mr. Salomon Reinach, "he suffered from one great fault: he was too witty." But how sweetly it reads, his comments on Professor Spingarn's *A Question of Academic Freedom*. A gentle surprise that such things can be; an incredulous lift of the eyebrows. He dips his pen in a rare ink. His traceries should be hung in glass frames in all committee rooms of our colleges, beside the diplomas of our Trustees. "Alas," he purrs in one passage, "it is very difficult, indeed, to persuade mankind that anthropologists are a deserving and useful set of men! An university bent on economising would probably begin by cashiering its anthropologists; not that any such thing was designed, as far as I know, at Columbia, though Mr. Spingarn seems to think that there was such a thrifty purpose in the air. Now comparative literature itself is a branch of anthropology, especially if it begins with the poetry of the Barkingi, Omaha, Zuni, Maoris, and other such peoples. Had I been a professor of comparative literature it would have pained, but not surprised me, if the Committee of Education abolished my chair."

Like that other Scotchman whose still precious name opened this paper, Lang loved France second only to Scotland and England. Indeed Richard Le Gallienne says Lang had the French mind. His letter to Ronsard [2] almost proves it: 'tis

[2] *Letters to Dead Authors.*

perfect; that on Gerard de Nerval [3] is nearly or quite so.   And how well he loved Molière!   Hear, ye scholars, nor be dismayed. "As I regard them," he says of those who hunt out each little detail about the Master, "as I regard them (for I have tarried in their tents) and as I behold their trivialities—the exercises of men who neglect Molière's works to write about Molière's great-grandmother's second-best bed—I sometimes wish that Molière were here to write on his devotees a new comedy, 'Les Molièristes.' "   At the same time, be it whispered, his translation of *Aucassin et Nicolette* is not perfect.   But neither is FitzGerald's *Omar*.

And speaking of France, hear further what Salomon Reinach said of Lang in the *Quarterly Review*, April, 1913: "If England did not do full justice to Lang, some Frenchmen would be ready to claim as their own the successor of Fontenelle, the admirer of French ballads and *contes* and the worshipper of Joan of Arc."   To controversialists, be it added, Lang recommended the rapier of Pascal in place of the bludgeons of Milton and Knox.   (See his *Impressions of Swinburne, Nation*, May 20, 1909).   Which leads us to add to his list of controversies, Lang's one-sided contest with Anatole France: for 'tis said that the latter profited from certain corrections on Lang's part of *La Vie de Jeanne d'Arc* and gladly incorporated them in a later edition.   But first Lang complained in several articles: then wrote rapidly his own book, *The Maid of France*, holding that "in Jeanne we see the warrior and the politician, not the ecstatic and the thaumaturge"—as he felt that Anatole France did. Moreover, just because Science cannot explain why Jeanne saw certain things, he declines to hold dogmatically that she didn't see them.   "Science may be able to explain them on some future day; at present she is not omniscient."   In his *Psychical Research of the Century*, in the Annual Report of the Smithsonian Institution, 1900, pp. 675–81, he continues, "On the whole, psychical research has, I think, shown that there is a real ele-

3 *Letters on Literature.*

ment of obscure mental faculty involved in the superstition of the past and present. It has also made some discoveries of practical value in hypnotism and the treatment of hysteria. It strengthens the opinion that science has not yet exhausted all attainable knowledge about the constitution of man." Earlier, in *The Book of Dreams and Ghosts*, Lang traced "the ghostly from its germs in dreams and momentary hallucinations of eye or ear, up to the most prodigious narratives which popular invention has built on bases probably very slight." But it is the anthropological that attracts Lang to psychism. In *Cock Lane and Common Sense* he is impressed with the ever-recurring testimony of savages, mediaevalists, and moderns to the presence among them of hallucinations, which, says Lang, they see, but whether through their own conjurings only or through transference from other minds, living or dead, he is not prepared to say.—Lang's book (to return to *The Maid of France*) is not so constructive a one as France's, but it is no less ardently desirous of truth; and, as is usual with Lang, really acts as a check on greater writers or scholars than himself. Yet to be quite fair, has either written so eloquently of Joan as Mark Twain in the Preface to his story of the Maid? "She was modest, and fine, and delicate when to be loud and coarse might be said to be universal; she was full of pity when a merciless cruelty was the rule. . . . She was perhaps the only entirely unselfish person whose name has a place in profane history." Not the fine touch of the Scotchman nor the friendly irony of the Frenchman, with all their respect for their heroine, can quite equal the love of the American. "Dr. Clemens' . . . researches into the biography of Jeanne d'Arc were most conscientious," Lang avers himself, in his posthumous volume, *Shakespeare, Bacon and the Great Unknown*.

That three hundred-page volume, says someone, was designed to lay once for all the Bacon bogey. One would think it had. Specifically, it attempted to answer, point by point, Mr. Greenwood's contentions, in his *The Shakespeare Problem Re-*

stated, that the Plays were written in part, probably, by Bacon; in part, without question, by an Unknown. The latter Lang decided to call Bungay. "I use Bungay," says he in his Introduction, "as an endearing term for the mysterious being who was the author if Francis Bacon was not. Friar Bungay was the rival of Friar Bacon, as the Unknown (if he was not Francis Bacon) is a rival of 'the inventor of Inductive reasoning.' " 'Tis good fooling! And indeed so is the whole book, with much irony, commonsense and truth between: and also words, words, words! But "in philology," he observes characteristically, "I am all unlearned, and cannot pretend to discuss the language of Shakespeare any more than I can analyze the language of Homer into proto-Arcadian and Cyprian, and so on." [4] Yet he concludes by meeting the possible objection of people who ask what it all matters, with the words, "We wish to give love and praise and gratitude where they are due; to that Achaean 'Father of the rest'; and to 'friendly Shakespeare.' "

His attitude towards the Homeric Controversy is nicely summed up in his little poem, *Homeric Unity*:

> "The dust and awful treasures of the Dead,
>   Hath learning scattered wide, but vainly thee,
> Homer, she meteth with her tool of lead,
>   And strives to rend thy songs; too blind to see
> The crown that burns on thy immortal head
>   Of indivisible supremacy."

In prose he devoted three volumes to the question: *Homer and the Epic, Homer and His Age* and *The World of Homer;* and an essay, *Homer and Anthropology*, in Marett's *Anthropology and The Classics*. The first held that a single Homer

---

[4] His curiosity was much intrigued, however, by Dr. George Hempl's account in *Harper's Magazine* for January, 1911, of his attempt to decipher the Cretan Disk. At first (in the *Independent* of February 9, 1911) Lang, though on his guard, was open to conviction; later (in the *Nation* of March 9, 1911) he found that he and another *amateur* could get quite other results than Hempl's even when reading the Disk according to the latter's method of letting the pictographs stand for Greek syllables.

cannot be argued away by pointing out inconsistencies in the
Homeric poems: there are inconsistencies in Thackeray. It also
criticized scholars who cut and rearrange texts according to
their prepossessions and was critical of such as took Wolff's
Prolegomena too seriously. The second and third volumes (the
latter also reverts to the Homeric Discrepancies) were concerned with Homeric civilization, as real a thing and as unified
to Lang (or more so) as that of any later and better-known
age. To quote his conclusion to *Homer and the Epic:* "The
Iliad and the *Odyssey* are neither collections of short lays, nor
expressions of an original brief epic, but, on the whole, they are
the composition of a poet . . . 'the golden poet, Homer' ";
and, from *The World of Homer*, "Homer surveyed the whole,
selected some situations, invented others, combined and fused
all in the furnace of his genius, just as did Milton and Shakespeare." And finally in his beautifully-written little study,
Homer and Anthropology, Lang, for Unity still, observes that
Homer is not rich in primitive survivals, is less barbaric, indeed,
than Hesiod and the dramatists, and is the poet of a short-
lived, gracious time. "I infer," says he, "that the *Iliad* and
Odyssey are prehistoric, the flower of a brief age of Achaean
civilization, an age when the society of princes and ladies had
a taste extraordinarily pure and noble." But though the
twentieth century has swung around to a considerable extent
to the theory of Unity, Professor Gilbert Murray does not feel
that Lang has settled or dismissed the Homeric Question. In
The Quarterly Review for April, 1913, he suggested that what
it needs most is clear stating. "And Lang," says he, "with his
great knowledge of literature and anthropology and history,
to say nothing of his powers of poetry and imagination, might,
perhaps, had he wished, have stated it better than anyone."
Meantime, as Professor Murray adds, he did some fine work in
his translation of and anthropological commentary on the *Homeric Hymns*. And he is the author, perhaps best of all, of
one perfect poem:

"Gladly, from the songs of modern speech
Men turn and see the stars, and feel the free
    Shrill wind beyond the close of heavy flowers,
    And through the music of the languid hours,
They hear like ocean on a western beach
    The surge and thunder of the Odyssey."

That gives one forever the same thrill that the hero got (in a novel of note) when he first came upon

"The isles of Greece, the isles of Greece,
    Where burning Sappho loved and sang."

In his General Essay on The Works of Charles Dickens [5] Lang observes whimsically: "It does not matter what a man calls himself; his 'aesthetic principles' do not matter. Homer had none, nor probably had Shakespeare; now we hear of them as if they were half the battle, and things highly precious." Yet with his *penchant* for Anthropology he writes of Dickens' animism! Rarely, indeed, was anthropology long absent from his thoughts. Whatever he was reading, even pure literature, anthropology was lurking in the background. "He was not unmoved by beauty," says M. Reinach (*Quarterly*, 218, 310), "but was ever anxious to detect the Red Indian or Australian under the helmet and armour of the hero, or the tiara and long robe of the priest." The wonder is that with so very real a specialty, he could write with apparently equal interest of cricket, golf, angling, Oxford and a dozen other things. He even attempted a novel or two.

"Lang's most signal contributions to anthropology fall in the domain of primitive sociology and totemism," says Mr. A. Goldenweiser.[6] In his *Social Origins* (1903) he propounded the jealous-sire theory of the origin of exogamy; while the totemic name theory of the origin of totemism received its de-

[5] Gadshill Edition, Vol. 34, p. xxxiii.
[6] *The Death of Andrew Lang* (*Journal of American Folk Lore*, 25, 372–3).

finitive form in *The Secret of the Totem* (1905).[7] Meantime
J. G. Frazer published *Totemism and Exogamy,* barely men-
tioning Lang. "Aroused at last," says Mr. Goldenweiser,
"Lang took terrible, albeit soft-gloved revenge in his article on
totemism in the eleventh edition of the *Encyclopaedia Britannica.*" [8]

In his *Custom and Myth* (1884), *Myth, Ritual and Religion*
(1887 and 1899), *Modern Mythology* (1897), *The Making of
Religion* (1898), *Magic and Religion* (1901), and in his article
Mythology in the *Encyclopaedia Britannica,* Lang sets forth
his views on religion, folklore and mythology. The part that
totemism played, together with his contention that very primitive peoples acknowledge, even when they do not worship, an
All-Father are among Lang's contributions to early religion.
But his particular controversial triumph was over Max Müller
(for which see his *Modern Mythology*). He opposed Müller's
philological method of explaining myths, setting against it the
anthropological procedure. He denied that myths were solar
survivals or diseases of language, showed that the repugnant
aspects of say the Greek myths were primitive survivals, maintained that myths came out of folklore, not folklore out of
myths, and held that folklore was based in turn on the prevalent
primitive belief in animism. A comparative mythologist of wide
range, he was naturally much impressed with the similarities of
the myths of different peoples, and held usually that they
showed similarity in men's minds, not transmission,—though Mr.

[7-8] "Man was at first, as Darwin supposed, a jealous brute who expelled
his sons from the neighborhood of his women." The sons "had to capture
mates from another herd (exogamy). The groups received sobriquets
from each other, as Emu, Frog, and so forth. . . . The rule was now that
marriage must be outside of the local group-name. Frog may not marry
Frog, or Emu, Emu. The usual savage superstition which places all folk
in mystic *rapport* with the object from which their *names* are derived
gradually gave a degree of sanctity to Emu, Frog, and the rest. They
became totems." Such is Lang's statement of his theories in his article
Totemism, in the *Encyclopaedia Britannica,* theories which "do not enjoy
the benefit of notice and criticism in Mr. Frazer's *Totemism,*" he adds.

Joseph Jacobs says [9] that Lang later came round to the latter theory.   That the man who has done as much as Lang has for Mythology "has conferred a benefit on the world of learning, and was a genius," is M. Reinach's final word on his friend.

The late Professor Flügel once told a group of us how Dr. Furnivall used to comport himself freely on grave occasions among scholars, fishing out nuts and eating them with unction. Lang was presumably too busy on like occasions taking every-thing in to emulate the great free lance scholar; but the incident recalls a story a young American professor told me of a visit to England with letters to several eminent men of learning. "They were cordial and kind," said he, "but I noticed that whenever I asked them if they knew Lang (the young professor combines English and Anthropology) a silence of uncomfortable proportions fell."   Good old days, when the battles of the world were the civil and international wars of men of letters and scholars!

[9] *The Journal of American Folklore,* Vol. 26, p. 372.

GRANT ALLEN, NATURALIST AND NOVELIST

AS a boy I remember Grant Allen as a writer of guidebooks:
then one Sunday afternoon at Stanford, calling, as I
so often did, at Professor Fairclough's, I learned that Mrs. Fairclough was Grant Allen's sister, and that about me were many,
many of Allen's books.

Now, years later, I have been spending a fascinated time in
the Fairclough library looking at these treasures of the past
—not treasures of rarest gold, if you like, but never tinsel.

Take *The Lower Slopes*, for instance, being *Reminiscences
of Excursions Round the Base of Helicon, Undertaken for the
Most Part in Early Manhood*: this copy, in Allen's fine hand,
is "For dear Mother, with Grant's love."

> "Mine is a fledgling of song, and
> its pinions are feeble to fly,"

says he in *In Night Watches*. Yet in this pleasant book of
verse Evolution is both seriously and humorously treated; the
Monad and the Absolute gently smiled at; Spencer set among
the gods, Woman repeatedly championed, erring and pure; Nature given her high place—her flowers and insects especially;
and France praised for what she has done and may do for
Liberty.

Grant Allen was an Englishman who was really a Canadian,
who was therefore American, albeit with an Oxford degree;
whose mother was a de Longueuil of the famous Le Moyne
family of Canada and Louisiana; who was connected with the
Coffins of Devonshire and Nantucket; whose full name, Charles
Grant Blairfindie Allen was due, in part, to his Scotch great-
grandfather, Captain David Alexander Grant of Blairfindie.
But his father was an Irishman whose forebears had been for

198

some generations settled in Ireland: Mr. Allen, Sr., however, was English in sympathy: he and his brilliant wife lived at Kingston, Ontario, and there, at "Alwington," Grant Allen was born, and there came people of attainment, even including Walt Whitman.   All this has some interest in itself: but a bearing, too, on Allen as poet, scientist and novelist.

For his father, J. Antisell Allen, wrote at least three things (there may be more) himself—a *Tercentenary Poem on Shakespeare*, *Day Dream* (verses that are cosmical enough to be almost scientific) and *The True and Romantic Love-Story of Colonel and Mrs. Hutchison*, a little play laid in the time of Charles I.   The pieces are pretty minor: Mr. Allen was also a minister, though, and philosophically minded, and Grant's mother was as sparklingly French as his father was solidly British.   Mr. Allen was a Unionist, whereas Grant was a Home Ruler. Grant maintained, wilfully, that the Celtic was stronger in the Isles than the Anglo-Saxon: his famous essay *The Celtic Fringe* expresses that and his enthusiasm for things Celtic.   *We* Celts shall win, says this Canadian Englishman.

Grant Allen throughout considered his real work to be scientific and philosophical and his fiction quite incidental.   It is really the other way round.   For though he said in his preface to *Twelve Tales* that he would be quite content could he gather up the crumbs that fell from the table of the Merediths, Hardys, Kiplings and Wellses, he did better than that and wrote some rattling good stories,—of which more in a moment.   On the other hand, his pleasant guidebooks have been succeeded by others; and his science—his science aimed at and accomplished little more than popularizing Darwin, Huxley and Spencer.[1]

---

[1] "I doubt if you do justice to his pioneer work in evolutionary science," Professor Fairclough writes.   "He was invited to lecture before the Royal Society, Darwin and others presented him with a beautiful and costly microscope, Herbert Spencer lived with him for months and turned against him only when Grant became prominent in the Fabian Society.   Spencer was too much of an individualist to tolerate Socialism, but he had asked Grant to be his biographer because he understood evolutionary philosophy so thoroughly."

In *Force and Energy*, it is true, he had a theory of Physics—something about the Energy of the earth and of the sun going together "to swell the energy of the ether, the great waste-heap of the universe."

Or are some of his science primers still read? "An excellent book," writes some kindly soul in the Los Angeles Library copy of *Flashlights on Nature*. Is his *Charles Darwin* still dipped into—and his *Common Sense Science?* The names of his nature books are pretty,—*The Evolutionist at Large, Moorland Idylls, Colin Clout's Calendar, The Colour of Flowers, Flowers and Their Pedigrees, Science in Arcady, The Story of the Plants.* He edited *The Natural History of Selborne*, too. A genuine love of plants and flowers and animals, a desire to see how and why they came to be, and why so varied and many-colored; a wish to share his knowledge and enthusiasm with others; a suggestion in *Science in Arcady* that we should all have our education in the Tropics where things really grow—show how his combined talents as student, poet, story-teller and *stylist* did him and his readers notable service. For he could write! Limpid and various, he moves—as a steady English stream flows.—and in sunlight.

In his guidebooks he says he doesn't aim at connoiseurship or the dialect of the studios, but at exposition, at appreciation of Europe's treasures—especially for Americans, who have come with honest and reverent desire to learn. *The European Tour* is all for substituting travel for college, for studying things on the spot, and for learning with joy. *Evolution in Italian Art* is a posthumous volume. *Post-Prandial Philosophy*—to continue with more of his versatility—includes among numerous essays the famous *Celtic Fringe;* also, *Is England Played Out?* and *American Duchesses.* The title paper of *Falling in Love and Other Essays* is sensible: he is not for eugenics: instinct selects well. His fiction supports this theory. His *Biographies of Workingmen* is of workingmen who climbed,—William Herschel, Bandman; James Garfield, Canal Boy, for example. When I opened the book, being of the twentieth century, I thought for a moment it would be about workingmen great in their own spheres.—It is only in America, he declares, that Garfield's rise is possible: "in old, settled and wealthy countries we must be content, at best, with slower and less lofty promotion"— this before (and after?) Russia and Bolshevism.

To aesthetics Allen contributed *Physiological Aesthetics* and *The Colour Sense*. But primitive religion and anthropology interested him (or shall I say interest us?) more. His *Evolution of the Idea of God*, with its sequel, *The Hand of God and Other Posthumous Essays*, are documented works,—but assimilated, and how simply presented,—a marvel, again, of clear thinking, of lucidity, of charm, of style. And he does sum things up neatly for the hasty reader! Take his final paragraph to *The Evolution of the Idea of God:* "In one word I believe that corpse-worship is the protoplasm of religion, while admitting that folk-lore is the protoplasm of mythology and of its more modern and philosophical offshoot, theology." Even his translation of the Attis of Catullus is accompanied by two essays— *On the Myth of Attis* and *On the Origin of Tree Worship*. The main idea is "that while all gods were originally ghosts, sacred trees and tree-gods owe their sanctity to having grown in the first place on the tumulus or barrow of the deified ancestor." In anthropology he is in the company of Frazer and Lang: the quotation shows him reconciling their views. And his story *The Great Taboo* pays his respects to both of them.

Allen and his charming wife were fond of company: everyone speaks of that. Among their friends were Andrew Lang, William Watson, Conan Doyle and George Romanes. In this connection, too, a word may be said of Allen and Meredith. They are mentioned together, for instance, in Le Gallienne's *Some Retrospective Reviews: George Meredith's Poetry* (in *Attitudes and Avowals*). "Grant Allen used to say," says he, "that Meredith was the most learned man in England, and that, whenever he was in doubt about some bird or flower, he would walk over and consult Meredith, for they were near neighbors." In 1881 Allen settled at Dorking, "finding among the Surrey hills and vales," in the words of Edward Clodd (*Memoir of Grant Allen*), "exhaustless wealth of material, and gathering round him at 'The Nook' an ever-widening circle drawn to him by a magnetic sweetness and old-world courtesy that disarmed the most prejudiced. And there, no light attraction and privilege was his in the neighborship of Mr. Meredith, who in a letter now before me says: 'You know how highly I prized Grant Allen's literary work, and the warmth of my feeling for him personally!' That love of Nature, with its penetration of many a secret, which suffuses all the writing of George Meredith, finding, as it seems to some of us, its fullest expression in his 'Poems and Lyrics of the Joy of Earth' (the title itself is for the 'besting of the nations'), and which, in the talks and gossipy essays of Grant Allen, invested every wayside weed with an interest and deep meaning, was a spiritual bond between them, as it is between all who draw inspiration of life from the Great Mother."

Clodd observes further in his *Memoir*, p. 154, that *Mylitta* and its allied group, together with articles of the type of *The New Hedonism* (*Fortnightly*, 1896), were preludes to the dramatic presentation of Allen's view in *The Woman Who Did*. Mr. Le Gallienne then points out the similarity of theme of this novel and Meredith's *Lord Ormont and His Aminta*. Allen's book raised a storm; Meredith's did not. But as Le Gallienne observes, "Meredith's style is a coat of mail which protects the most innovating idea"; and that moreover Meredith dealt with adultery in the concrete; Allen in the abstract. *The Woman Who Did* is apparently the only one of Allen's stories that is remembered at large. It gave him a "black eye," and probably deserved to do so. When I read it some years ago I thought it uncalled for. Professor Fairclough declares in his interesting paper, *Grant Allen's Personality*,[2] that the book is an

[2] *Montreal Life*, Nov. 17, 1899.

academic exercise: a problem stated and solved; a protest against loveless unions; a proudly rebellious document. Grant Allen *was* a rebel, says Mr. Fairclough: "though connected by birth with families of distinction, he prided himself on his democratic and radical proclivities." But if his muse was wanton in this book, his life was pure. Yet every other person one speaks to about Allen thinks he must have lived an unconventional life himself because the Woman did.[3] Briefly, this feminine innovator, for no better reason than that she honestly believed the marriage bond antiquated, took a lover "honestly" and honestly had a child. But when the child realized she had no father like other girls, she rose mightily against her honest mother and honestly damned her. Her mother wrote her an honest letter of explanation and then made away with herself. If there is rhyme, reason, beauty or even real pathos in the book, I don't get them.[4] But the daughter's reaction is real. Indeed, there's the answer, the excuse for writing the book at all—what the child of such a union pays,—and says. And there Life and Art triumph after all. In short, Allen chooses to stand by the mother in the story. Some of us are essentially for the child.

A chip off the same block, in a sense, is *The British Barbarians*, a satire on British taboos. A stranger—a twentieth century non-barbarian anthropologist—so enchants Frieda, an English wife, in three hours, that when he gives her back to her husband, who is her chief taboo, she kills him (the stranger) and herself, rather than return to British bondage. Allen called the piece a Hill-top novel, so H. D. Traill parodied it in *The Barbarous Britishers*, a *Tip-top Novel*. The Introduction (at least to the third edition) is illuminating: "Not to prove any-

---

[3] See, for example, Frank Harris in *Contemporary Portraits,* Fourth Series.

[4] Ernest Boyd, in his Introduction to the 1926 "reincarnation" of the book writes no defense of it, but contents himself with quoting ironically from the Storms of Protest which greeted it on its initial appearance in America.

thing, but to suggest ideas, to arouse emotions, is, I take it, the true function of fiction. . . . Women, in particular, are the chief readers of fiction and it is women whom one mainly desires to arouse to interest in profound problems by the aid of this vehicle." Profound problems, indeed! Follows, however, a picture of lovely Surrey from his Hill-top—and the blur of London in the distance.

In a Preface to *Twelve Tales* Allen tells how he blundered into story-writing: one of his scientific chats was more or less narrative; whereupon "Fate (or an enterprising publisher) turned me from an innocent and impecunious naturalist into a devotee of the muse of shilling shockers," he continues in his preface to *At Market Value*. He refers to his well-known short story, *The Reverend John Creedy*, "a tale of a black parson who reverted to savagery"; but says he prefers *The Curate of Churnside*. He discourses on the original of his novel *Philistia*, which disclosed the struggles of a Socialist ahead of his time, and whom he had die. But he says he had to change all that. *Philistia*, a farcical picture of Socialism, is the description of it in Baker's *Guide to Fiction*. "The education of an English novelist," says Allen, "consists entirely in learning to subordinate all his own ideas and tastes and opinions to the wishes and beliefs of the inexorable British matron. . . . Don't take to literature if you have money enough in hand to buy a good broom and annex a vacant crossing." In an essay, *Natural Inequality*, he makes an earnest plea for Socialism as a system that recognizes and endeavors to preserve differences in native ability.

At Market Value itself tells of a young English lord who has his face altered, becomes a sailor-painter and writer, wins the world's regard, in a modest way, and marries a nice wife. There is fun over the social game, English and American. Mortimer, a rich American, makes the most of *his* standing. 'Tis a bright book,—Allen at his best and most natural; for gayety, healthiness, the normal, were natural to him. Somewhere in this book the sailor-man distinguishes between cynicism and knowledge of the world. The cynic is censorious, says he; the worldly person is genial and tolerant, knows what men and women are, yet owes them no grudge; and realizes that we are all much the same. At once one appreciates Allen's own bantering, dancing manner, his ever-ready smile: he vibrates, normally, with happiness over this world and the people in it. Mr. Mortimer, too, is Allen. "The rich young American," says the author, "had all the piquant frankness and cordiality of his nation, with all the grace and tact of Parisian society." In *Linnet*, too, Florian Wood is Allen; for Florian "was a young man of delicate habit of mind and body—a just and pleasing compromise between a philosopher and a butterfly. . . . He played with science as he played with everything else." Florian is Allen dandified.

Indeed the two of his novels that stand out preëminently for this naturalness are *The Tents of Shem* and *Linnet*. Both are melodramatic in spots, but both have delightful heroines. Meriem and Iris of the former are charming and unselfish girls; and Linnet of the latter is good, faithful, winsome and conventional, yet without one trace of priggishness. Linnet is a Swiss girl, a talented singer who is loved by Will Deverill, a poet, but marries Andreas Hausberger, who is later slain by Franz Lindner, a former suitor. Linnet then, by Papal dispensation, marries Will, who gives up Rue. At the end Will, in a well reasoned discourse, shows Linnet she's his, Pope or no Pope, married or free—but she, in her charming way, is glad of the dispensation. Our bald statement does the book slender justice: I can assure the reader that Linnet is a creation. And the sunlight over the Alps and the whole book! The speech, the style, glisten and sparkle.

The Tents of Shem I have had the pleasure of seeing in manuscript and in book form. Mrs. Allen presented the former, after her husband's death, and, as a memento of him, to the Faircloughs. On and on flows his exquisite clear script, with frequent insertions but relatively few alterations or excisions.

As for the story, Meriem, a Kabyle, is daughter of an Englishman and a Berber.   She turns out to be cousin to Iris, who
wins a First at Cambridge, but goes to Algiers, where the girls
meet.   A male cousin tries to get the family money, but is foiled.
For a time both girls love the same man, but in the end each gets
one of the two with which the story opened,—a painter and a
naturalist.   Insurrections against the French enliven the course
of true love.

Allen likes exciting plots.   Take *The Duchess of Powysland.*
Here we have Linda, a superior sort of housekeeper to Basil
Maclaine and Douglas Harrison, a briefless barrister.   Basil
treats her badly, she marries a Duke, is accused of poisoning
him, is freed by Harrison and marries this worthy man.   *Under
Sealed Orders* has love and a vow to kill the Czar conflicting
—the solution being left to the reader.   *The Cruise of the Alba-
tross*, a little adventure story, pure and very simple, is told by
a pure and simple sailor, captain of a simple ship that cruises
in the South Seas.   He picks up two boys in a boat, rescues
their parents from savages on a distant isle and makes all happy
ever after.   How Allen enjoys all this!   *The Devil's Die*, too,
is full of action: a young doctor, who is experimenting on a
patient, kills him, etc., etc.   And speaking of doctors, *Hilda
Wade* is a doctor book, adventure book, travel book, all in one.
Hilda becomes a nurse in order to watch Dr. Sebastian, whom
she suspects of the death of her father.   In lighter vein are
Miss Cayley's Adventures—some of them: she is a Girton girl
(so is Iris), capital twopence, who sets out around the world
for adventure, finds them, achieves a career and marriage.   More
of a skit is *Blood Royal*, in which a youth named Plantagenet,
who has been flattering himself that he is royally born, turns
out not to be.   An episodic piece is *An African Millionaire*, said
to contain an entertaining scoundrel in Colonel Clay.

The Incidental Bishop is a farcical thing gravely told.   The
story starts in Australia, where a young man falls in love and
becomes a clergyman; then returns to England, where we find

him a bishop, though he has never really taken orders.   Tortured by conscience, he confesses to a priest, but to his dying breath he is holy to his family and his secret is kept by his friends.   Allen likes to have his fun with religion.   A really masterly little story is *Longulula* in *Twelve Tales.*   It tells how a savage chief becomes a Christian, first killing a man to get his wife, then killing her in the morning, and keeping of his own many wives only his first, that he may fulfill all Christian requirements.   'Tis grim, mocking and cruel, but again the author seems to be having a grand time.   The *Twelve Tales* are varied and arresting.   On the other hand his novel *A Splendid Sin* is more serious.   Here the woman who did, has done well— even for her child.   For her prospective daughter-in-law is in danger of being lost to the family because of the boy's reprobate father: whereupon the mother discloses the secret that he is the son of herself and a poet.

Allen was professor for a time in a government school for the colored in Jamaica and his sojourn there added to his equipment as a naturalist and a story-teller.   *Ivan Greet's Masterpiece,* for example, is laid there.   Ivan dies, his mistress tries to get his manuscript printed, and she and their child perish in a storm.   But his novel *In All Shades* is the outstanding result of his visit in the West Indies.   Its habitat, however, is not Jamaica.   Edward Hawthorne marries Marian and goes out to Trinidad, where they are received coldly, though his parents live there.   The difficulty is a strain of negro blood.   Harry Noel, a dandy, comes out and marries Nora Dupuy, who is also "tainted."   Native rebellions enliven the book and even motivate it; for Edward wins favor both with whites and blacks and is honored by the government.   The Dupuys go to live in England, where Mrs. Dupuy's unhappy tincture will not matter.

In *Karen* Allen lays a Russian romance in his own country, Canada.   But Americans figure more often, if usually incidentally, in his novels.   His Mrs. Palmer in *Linnet* is clever and life-like; so, in *The Scallywag,* is the amusing girl Isabel Boynton, from Philadelphia. Allen is the only Britisher who can make Americans talk naturally, I fancy. Indeed his ear is equally sensitive to English, Cockney and American accents. *The Scallywag*, though, is English. Rea marries young Sir Paul, and Faith, Thistleton; while a rich Jew leaves money for Paul and Rea.—A story, however, in which an American is one of the heroes is *Babylon*. Here Allen's favorite device of two pairs is extended to include an American. The story passes back and forth across the Atlantic, now following the fortunes of a New York State boy of New England descent whom Mr. Audouin, a New England naturalist, is persuading the boy's Yankee father to educate,—now directing our sympathy and attention to an English country boy, who is destined to be a sculptor. The American becomes a painter, the two meet in Paris, a love affair is provided for each, the American and his wife settle in Wales, the Englishman and his in France, and Mr. Audouin circulates between them.

'Tis said that Allen wrote thirty or more novels in all. Some others of that great plenty are *Rosalba*, *The Typewriter Girl*, *What's Bred in the Bone*, *A Terrible Inheritance*, *Michael's Crag*, *A Bride from the Desert*, *This Mortal Coil*, *Dumaresqu's Daughter*, *An Army Doctor's Romance*, *For Mamie's Sake*, *Kalee's Shrine* and *Recalled to Life*.

Of these *A Bride from the Desert* is a long short story in which Wilfrid rescues Mona somewhere in Africa, is promoted and marries her; while *An Army Doctor's Romance* (93 pp.) has Oliver Cameron and Wilfred Burgess getting tangled over Muriel Grosvenor; but Oliver gets her and Wilfred marries another. *Dumaresqu's Daughter* is Psyche, and her father is a poor but noted philosopher. She loves Austen Linnell, an American, and he loves her, and in the end they marry, though things look dark for a time—while Austen is lost on the African sands. *Kalee's Shrine* (written in collaboration with Mary Cotes) receives as a living votive offering, in India, a child, Olga Trevelyan, who, after strange adventures, marries the heroic Alan Tennant. *For Mamie's Sake, A Tale of Love and Dynamite* (all mixed up with advertisements of Pearline, Pear's Soap, Sapolio and Ball's Corsets), adorned The Seaside Library, 712, Double Number, Price 20 cents. Mamie is baby-faced and infant-minded, not very bad, not so good—just trying to get along. She marries Sydney Chevenix and Adrian Pym; so Sydney drowns himself—for Mamie's sake. First, though, Mamie thinks Sydney is dead: he was always fooling with experiments and dynamite. *What's Bred in the Bone* is an absorbing story of English high life. Twin brothers are acknowledged by their noble father and become joint heirs with his always acknowledged son. A pretty love story between one of the twins and Elma Clifford, and the suspicion of murder that is fastened upon the other, occupy the greater part of the book. *Recalled to Life* is "a wild one" about a girl who lost her memory, except of the seeing of the fatal shooting of her supposed father, a heavy villain. It turns out (when she regains it) that her "father" was about to chloroform her lover and that she, to save the one, shot the other. There is a lot about a flashlight picture, too, which corresponds to the mental picture the girl carries about with her. *The Typewriter Girl*, Arrow Library, No. 101, 10 cents, and therefore a dime novel! was published under the pseudonym of Olive Pratt Rayner. But it is Grant Allen at his better, if not his best. The heroine is a Girton girl whose fortune has disappeared, who is greatly independent, joins anarchists for a time, meets her Romeo, follows him to Italy, loses him to the girl he is engaged to, and continues typewriting. The book is full of talk about Butler's theory that the *Odyssey* was written by a woman, though the author says she (i.e., he) doesn't believe it. *Rosalba, the Story of Her Development*, which also appeared as by Olive Pratt Rayner, is a girl of Italian and Irish parentage who dances, is adopted by upper class English people, is engaged to one of her patrons, but marries someone else, as does the other patron also. But first she supports herself for a while and later writes a successful book. Economic independence for women is very much in Grant Allen's mind here and elsewhere. In *A Terrible Inheritance* a young man thinks he is the son of a poisoner, and breaks off his engagement; but later his father is shown to have been innocent of the murder charge against him. *Michael's Crag* is a story of Cornwall and of two young men, one of whom marries Ellen, the other of whom has been the accidental murderer of her brother.

And the upshot of it all? Allen liked to "start things," to arouse interest and discussion, to popularize and interpret Science; but he fell back on fiction, on action, on plots and more plots, on "much plots." Yet his charming young men are charming, and several of his girls are living and delightful. But 'tis his Gallic clarity, warmed by Jamaica suns, made sunnier by Switzerland, sweetened by England, kept human and humorous by America that delights one. I long to shout to the hurrying world to go open a Grant Allen story and gaze into its crystal deeps and shallows. His superb style! it makes even the lauded manner of Howells seem prosy. There is the most utter lack of strain in it. How he and Meredith could even understand each other— His stories are just talked off, yet his style is a written style, not an oral one. However, he "wrote as he spoke," declares Mr. Fairclough. Therefore he spoke an exquisite written style.

And now, given our way, what would we have had of all this "wasted talent"? At one moment one thinks that Allen would have written better novels if he had taken novel writing really seriously; at others one feels that he would have lost something of his lightness and verve if he had. Were pressure of money and orders all that caused him to write novels at all? At times he said so.

Here, to state the matter baldly, was Talent placed, without Theory, at the service of Fiction. Normally some distinguished anthropological novel, some religious novel, some philosophical or psychological novel should have resulted from an education surely superior to most novelists. But such a masterpiece just didn't come from him: great novels don't grow that way; and Allen died an expositor in science, an entertainer in fiction. For one, I do not weep that this is so. He did what he liked to do; he had a charming wife and home; he adored his family in Canada and America; he knew Meredith; he had many other friends; he helped young writers along and he labored for the unlucky and the oppressed. Le Gallienne puts him among the many martyred men of genius who have fertilized English soil. Happy the man whose soul or bones have added to that rich loam. I think his memory is green. I am happy to do my bit to keep it so. Better still, the brilliant Thomas Beer has just given "the curious Grant Allen" a shimmering page and a cameo bibliography in *The Mauve Decade*.

TOLSTOY'S RE-ASSERTION OF CHRISTIANITY

IN 1908 the members of Mr. Robert Herrick's course in the Novel at the University of Chicago were reading Tolstoy's *Anna Karénina*, and that, I think, was my formal introduction to the greatest of the Russians. Before that time, though, I had been reading the beautiful, artistic stories of Turgenieff.

Then the War came, and after it was well under way I went one day to a Los Angeles High School to hear Tolstoy's son lecture on his father. "Everyone in Russia," said he, "is reading *War and Peace*." I followed suit. I found it the most amazing work of fiction of the modern age, in size, richness, power. It painted the Russian aristocracy for all time; it burlesqued Napoleon, condemned war, declared for Christianity and ridiculed History.

Then the War closed and I found myself, if not in Moscow, Russia, at least in Moscow, Idaho. Thither again came Tolstoy's son, this time, even more democratically, on the Chautauqua platform. After saying in a most Christian manner to several little boys in the front row, "Children, won't you be quiet, please, and let me finish my lecture?" he discussed conditions in Russia and reiterated Tolstoy's principles of love and peace for his own country and the world. "The Bolsheviki cannot endure," said he, "because they use Force."

After he was through, some of us lingered about, for he came forward and welcomed talk. He is an aristocrat; his manners are sincere and simple. Besides, he is a Christian aristocrat! He said something, I forget what, about colleges and universities, so that gave me an opening. Presently we were on our way down town to the Hotel and I found myself saying, "Your father and Turgenieff were friends, weren't they?"

His face clouded, then cleared. "At first," he said, "my. father and Turgenieff were not friends,[1] but after my father's religious experience, he wrote to Turgenieff, who was in Paris, and begged him to visit him in Russia, and Turgenieff came readily, and their affection and admiration for each other continued thereafter." On his death-bed Turgenieff begged Tolstoy to return to his novel writing; and in due time Tolstoy produced *Resurrection*, a great novel and a great tract.

What was this religious experience of Tolstoy, this conversion of the year 1881? Well, that is a large question, and one not yet fully written up. But in brief, Tolstoy repented of his youthful follies, of his inherited tendencies, properties, ideas, creeds, politics and military activities. He determined to arrive at a real religion, to discover his relation to God, to still the insistent questionings of his conscience.

He first consulted priests, monks and theologians, but found their lives at variance with their professions. He then talked to peasants as they passed his estate as pilgrims to Kiev or Jerusalem. He saw that Faith was the power of their lives. Then he decided that he could find God only by changing his mode of living, through prayer and labor and consecration. Meantime he studied Mohammedanism, Buddhism and books about Christianity. Finally, he threw them all aside and attached himself heart and soul to the four Gospels, and especially to the Sermon on the Mount. Then his troubles began, for he found the Church and State supporting organizations that cramped the individual and wars that made away with him, thereby interfering with his divinity, and discountenancing Christ's injunction to love. The Church excommunicated him, the state feared and distrusted him, the censor blotted his writings. But he went gravely on. His wealth, his high birth and his watchful wife preserved him from want and

---

[1] For their quarrel, see the *New York Times Magazine,* Jan. 2, 1927; or Avrahm Yarmolinsky's *Turgenev* (1926).

exile. People made pilgrimages to him. Edward A. Steiner,
Professor of Applied Christianity at Grinnell College, was
one of these   Mr. Steiner writes in *Tolstoy the Man:* "The
Jews came to Yasnaya in goodly numbers to see a man
who was really living the Christian life, not merely preaching
it; and under the influence of that life they accepted the Christian faith. At first Tolstoy encouraged the baptizing of one
or two of them into the Greek Church; but he always expressed
himself as regretting this act. If he had had Jewish blood in
his veins, he would have found it difficult to prevent his being
declared the Jewish Messiah. But Tolstoy was neither the
organizer of a movement nor a zealous propagandist. He did
not care whether he had followers or not; and when men and
women came to worship him he would say in the language of the
Angel of the Apocalypse, 'See thou do it not,—worship God,'
and when they called him Master he said: 'One is your Master,
even Christ.' When they called him Teacher, he answered: 'Call
no man Rabbi.' He did preach to every man who came; if he
were rich he took him into the woods and looked into his soul
with his piercing but kindly eyes, saying repeatedly and in-
sistently: 'Sell all thou hast and give to the poor.' When the
mighty and strong came and asked what to do to be saved, he
would tell them: 'Thou shalt not kill.' When the spiritually
blind came he repeated Christ's words: 'Blessed are the pure in
heart, for they shall see God.'

"To the Socialists, with their grievances and schemes, Tolstoy said: 'For man shall not live by bread alone.' He was indeed a 'Gospel Preacher, so narrow that he saw salvation for
all who followed the Christ, no matter to what church they belonged, or whether they belonged to any. While he did not
shirk from accepting the consequences of his teachings for himself, he did not force others to do so, and to a friend who
found it difficult to part from his land he writes thus: 'Do not
mind what the world will say about your retaining your property; it is a question which concerns you alone; and if your

conscience does not condemn you, do just as you have planned.' "

Tolstoy drew up *The Gospel in Brief*, a running summary of the Christian teaching as he understood it.   Out of it he educed five commandments: (1) Be not angry; (2) Lust not; (3) Swear not; (4) Resist not evil with evil; and (5) Love your enemies.   Follow these, sacrifice yourself, put the spiritual ever before the material and God's kingdom will be realized within you and upon Earth.

In his *The Christian Teaching*, again, he warns us all against Sins and Snares.   The Snares are interesting and characteristic.   They are the Personal, the Family, Activity, Fellowship and the State.   Give not thyself wholly to any or all of these.   They will wean thee from God and thy great duty to mankind.

Tolstoy has been criticized for his views by artists, musicians, churchmen, kings, warriors, economists, historians and political scientists.   His family, his friends, the literary world regretted his defection from his great work of picturing Russia in fiction.   Yet this novelist, aristocrat, soldier and landholder chose to reassert the integrity, the soundness of primitive Christianity.   At the end he could say, "Not only have I no regret, but I rejoice at the thought of the passage which awaits me.   'Into thy hands I commend my spirit.' "

Tolstoy's theories have grave practical defects that, be we for or against them, we detect at a glance.   But his name will never die from among us as long as men live or endeavor to live the Christian life, and as long as they labor to rid the world finally of War.   If only, to return to the Old Testament, no man coveted what was his neighbor's!

Tacoma, 1921.

MORE ON TAGORE

IF I may presume to say so, I deplore Mr. Paul Elmer
More's hostility in *The Nation* of November 30th, 1916,
to Rabindranath Tagore, especially since a local paper, if
Mr. Mencken will pardon me for citing it, gave local
celebrity to Mr. More's article, adding a portrait of the
poet, with a selected phrase under it,—slightly altered to be
sure; namely, "a puddler in sentiment." In *The Nation* of
January 4th Mr. More said flatly, in reply to a letter of mild
protest and of gentle explanation of Tagore's purposes as a
poet from Lajpat Rai, that both Tagore's poems and his
philosophy are "saccharine imitation." Mr. More believes that
a poet should be a sound philosopher; Mr. Rai declares that
"a poet is a poet first and anything else afterward." It is the
eternal conflict of Art for Art's Sake and Art for Conduct's
Sake.

Mr. More is rightly impatient of ill-advised persons who
seek messages in Tagore; but he somewhat illiberally condemns
him also on the score of puddling in sentiment in days of war.
For was not his chief puddling—if that is what his divine *Chitra*
and his exquisite *Post-office* are, for example,—both of which
have been produced unforgettably in Los Angeles,—done before
the war; and has he not disappointed his literary audiences at
times by talking about Nationalism instead of reading love
lyrics? As Mr. Rai holds, is he not only a great love poet, but
also a patriot? And if many persons in stricken England drew
solace from Robert Bridges' *Spirit of Man*, an anthology compiled of fine things by a fastidious poet to comfort them, who
shall say that prosperous America is wrong-headed in finding

something to carry away from Tagore's mysticism and idealism?

Of course one unpardonable fault with Tagore in Mr. More's eyes is that Tagore is a romanticist. In his *Drift of Romanticism* Mr. More said severe things about Pater, Beckford, Fiona Macleod and the rest. He admitted as much in his Preface. Mr. More's pet aversions are the Celtic school and the new mysticism of the Orient. According to him the Celtic Renaissance is a pseudo-Renaissance because it does not revive accurately the simplicities of Old Irish, and Tagore is not a great poet because he does not write after the manner of the early Indian sages. We have all heard at some time or other the same about Tennyson, who is out of favor in our time because he did not write like Malory.

What is the use of this sort of criticism? The past should not raise insuperable prejudices in the present: it should afford standards, it is true; but growth and decay—new forms, at least,—are inevitable. Why not appreciate Tennyson and Malory, Yeats and Old Irish, Tagore and the *Bhagavad-gita?* If there is much that can be spared, in time of war, from Tennyson, Yeats and Tagore, there is not a little that one does omit, whether he should or not, in days of peace, from Malory, Cuchullain, and the *Bhagavad-gita,*—to say nothing of the last books of the *Aeneid* and portions of the *Iliad,* as Cowper observed in his generation.

And with that I should "cease": instead I may be permitted to add that sometime in 1915 Mr. Joyce Kilmer anticipated Mr. More in an American attack on Tagore, as one may learn from *The Literary Digest* of August 21st of that year. In the *Westminster Review* for December, 1913, too, E. G. Gilbert-Cooper found fault with Tagore's *Problem of Evil* (*Hibbert Journal,* July, 1913) for its want of philosophical grasp. And in *A Hindu View of Tagore* (*The Literary Digest,* December 6, 1913) we learn that some of Tagore's countrymen do not feel that he has supplanted their poets and prophets.

Strange! Other writers hold, more justly, that he is to India what Yeats is to Ireland,—the leader of a literary revival. Still others, sentimentally, perhaps,—but why so?—emphasize his service in bringing the Orient and Occident together, as Yeats has brought Ireland, ancient and modern, to many another land and people.

Tagore is not a profound philosopher or a poet of the foremost rank. He is not Plato or Shakespeare. But I insist with several reviewers that he has qualities as a man and writer that are an inspiration to his own country and to ours. He is a visionary and an idealist, it is true, but out of his creed comes a gospel of contemplation, which, since it is not carried to the excess of dreaming ecstasy so much abhorred by Professor Babbitt, is good for India and America. For everyone knows that Tagore does things: he preaches work and works himself. And if, as Mr. More feels, he works the public as well, let us recall with Mr. Le Gallienne in his *A Memory of Frédéric Mistral*, that there are many signs that poetry has come into its own again—"even now in America, which, while actually one of the most romantic and sentimental of countries, fondly imagines itself the most prosaic."

Tagore heads a school; he is a lecturer and a musician; he is a patriot; he is a great love poet; he believes in education for Oriental women; he is a mystic who soothes but does not enervate; he is a Hindoo who takes account of the best in Christianity. Indeed, "there is no English poet in all the annals of our literature," writes Odell Shepard in an article on *Christianity and the New Orient*,—"not George Herbert or Richard Crashaw or Francis Thompson—whose verse gleams and glows with religious passion as does that of Rabindranath Tagore." And if his philosophical conception of the problem of evil is weak, the following passage on Optimism is strong, good alike for Indian quietists and Mr. Hardy. "Our pessimism," writes Tagore, "is a mere pose, either intellectual or sentimental; our life itself is optimistic; it wants to go on. Pessimism is a form of mental dipsomania, it disdains healthy nourishment, indulges in the strong drink of denunciation, creates an artificial dejection to fall back upon, a stronger draught to drink."

LOS ANGELES, 1917.

"TRADITION AND JAZZ"

PROFESSOR PATTEE (a student has just spelled it Patti), careering through American literature and tilting at it and for it, is a veritable Don Quixote among our Shermans, Mores and Menckens. Indeed in *Tradition and Jazz* he writes an impassioned defense of the knight and denounces Cervantes for ridiculing him. He is the most agile and growing of critics, and some of us watch him still, as we have for years past, breathlessly, fascinated. His *American Literature Since 1870* was and is a "wonder": a glamorous thing, wrong about Henry James, but otherwise chiefly sound and always entertaining. But it omitted Jack London. So *Sidelights on American Literature* followed, with London studied and then lauded, as no one else—but a Mencken—could beat the bass drum for him; and with O. Henry amazingly badgered and comprehended. Then came *The Development of the American Short Story*, with Henry James admirably apprehended and with only seven James titles mis-spelled in the Bibliography.

In *Tradition and Jazz* Mr. Pattee pictures himself as withdrawing from the hurly-burly of, let us say, Penn State, and fleeing to the New Hampshire Hills, to his Sabine Farm. There he reads Eugene Field's *Horace* and restores his reason; then Horace himself, then Virgil, Walton and Sir Thomas Browne. Next he meditates on the *Ars Poetica* and modern American Scofflaw Poetry. He gives ear to Lindsay, laureate of the Saxophone Age, and Amy Lowell, singing feminine bass in the Masters-Sandburg-Lindsay-Lowell quartet, and pushes them all, along with others of the Untermeyer choir, over the mountainside. (Ladies, pardon him, for those in the Pattee secret know that in a later volume he'll drag you all back up again—

the boys, too—and do you brilliant justice in a vocabulary so rich, pungent and new that you'll swear it's never been to college and got educated. Note: in this volume he admits Longfellow—him of the Sonnets—to his Farm. Read his preceding books for the wonder of that).

But we have only scratched rich soil. For delightful inconsequence watch him flay the gentle, genial Harry Hansen and *Midwest Portraits*—then hear him inditing a letter to Hamlin Garland, bidding Garland and himself get on the bandwagon of the Youth Movement: in *The Old Professor, an Autopsy*, pointing out that the old fellow's well dead since most of our leading young writers to-day are products of our younger professors. Then in *The Log Unseats John Hopkins* he administers a drubbing to University administrators and whangs away at our hard-working young instructors,—our great teachers being snatched off by administrative duties. Then, in his final essay, behold him return to his Field, to his *Love Affairs of a Bibliophile*, and decide that essays alone in our output to-day possess that repose, that classic calm, we need. But first, O lovers of American letters, read his call for a History of American Literature—a real one, an interesting one, drawing a hint, rightly, from D. H. Lawrence's amazing *Studies in Classic American Literature*, and warning its maker against provincialism, sectionalism, academicism and exclusivism.

The professor shakes a glorious mixture. Draw near, ye men of old, and drink with the new.

And speaking of that, Professor Pattee is not a critic only, for *The Wine of May and Other Lyrics* (1893), is a presentable book of verse, chiefly of Nature, some of it foreign, but most of it New England, with just a hint of love, but a greater passion for birds, flowers and the seasons. *Elements of Religious Pedagogy*, on the other hand, is a closely printed volume of two hundred and twenty-four pages, witnessing to the author's great interest in children and Sunday School, and attesting the influence of Pennsylvania. More of the last is in *Compelled Men* (1913). Here one is bidden get a vision of the Master: though compelled by what we are, He will constrain us. Our author tells of a small college instructor so compelling that students' cigarettes automatically came out of their mouths when Mr. Prim passes by. But more of religion in a moment, for we now approach Mr. Pattee's three novels. The first, *Mary Garvin, the Story of a New Hampshire Summer* (1902), tells how Luke, a young lawyer, is in danger of being carried off by Miss Biddle, from Boston, but isn't, and marries Mary, his country sweetheart. There is much atmosphere of Mr. Pattee's native state. *The House of the Black Ring* shifts to his adopted land, with the Pennsylvania mountains and valleys, and the Pennsylvania Dutch and their superstitions for subjects. Squire Hartswick controls the valley, but a newcomer, Allen Farthing, becomes his rival. His daughter Rose, however, whom the Squire intends to marry to Karl, falls in love with Farthing's son, Jim. Karl is murdered. The Squire tries to put the guilt on Jim, is shown, moreover, to have framed a robbery charge, and dies of apoplexy. Rose supplies an alibi for Jim (they were away the night of the murder getting married) and the curse upon the Farthing house—really the Heller house, since the Farthings are the Hellers returned,—is shown to be mere moonshine and is removed. Then in *The Breaking-Point* (1912), our author moves into town and writes of a young minister, righteous but somewhat bloodless, who preaches in behalf of Mary Magdalens, rescues one from suicide, has trouble with his church, founds a M. M. Mission, is killed by an automobile and has his work carried on by the woman he saved and who deeply and purely loves him.

Long live our professor-critic-novelist!

WILLIAM PENN, AMERICAN

WHAT I didn't know about Penn when I came from my state to his would be a chapter in itself. I must have been in like case with the gentlemen in New York lately who denied Penn (for the present) a place in their Hall of Fame. Like Nicholas Murray Butler he must now wait his turn; till such time as New York snatches time to read of him and from him, or drops down to the country to hear of him.

Penn was born October 14, 1644. He is thus nearly three hundred years old, and very much alive. For if Penn's spirit, politicians notwithstanding, isn't still abroad in his beloved Sylvania (Penn is in front of it in honor of his father) then my sense of time and place and Penn are badly muddled.

Indeed, for Pennsylvania politics, Christopher Morley, in his bland *Travels in Philadelphia*, suggests a palliative. Morley has just been guided up into the heights of the Philadelphia City Hall, whence Penn, in Quaker garb, and with his hat on, gazes gravely down on his city. Let Pennsylvania install an oracle at Penn's feet, says Morley, and let the politicians come and consult it, inspired, as the soothsayer would be, by the great spirit above it. Or, more accurately, let the oracle sit reading Penn's *Fruits of Solitude* (of which more in a moment) and throw down quotations from it weighted with pebbles. And when Penn didn't like a candidate, let him be seen to frown visibly.

I have never read of any mortal man who so cherished his fellow-man as Penn. Certainly mere gods and goddesses pale before him. Take almighty Zeus, for instance— Penn gave his voice, his person, his money, his land and his very reason, to others. Once a friend, a friend to the death. A friend to the maligned and persecuted Quakers in England, a friend to the oppressed in Germany, a friend to the plundered Indians, nay a friend to Peter the Great of Russia and the unhappy Catholic James II of Great Britain.

In Pennsylvania his friends and colonists and enemies deceived him and robbed him and reviled him. He fathered them, he bore with them, he forgave them; he swore not, neither took up arms against them. But at the last he took up his pen. He wrote at length to his children. He asked them how he had harmed them, and why he deserved harsh treatment from them; and he pointed to the present and the future of their great land. Let Mr. Morley advise politicians also to read Penn's *Expostulatory Letter to His Colonists*. It should never die; it will never die; but lo, it slumbereth.

I love, too, to read of Penn's youthful activities in England and to watch his British independence and Christian humility mingling. His father was an admiral; nevertheless Penn was early hailed into court for addressing a religious meeting. True, such meetings were forbidden. After measures had been taken to get Penn's hat off (he had an annoying way of keeping it on in courts and courtrooms), the Judge instructed his jury to *do* something. Whereupon they brought in a verdict of Guilty of Addressing a Meeting. "His Honor" was dissatisfied and returned them to the jury room. So they brought in a verdict of Not Guilty. The Judge was seriously annoyed and fined them. As for Penn, he clapped him into jail, or if he didn't, someone else did soon. Penn was always getting locked up for thinking right, acting justly, and giving away his money. Yet when he was young he had his portion of his father's fighting talent. For what Englishman ever lets another Englishman thoroughly impose on him? An Englishman may oppress the heathen; but the long bitter fight for liberty in England, and the Revolution in America show clearly enough what happens when one Englishman treads on another.

I shall now say my word for Scotland and California, since

I am one half one and all the other. Robert Louis Stevenson, Scotchman, wandered to California, you remember. There he was cold, hungry and lonely, it being San Francisco instead of Los Angeles. One day in a bookstore he picked up Penn's *Fruits of Solitude*, and he bought it cheap. But it was food and gold and raiment to him. He read every word of it, so he must have read the following sentences among the rest:

EDUCATION

It were Happy if we studied Nature more in Natural Things; and acted according to Nature; whose rules are few, plain and most reasonable.

APPAREL

Chuse thy Cloaths by Thine own Eyes, not another's. The more plain and simple they are, the better. Neither unshapely, nor fantastical; and for Use and Decency, and not for Pride.

RIGHT MARRIAGE

O how sordid is Man grown! Man, the noblest Creature in the World, as a God on Earth, and the Image of Him that made it; thus to mistake Earth for Heaven, and worship Gold for God!

FRIENDSHIP

There can be no Friendship where there is no Freedom. Friendship loves a Free Air, and will not be penned up in straight and narrow Enclosures. It will speak freely, and act so, too; and take nothing ill where no ill is meant; nay, where it is, 'twill easily forgive, and forget, too, upon small acknowledgments.

RULES OF CONVERSATION

In all Debates, let Truth be thy Aim, not Victory, or an unjust Interest: And endeavour to gain, rather than to expose thy Antagonist.

POSTERITY

If we would amend the World, we should mend Our selves; and teach our children to be, not what we are, but what they should be.

A COUNTRY LIFE

The Country is both the Philosopher's Garden and his Library, in which he Reads and Contemplates the Power, Wisdom and Goodness of God.

OF PRAISE OR APPLAUSE

We cannot be too Circumspect how we receive Praise: For if we contemplate our selves in a false Glass, we are sure to be mistaken about our Dues; and because we are too apt to believe what is Pleasing, rather than what is True, we may be too easily swell'd beyond our just Proportion, by the Windy Compliments of Men.

And now, with Locarno ringing in our ears, and with the first important world victory of the League of Nations fresh before us, let us recall in conclusion Penn's plan for World Peace, 1693–4, "An Essay Towards the Present and Future Peace of Europe, by the Establishment of an European Dyet, Parliament or Estates." Briefly, Penn proposes an Assembly "before which should be brought all Differences depending between one Sovereign and another, that cannot be made up by private Embassies, before the Sessions begin"; and that if any member of the Assembly refuse to abide by the decisions of the rest, or delay, or take up arms, that member shall be constrained to do the will of the Diet, and assessed Costs.

I am not sure that Penn is not our greatest American— greater than Washington, Lincoln, Lee. At least no blood was on his sword, for no sword was in his hand.

ALBRIGHT COLLEGE, 1925.